Main Concepts of Russian Politics

Oleg Kharkhordin, 1964 -

UNIVERSITY PRESS OF AMERICA,® INC.
Lanham • Boulder • New York • Toronto • Oxford

Copyright © 2005 by
University Press of America,® Inc.
4501 Forbes Boulevard
Suite 200
Lanham, Maryland 20706
UPA Acquisitions Department (301) 459-3366

PO Box 317
Oxford
OX2 9RU, UK

Library of Congress Control Number: 2005924389
ISBN 0-7618-3143-6 (clothbound : alk. ppr.)
ISBN 0-7618-3144-4 (paperback : alk. ppr.)

Contents

Foreword

This book is very pragmatic in its intentions. While teaching political theory and Russian studies for the last ten years in different universities of Europe and the USA, I wrote a number of articles that employed interesting ideas from classic and modern political theorists to analyze different aspects of Russian politics. However, being put together in the framework of a single class, this motley assemblage of articles followed its own logic, having gradually transformed itself into a more or less systematic attempt to cover some key concepts of politics in Russia. Hence the structure of this book.

The one thing that can be surely said about this assemblage is that it lacks a common theoretical approach to treating political phenomena. Some chapters, like the one on the state or the first of the two devoted to the subject of friendship, rely heavily on the history of concepts approach. Others, like the chapter on nationhood, draw on some conceptual history as well, but are more concerned with the elaboration of the thought of individual theorists, e.g. Hannah Arendt. Still others, like the second chapter on friendship, as well as a chapter on the concept of virtue, are concerned with many theorists simultaneously. In all cases, these separate chapters emerged as the result of tinkering with something with the help of different theorists: my concerns, as I once noted in my book on Foucault, were more appropriate to an artisan rather than to a well-disciplined political theorist.

My thanks go first of all to the Academy of Finland, which made this publication possible. Research on self-governing associations in Russia, conducted under the auspices of this Academy (project # 208170), gave me a unique opportunity to think through the logic of civil society and republican leanings in Russia. Risto Alapuro receives special thanks for encouraging me to publish: without this encouragement, this collection would not have appeared.

From the ranks of my friends, I would like to single out Hanna Pitkin, Vadim Volkov, Jeff Weintraub and David Woodruff as main theoretical influences and sources of inspiration and advice. David Montgomery sought to extend ideas of friendship and virtue into the realm of practice by providing some last-minute assistance with editorial issues and the challenges of purging occasional renegade Russianisms from my English text. And my colleagues and students at the European University at St. Petersburg are unintentional contributors to this book as well – many debates in public spaces, classrooms and administrative offices inscribed themselves into the text, frequently—even without me reflecting upon that.

I gratefully acknowledge permissions to reprint texts of my previously published articles. Some of these texts have been slightly modified and updated for the present edition, but no major corrections were undertaken.

Chapter 1 initially appeared as "What Is the State?: The Russian Concept of *Gosudarstvo* in the European Context," *History and Theory*, vol. 40:2, May 2001, © Blackwell 2001.

Chapter 2 initially appeared as "Civil Society and Orthodox Christianity," *Europe-Asia Studies*, vol. 50:6, September 1998, © Taylor and Francis Ltd, http://www.tandf.co.uk/journals.

Chapter 3 appeared as "Reveal and Dissimulate: A Genealogy of Private Life in Soviet Russia," in Jeff Weintraub and Krishan Kumar, eds., *Public and Private in Thought and Practice*, Chicago: University of Chicago Press, 1997.

Chapter 4 is reprinted by permission of Sage Publications Ltd, from Oleg Kharkhordin, "Nation, Nature and Natality: New Dimensions of Political Action," *European Journal of Social Theory*, vol. 4:4, November 2001 (© Sage Publications, 2001).

Chapter 6 first appeared as Oleg Kharkhordin, "The Politics of Friendship: Classic and Contemporary Concerns," in Yehuda Elkana et al., eds., *Unraveling Ties*, Frankfurt: Campus, 2002 (© Campus Verlag GmbH).

Chapter 8 initially appeared as "Things as *Res Publica*: Making Things Public," in: Bruno Latour, Peter Weibel, eds., *Making Things Public*, Cambridge, MA: Zentrum für Kunst und Medientechnologie Karlsruhe / The MIT Press, 2005.

Chapter One

The State

A state exists chiefly in the hearts and minds of its people; if they do not
believe it is there, no logical exercise will bring it to life.[1]

If we ask what in empirical reality corresponds to the idea of the state, we
shall find many diffuse and discrete human actions and passive reactions,
practically and legally ordered ties either of a singular character or of a
regularly recurring kind, united by an idea which is a belief in effective
. . . norms and in relationships of domination among people.[2]

What is the state? As linguistic analysis demonstrates, this question may
hardly make sense. Alf Ross was the first to consistently apply a Wittgen-
steinian approach to analyzing statements that described state actions, or,
more accurately, to analyzing the fact that certain acts performed by individuals are spoken of as if they are performed by the state. Indeed, when we
speak of the German state declaring war or building a highway, we are fully
aware that it was a certain civil servant who pronounced a declaration of war
or that there is a multitude of construction workers who are actually building
the highway in question. We are aware that we cannot empirically see, hear,
or touch an entity called the state, while individuals appear in their full empirical splendor. However, noted Ross, in modern English it generally made
sense to speak about state actions in the following two cases: "when the act
represents the exercise of public authority or official coercive power" and
"when the act is the performance of a certain piece of work which is paid by
the 'public treasury.'"[3]

Even if statements that mention state actions make sense, they are systematically misleading since we often intuitively presume that we can find a logical subject of action mentioned in the statement by means of pointing to reality. This search for an empirical referent for "the state" will not help,

1

however, because statements that describe state actions have only grammatical subjects (that is, the word "state" is a grammatical subject to which a predicate is attached,) but do not have logical subjects as in the statement "Peter built a house," which has both grammatical and logical subjects. When we say "the state is constructing this building," implied are some individuals authorizing expenditure and directing the whole project or a set of individuals physically assembling the building, while the "state" to which the act of building is linguistically ascribed is not found in empirical reality. As Ross concluded,

> It is not possible to replace the word "state" by other words, so that a certain substance, occurrence, activity, quality, or anything else is designated, which "is" the state. . . . The question whether the state is a reality, . . . a fiction, a sum of psychological processes is also a fictitious problem—in any case in relation to the usage that we have been considering. The state "is" nothing because the statements of the structure "the state is . . ." cannot properly be made.[4]

Ross also described the four conditions that enabled statements that describe state actions to make sense. We are able to speak of some individual's actions as if they are being performed by "the state" when, first, authority is not vested in this private individual but in his or her capacity as the present holder of office; second, if this authority entails giving orders to others; third, if this authority is not exercised in the holder's own interest, but in the interests of a duty-bound office established for the common good; fourth, when this authority is part of a systematic unity of authorities. In short, to speak of the act of an individual person as being performed by the state we have to believe that this individual currently holds an office, legally regulated to promote the common good, and part of similar offices that together constitute public government or civil service.

If Ross is correct and we cannot meaningfully talk about the question "what is the state?" we can at least posit a question about the historical conditions that made it possible to talk meaningfully about state actions, being at the same time fully aware that one cannot find an entity called "the state" in empirical reality. In other words, how did these four conditions for validating a speech act mentioning "acts of the state" develop? What were the reasons for adopting such a convoluted usage and how did it actually happen?

This question is all the more interesting since speaking about the state as a subject of action is definitely a modern invention. For example, even Machiavelli, who is usually credited with having first elaborated the modern concept of the state, rarely if ever speaks about the state as an active agent. Jack H. Hexter in his 1957 article—now almost a classic in Machiavelli studies—analyzing the usage of *lo stato* in *Il Principe*, found that "*lo stato* is never worked for, helped, served, revered, admired, feared, loved; it is added to, assaulted, possessed, occupied, seized, taken, acquired, kept or lost."[5] In short, it is up for grabs, not an organized body politic, ready for action, but an "inert lump." Out of 110 instances when *lo stato* appears in *The Prince* in connection to politics, thirty-five times it appears with only five verbs—*acquistare, tenere, mantenere, togliere* (to take), *perdere* (to lose). Furthermore, the majority of other uses of *lo stato* is also "exploitative." The state "is likely to be being bossed by someone . . .; or created or increased . . .; or defended and conserved."[6]

The explanation for this curious usage may lie in the fact that Machiavelli's advice to princes is concerned with their main goal—*mantenere lo stato*—that is, to maintain their estate and state of domination, and hence Machiavelli rarely talks about *lo stato* outside of this context. Thus, out of 110 uses, Hexter found only eight where *lo stato* may be said as being unambiguously active; these are phrases that may imply our contemporary perceptions of the state—*lo stato* is said to have foundations, take root, and so on. However, we may be just reading our perceptions into these lines, since the modern concept of the active state was hardly available in Machiavelli's time at all. Hexter elucidates the context for each of the "active" uses of *lo stato* and shows that all of them may also be interpreted as dealing with the roots and foundations of personal domination of the prince over men, rather than with actions of the separate entity called the state, or even with actions of the prince's governing apparatus. For example, the first sentence of *The Prince*, even if employing *lo stato* in the active sense, clearly reveals the main feature of this term, in Hexter's opinion: "All states, all dominions (*tutti gli stati, tutti i dominii*) that have held and do hold empire over men have been and are either republics or principalities."[7] Following the usage of his day, Machiavelli is concerned with "empire over men," *imperio sopra li uomini*, or in Hexter's term, with "tenancies of command over men." His book does not deal with the operation of an abstract entity called the state, because this conception had not been formed yet.[8]

To restate our initial puzzling question: how did we come to imagine the state as an entity that actively influences the world, even if we cannot verify this belief empirically and if the early moderns could hardly think of the state as an actor either? What made possible such a radical reversal from the early modern concept of the vulnerable state, on which everybody feeds, to the active and overpowering entity that we now imagine? What made it possible to think of the existence of an almost mystical entity—"the state"—that nobody sees but that everybody presumes to exist and to act, frequently in an overwhelming manner, on our individual lives?

In order to answer these questions, I shall first survey the well-researched history of the concept of the state in major western European languages, and

particularly in English. Then I shall examine the history of its Russian equivalent, the concept of *gosudarstvo*, which will supply a good contrast to the results obtained from research on the word "state." Generalizing from both conceptual histories, we might be able to provide a hypothesis on the reasons for
the appearance of a puzzling contemporary usage that systematically mis-
leads us to perceive "state acts" carried out by individuals as actions of a mystical entity called "the state."

I. HISTORY OF THE CONCEPT OF THE STATE

The English word "state" has a very rich history. The *Oxford English Dictionary* enumerates about forty senses of it. Coming from the Latin word *status*,
it carries connotations of something standing or established, of a condition or
manner of this standing. Quentin Skinner has provided a most comprehensive
history of the political uses of the term, and we shall follow his exposition
rather closely.[9]

Harold C. Dowdall, who first wrote in English on the development of the concept of the state, emphatically asserted that from Cicero to Grotius he had found
not even one use of the term *status* in the sense of modern political state.[10] Skinner finds two important medieval Latin predecessor expressions that supplied
grounds for the development of the modern concept of the state. The first is *status regis* which meant "status of majesty, high estate, condition of stateliness."[11]
Justinian's code, the vocabulary of which provided terms for many of the key
medieval categories, starts with a section called *De statu hominum* which deals
with the problem of *de personarum statu*, the status of different persons. This usage proved to be very convenient after the rebirth of Roman law in eleventh and
twelfth century Europe. Since in the medieval worldview each vocation had its
own station or status, the vocation of princes or kings had a corresponding status appropriate to them, called *status regis*, *estate royal*, or *estat du roi*. As Dowdall first noticed, this status implied not only a set of duties and qualities appropriate to a magnate, but all "the trappings of exalted station" as well.[12] Skinner
explains this attention to the external signs of princely stature through Clifford
Geertz's theory of the majesty of the sovereign residing in the "ordering force of
display"—a feature of sovereign power, about which we have almost completely
forgotten but which constituted a very important part of *status regis*. Only a man
of the stature and stateliness appropriate to a prince, with respectable physical
comportment and posture that inspired awe, could successfully claim *status
regis*. We can still register residual elements of this understanding in Milton,
when he writes about Canute in *The History of Britain*: "with all the state that
royalty could put into his countenance."[13]

The second important medieval expression that contributed to the rise of the modern concept of the state is *status regni*, or, better, *status rei publicae*. It also came from the vocabulary of Justinian's code, which in turn quoted the famous statement of Ulpian: "Public law pertains to the *status rei Romanae*; private, to the utility of individuals. Public law relates to religion, priests and magistrates."[14] *Status rei publicae* thus designated a state or a condition of the realm or of the commonwealth—a sense still retained in the US President's State of the Union address—and most often was treated as a specific object of concern for princes. A prince was expected to keep the *status regni* in good condition. The expression *optimus status rei publicae* dates back to Cicero, but it also became part and parcel of numerous writings on *bonus status* during the Middle Ages, one of the last most telling examples being the Latin title of the famous *Utopia* of Sir Thomas More, or as it was translated in English, "A fruteful and pleasaunt worke of the beste state of a publyque weale."[15] Of course, frequently the two predecessor categories appeared together: the glory of the magistrate's vocation consisted in attaining or furthering the good standing of the commonwealth. Analytically, however, these were distinct categories, since the first primarily indicated the specific status of one estate among others within a given realm, while the second pointed to the common welfare of this realm.

Neither of these two terms, however, signified the modern concept of the state as an autonomous governing entity, distinct from both rulers and the ruled. It was the advice books to Italian princes—the earliest example of "popular" literature that used these categories and translated them from Latin into vernacular Italian—that gradually extended the meaning of the term *status* in the direction of the modern concept of the state.[16] Generally, answering Machiavelli's question—how can the prince *mantenere lo stato*?—advice books made three types of recommendation. First, in order to maintain one's dominant status and the good state of the entrusted realm, a prince must maintain the character of his regime, the type of government. It is in this sense of regime that the first sentence of *Il Principe* uses the term *lo stato*: *Tutti gli stati . . .* and so on.[17] The second way to maintain *lo stato* was to allow "no loss or alteration in the range of territories given into one's charge."[18] Hence *lo stato* came to designate the territory over which princely domination was exercised.

The most decisive innovation was the idea that in order to maintain both regime and territory, one had to command "the institutions of government and means of coercive control that serve to organize and preserve order within political communities."[19] Machiavelli talks about *lo stato* in this sense, even if he makes the very first steps in this direction, departing from old usage. Indeed, it was easy for Hexter to interpret all instances of the use of *lo stato* as dealing with the personal command of the prince over his subjects since the new meaning had not yet separated itself from the old ones of regime and territory and could be easily overlooked in expressions which combine many connotations. *Lo stato* at that time, as we have already said repeating Skinner, almost always meant *il suo stato* of the prince, the condition of his personal domination rather than a state apparatus serving him. In western European literature as well, until the mid-sixteenth century "there will be found scarcely any instance in which *état*, *staat*, or state in question is unequivocally separated from *status* or standing of the prince himself."[20] One could add that the "state" in question most frequently was his lordly stature or his standing domination.

Two developments in political theory in the sixteenth and seventeenth centuries separated the state, as an entity with a life of its own, from the person of the prince on the one hand and from the prince's subjects and the territory they inhabit on the other. First, the republican tradition of European thought contributed to the separation of the prince from the state. This was a well-established point in a stream of republican thinking from Dante to Contarini (best exemplified in his *De republica Venetorum*, 1543): a city can hardly hope to remain free unless it succeeds in imposing strict legal conditions on its rulers and magistrates. However, this idea of the need for a framework of laws and public power independent of the prince could be easily expressed by Italian republicans in traditional terms, rather than by introducing a new and unnecessary term *status*. Thus, "although Contarini has a clear conception of the apparatus of government as a set of institutions independent of those who control them, he never uses the term *status* to describe them, but always prefers in a similar way to speak of their authority as embodied in the *respublica* itself."[21]

Second, absolutist thought in the sixteenth and seventeenth centuries contributed to separating the figure of the prince from the multitude of the ruled, and here the word "state" was called for in order to express this not-so-subtle distinction. Fighting against the fiduciary theories of sovereignty, where the prince was considered to be a trustee or a minister of the people, and who could be recalled under certain conditions, the absolutists strove to impose a vision of sovereignty endowed with irrevocable powers. The powers of civil government may initially depend on the power of citizens, in this line of thinking, but once established, they belong to an independent sovereign and cannot be reclaimed. Neither the word *respublica* nor its English or French equivalents fared very well in expressing this idea. For example, Raleigh lamented the fact that the word "commonwealth" did not successfully describe the source of sovereignty since it became "an usurped nickname" and frequently referred "to the government of the whole multitude."[22] Hence he employed the term "State" which he defined (in 1618) as "the frame or set order of a Common-wealth, or of the Governours that rule the same, especially of the chief and Sovereign governour that commandeth the rest."[23] Hobbes, wrestling with the same problem in his early treatises, used the word "city," the old English equivalent of Latin *civitas*: "A city therefore (that we may define it) is one person whose will, by the compact of many men, is to be received for the will of them all."[24] This, Skinner suggests, was so awkward and alien to colloquial usage of the word "city" that when he published *Leviathan*, he opted for another term: "that great Leviathan, called a Common-wealth, or State (in latine Civitas)."[25] As many have noted, in *Leviathan* sovereignty resides in an artificial soul, neither in the ruler nor the ruled. This allows Hobbes to distinguish the state, or "the Seat of Power," as he calls it at one point,[26] from both the people and the person of the prince. The term "state" itself is very convenient since it does not carry the connotations of popular rule that "commonwealth" has, nor does it directly imply the personal rule of the prince, as the word "sovereignty"—interpreted as the domination of a feudal sovereign—could have done.

II. HISTORY OF THE CONCEPT OF *GOSUDARSTVO*

Let us juxtapose this account to the conceptual development of the term in the Russian language. The movement away from *il suo stato* to "the state" conceived as different from both the person of the ruler and the body of the ruled is obvious in the Russian case as well. However, there are significant differences that may shed light on the historical reasons for the peculiarities of the conceptual development in western European languages. A comparison will also allow us to formulate a hypothesis on what made it possible, in both English and Russian, to speak of "the state" as an independent entity with a capacity for action. I apologize for the somewhat extended treatment of Russian matters, but since no extended conceptual history of *gosudarstvo* has been produced so far, I shall have to be tediously meticulous at times, assembling bits and pieces of evidence that have been heretofore produced by scholars in various disciplines.[27]

The first obvious difference between the conceptual developments in the two languages is that Russian did not adopt the Latin term, or its western European equivalents, to designate the state. The Latin word *status* was incorporated into Russian only to designate the social rank or high esteem of a person, while the phonetic copy of the German word *Staat* came to signify units within a federal state, as in *Soedinennye shtaty*, "the United States." The main Russian term for the state, *gosudarstvo*, is a derivation from *gosudar'*—meaning prince or master of a household, the obvious equivalent of the Latin *dominus*—which led Richard Pipes to suggest that *gosudarstvo* could be more accurately translated as "domain."[28]

A conceptual history of *gosudarstvo* thus seems at first sight rather straightforward. Ancient Slavonic had a word, *gospodar'*, linked to the root term *gospod'* or *gospodin*, meaning "head of the household, property owner, male spouse" (also later—"Lord, meaning God") while a related early word, *gospoda,* meant a household or a land estate.[29] The word *gospodar'* is already found in Novgorod birchbark charters from the eleventh century.[30] Somewhat later, *gospodar'* gained preeminence in political usage because it became the official title of some Russian princes. This happened due to the Latin influence on the chancery language of Russian princes through the official language of the Polish Kingdom and Lithuanian Russia. The first registered usage of *gospodar'* appears in 1349 in the Slavonic version of the princely title of Casimir III of Poland, who is called *gospodar' ruskoe zemle*, that is, *dominusque terre Russie* in its Latin version.[31] Poland at that time gained the principality of Galicia-Volhynie, the prince of which, Andrei, called himself *dux Ladimiriae et dominus Russiae* in Latin already in 1320.[32] After Galicia was ceded to Lithuania, *gospodar'* became part of the title of the grand duke of Lithuania, and the knowledge of this title eventually spread to those Russian princes who closely interacted with Lithuanians and Poles. In 1427 Bishop Kirill of Beloozero applied the title *gospodar'* to the great prince of Muscovy and in 1431 Photii used for the first time the derivative *gospodarstvo*.[33]

The term *gosudar'* eventually appeared and squeezed out *gospodar'* for reasons that are not yet entirely clear.[34] In the opinion of Russian historians, the main distinction, however, lies not between the terms *gospodin–gospodar'—gosudar'*, but between these terms and the previous term for great princes, *velikii kniaz'*.[35] For example, in 1477 Ivan III demanded that the republic of Novgorod accept him as their *gosudar'*. *Velikii kniaz'*, the hereditary title of Muscovite princes heretofore, implied *primus inter pares*, one prince among many, while the title of *gosudar'* implied that the subjects of Ivan III could be treated like serfs or other personal property of the *dominus*. With the expansion and centralization of the Muscovite principality that followed the fall of Novgorod, the title of *gosudar'* became predominant, and czars later could simply perceive their realm as *gosudarstvo*, their exclusive domain where everything, including the property of the subjects, belonged to the czar personally.[36]

Furthermore, some scholars assert that *gosudar'* in the seventeenth century, particularly after the crowning of the first czar of the Romanov dynasty in 1613, really came to mean what the title said—*gosudar' vseia Rusi* ("of all Russia")—since a special perception of a deep personal connection between each subject and the czar developed after the extensive search for and enthroning of the new dynasty. Service to the czar came to be regarded as a direct personal relationship between the sovereign and the subject. People handling what we might call "state affairs" were considered and regarded themselves as actually handling *gosudarevy dela*, "affairs of the czar," and thus carried in themselves part of his person and status. For example, Russian ambassadors abroad held that they would directly affect the personal stature and standing of their *gosudar'* if they were not treated with all the pomp pertaining to his dignity.[37]

The term *gosudarstvo*, as a consequence, came to mean both a feature or quality of being a *gosudar'*, and the territory of his rule. In the fifteenth century, the term mostly designated a general condition of being *dominus*, what one might call in Latin *dominatio*—a regime of domination—and only with time did the sense of *dominum* (in Machiavelli's Italian—*dominio*), a territorial domain, emerge to equal importance. Thus, Ivan III, in a famous exchange with a Novgorod delegation in 1477, insisted that they came under his total domination and could not curtail or regulate it: "We desire the same rule (*gosudar'stvo*) in our patrimonium (*otchina*) of great Novgorod as we have in the Low Lands of Moscow. . . . And you are trying to tell me what my rule (*gosudar'stvo*) should be? But what would this rule (*gosudar'stvo*) then amount to?"[38] Thus, *gosudarstvo* in the fifteenth century was close to the Italian *lo stato* in that both appealed to *dominio*. But while *lo stato* in the first sentence in *Il Principe* meant a *dominio* that had *imperio* over men, the Russian language did not know this distinction between *dominio* (feudal household) and *imperio* (sovereignty, command over free men, meaning non-slaves).[39] *Gosudarstvo* was rule and command, but rule and command as practiced in one's patrimonium over serfs and members of the family.[40] Also, the term *gosudarstvo* at the time seems not to have had the connotations of kingly stature, the ordering force of display, that *status regis* and *lo stato* had.

Zoltan tried also to trace the development of the second meaning of *gosudarstvo*—"the territory which *gosudar'* rules." Although the meaning of territory may be said to appear already in the epistle of Photii in 1431,[41] its widespread use in this sense followed later borrowing from west-Slavonic (Belorussian and Ukrainian) scribes who translated the Polish word *panstwo* with the term *gosudarstvo*. Under their influence, Russian scribes implanted the territorial meaning of the Polish *panstwo* in the Russian *gosudarstvo* as well. Since the Polish term meant both *dominatio* and *dominum*, this importantly extended the meaning of the Russian term.[42] Thus, in 1536 the term was already used in the plural, meaning multiple lands,[43] while Ivan IV had no problem recounting in 1543 all *gosudarstvy* that were part of his title.[44] Residual evidence of *gosudarstvo* primarily conceived as *dominatio* rather than domain comes from as late as 1570, when Ivan IV wrote to queen Elizabeth of England on his disillusionment over the character of her rule which he considered not appropriate to an autocrat. His letter can be paraphrased as follows: "And we thought that you are a *gosudarynia* [the female form of the title] in your domination [*gosudarstvo*, but interpreted as an activity] and that you yourself own and look after your sovereign [*gosudarskoi*] honor and the augmentation of your domination [*svoemu gosudarstvu pribytka*]." Pipes supplies the translation that was made by the English chancery—"We thought that you lord it over your domain, and rule by yourself and seek honor for yourself and profit for your realm"—and notes that English interpreters were baffled by the Russian text and rendered Russian *gosudarstvo* by "rule," "land," "country," even though these terms hardly corresponded to the Russian word that frequently implied personal possession.[45]

Summing up the early development of the Russian term for the state, one sees a parallel emergence of both connotations that one finds in *lo stato* or "the state" in early modern Europe. Both *lo stato* and *gosudarstvo* signify aspects of the personal domination of the prince, *il suo stato* (though the Italian *principe* commands free men in the sense of non-slaves while the Russian *gosudar'* rules his subjects like serfs). Both words also signify territories that sovereigns control. The most decisive innovation, however, was one that happened, according to Skinner, in the beginning of the sixteenth century in Italian, and in the beginning of the seventeenth in English—the designation by *lo stato* and "the state" of an apparatus of government, independent of both the rulers and the ruled. This happens in Russian as well, but only in the early to mid-eighteenth century. This extension also occurs in Russian in a different manner than in Western Europe, because of the absence of long-established republican or absolutist traditions of political thought. Nevertheless, a comparison of the Russian and western European cases may help us understand what was at stake in the appearance of the idea of the state as an independent and active entity.

III. THE STATE OF THE COMMON GOOD

The first and decisive distinction that led to the formation of the familiar triplet ruler/state/ruled in Russia, was the distinction between the ruler and the country, perceived as some kind of a union of kin, of a multitude bound by a common lifestyle and origin. Personal service to the czar gradually came to be interpreted as a service to the country, or better, to the fatherland, and this altered emphasis helped for the first time to separate state affairs from the personal affairs of the czar.

Some leanings in this direction are found during the rule of czar Alexei Mikhailovich, the father of Peter the Great. Russia at the end of the seventeenth century was largely perceived by the czar as a patrimony, as his personal domain, and he called it *edinogo gosudaria gosudarstvo*—"the territory of a single *gosudar'*," or an estate, if you like.[46] This has been compared by Russian historians to the "l'état, c'est moi" of Louis XIV—a far-fetched comparison, indeed. When *le roi soleil* expressed this thought, it was plainly paradoxical because the separation of a distinct bureaucratic apparatus and the person of the king was by then largely completed in France. In Russia, the statement of Alexei Mikhailovich presupposed no such separation: *gosudarstvo* of the czar was still generally interpreted as *il suo stato*.

Even the nascent bureaucracy functioned sometimes just to satisfy the czar's personal wishes and needs. Given that affairs of the state and affairs of the czar were not separated, generally the proto-bureaucracy conceived of itself as serving the czar, not any other entity. As Pipes claims, the system of chanceries (*prikazy*) that appeared under Ivan the Terrible in the sixteenth century had its origins in the households of appanage princes that were moved to Muscovy after the capture of their principalities, in order to help *gosudar'* rule their conquered domains.[47] Other, functional rather than territorial, chanceries were established on an ad hoc basis to service the various needs of czardom and the czar personally, their objectives overlapping and jurisdictions frequently conflicting with one another.

The Secret Chancery established in the seventeenth century to deal with the czar's most personal affairs may be a case in point. After 1662 its functions underwent a phenomenally swift transformation and expansion. Instead of conducting its usual investigations, the chancery engaged frantically in food procurement and land accumulation through requisitions and acquisitions. This is explained by the czar's resolve to supply munitions and alimentation to regiments of musketeers that helped him smash the rebellion of 1662. Heretofore the musketeers had had to procure their own maintenance. Now the czar, having recognized the advantages of a standing army, wanted to put it on a firm basis through state supplies. Hence the chancery that dealt with what we might call today the czar's personal affairs started to deal with army maintenance as well. Interestingly, with the death of Czar Alexei in 1676, this chancery was immediately disbanded, and its property was divided among other chanceries. The heirs apparently did not consider army maintenance their personal affair, or did not see any need to maintain a special chancery for the personal affairs of the czar. Scholars conclude: "In the epoch when they did not distinguish at all between the state and the form of government, the concepts of belonging to *gosudar'* and of belonging to *gosudarstvo* completely overlapped. The state and state interest were thought of only as concretely embodied in the living person of the *gosudar'* and his affairs."[48]

Yet a nascent tradition of what one might now call "state service," what until the middle of the seventeenth century was still generally called "service to the czar," provided opportunities for new formulations. Even if the czars themselves had only once thanked their subjects for service to *gosudarstvo* in a written legal document,[49] some of the servicemen in their patrimonial bureaucracy started to entertain thoughts that they might be serving something other than the czar. Thus, already in the 1550s we find an instance when a chronicler laments the fact that the boyars each "look after their own [welfare], rather than after that of the *gosudar'* or of the land."[50] A hundred years later, Ordyn-Nashchokin, one of the top chancellors of Alexei Mikhailovich, could sometimes—amid the usual assertions that he was working in the interests of the sovereign—proclaim that he was also working for *ustroenie svoego gosudarstva*, "the arrangement of his state."[51] This, of course, could not mean the personal domination of the chancellor (a crime and a blasphemy), but implied that Ordyn already regarded himself as part of some larger community, as someone serving its interests as well as the czar's personal ones.

The decisive shift in discourse, however, happens with the ascent of Peter the Great who introduced a notion of the common good and attempted radically to distance the person of the czar from the body of the country. In the words of one astute commentator: "a hierarchy that existed in the medieval Russian idea of the state—the czar serves God and people serve the czar—has been replaced by a new relationship: both czar and subjects serve the fatherland, the 'common good' of the state."[52]

Historians argue about when this doctrine of the common good was first enunciated. Chernaia takes 1700 as a point of departure, when Peter ordered that books be printed in Amsterdam in the Slavonic language "for the glory of the great *gosudar'* . . . and for the common utility and growth of the people."[53] Pavlenko singles out the 1702 manifesto (on recruiting foreigners for state service) where Peter claims to govern so that "each of our true subjects may feel that our only intention is to procure their well-being and their augmentation."[54] However, most agree that the most famous formulation appeared in Peter's speech before the battle of Poltava, in which Russia defeated the Swedish army and became a European power, in 1709: "Warriors! Here is the hour that will decide the fate of the fatherland [*otechestvo*]. You should think that you are fighting not for Peter, but for the state [*gosudarstvo*], entrusted to Peter, for your kin, for fatherland. . . . And know of Peter that he does not care about his life but only that Russia lives in bliss and glory for your well-being."[55]

Two points should be stressed here. First, Peter presents himself not as the owner of the domain called Russia, but as a caretaker and curator. Second, the community whose interests he serves is not necessarily *gosudarstvo*, it is also a community of blood lineage and common ancestry. The state understood as "fatherland" moves into the forefront of discourse, since this word more felicitously connotes the desired commonality than the word *gosudarstvo*, which is far too obviously linked with the might and oppression pertaining to *gosudar'-stvo*, a word which could be literally taken as "prince-ness," a general quality of domination and domain.

The Russian word for fatherland—*otechestvo*—in ancient Slavonic initially meant extended kin rather than nuclear family, then came to designate the place of birth, *pays natal* as the French would say; only very late did it come to designate the lofty ideal of the nation, worthy of self-sacrifice.[56] Historians tend to ascribe the appearance of this third meaning of the term to the Time of Troubles (the 1610s), when militia from different parts of Russia united to liberate Moscow.[57] The lofty ideal of *pro patria mori*, however, could not easily appear in Russia—as it did in western Europe—through the translations of Roman literature or through the development of the medieval notion of *patria* of Christians in the city of Heaven.[58] Rather, it came through the borrowing of the Greek models, particularly with the help of the vita of St. Dimitrius of Thessaloniki, a Greek martyr prince who sacrificed himself for the community of the *polis*, a small fatherland.[59] Still, being linguistically linked to the notion of the father (*otets*), *otechestvo* could have the connotations of the patrimonial household structure and of the founder of extended kin[60] that thus served the role of a successful transitional term, which eased eliciting support for some impersonal stance from Peter's largely traditional audience.

Generally, commentaries now assume that belief in the common good and service to the fatherland was personally important for Peter I: "the idea of serving the state, into which the czar came to believe deeply and to which he subordinated all of his activity, was the essence of his life."[61] He visibly separated his private person and his body politic by playing two roles, that of the common soldier, bombardier Peter Mikhailov, standing in the ranks with others in military marches and exercises, and that of the sovereign towering over the rest on his throne during official receptions. By playing Mikhailov, he offered a model of service as appropriate to a true son of the fatherland, and thus preached by example. His personal spending was very modest, as befitted his army salary. On receiving these payments, he was recorded to say: "This is my personal money: I have earned it and will use it as I please: but with state income (*gosudarstvennye dokhody*) one should be very careful." In his own words, he was serving "this state" (*semu gosudarstvu*) rather than "his state," and viewed it as an entity that had independent existence and interests of its own. Thus, an order establishing the Senate (effectively a council of ministers) in 1711 obliges this new body to "control expenses in all of the state and curtail unnecessary, and in particular, vain ones." A reform of the Senate some time later stated: "it is always appropriate for the Senate to relentlessly be in charge of the benefit of the state and of the monarch."[62]

The intention to draw a distinct line between the person of the czar and the body of the state is clear. However, this was not always easy to carry out.[63] The main reason for these difficulties was the self-undermining character of Peter's introduction of the notion of the common good: as many commentaries were quick to notice, the segregation of the body of the state from the person of the ruler was ordered and implemented by a personal whim of an autocratic ruler who controlled this body completely. Indeed, Peter's other reforms that had introduced numerous innovations in customs and everyday life—spheres that were rarely touched by Muscovite princes—probably succeeded only due to the mechanisms of traditional domination that helped overcome huge resistance. In the latter case, Peter's ideologists appealed to the czar's divine sanction to change mores, rather than to his sovereign will.[64]

Thus, inconsistencies pervaded the intended introduction of the notion of the common good that allegedly united the ruler and the ruled in service to the fatherland. In 1721 Peter was proclaimed "the father of the fatherland" apparently in imitation of *pater patriae*, a term for Roman emperors, which since the collapse of Italian medieval republics designated, in the words of Skinner, "a wise prince . . .whose actions will be governed by a desire to foster the common good and hence the general happiness of all his subjects."[65] But by accepting this title Peter stopped being a son of the fatherland, Peter Mikhailov, marching in rank with other officers of the army. In 1721 he also officially became emperor. This visibly strengthened the autocratic pretensions of Russian czars. As a result, Feofan Prokopovich, one of the chief ideologists of Peter's reforms, frequently could not decide which terms to use in lauding the czar's works after his death, whether to dub Russia "our fatherland" or "his (Peter's) fatherland." For example, Prokopovich proclaims that what Peter "made *his* Russia, such it will be" and discusses "what power a *gosudar'* needs to have to rule and correct *his* fatherland." Both uses strongly remind us of the concept of the state as a personal possession of *gosudar'*. A little later, however, Peter is said to have copied good foreign laws to "improve *our* fatherland."[66] The secret of this confusion is perhaps revealed by the clear exposition in the political treatise *On the Truth of the Monarch's Will*, written by Prokopovich: "A monarch may lawfully order people to do not only what is necessary for the good benefit of his fatherland, but also whatever he may wish, as long as it does not conflict with the common weal and God's will."[67]

Autocratic will is the ultimate mover of the Russian state, and no matter how much is said about the public good to which czar and people commonly aspire, a common "fatherland" is instituted only on the order of the czar who must be obeyed due to the total patrimonial power of the *gosudar'* in his domain. Thus, the word "fatherland," even if a bit more felicitous linguistically than the word *gosudarstvo* for the point of common allegiance of potentially equal citizens, was frequently used synonymously with "the state." Most commentaries notice the essential interchangeability among Russian words for fatherland, state, and society until the end of the eighteenth century. Their shared connotation then was a "lofty, mighty, and radiant union of the reborn society-state with its members."[68] Also, in terms of natural-law theorists, who had been extensively translated into Russian in the eighteenth century, civil society was synonymous with the state (as in Locke, for example), while entering this " civil state" was achieved simply by means of instituting a common umpire and common defense among naturally separate humankind. Thus, even radical thinkers initially shared the vision that equated society, state, and fatherland. Radischchev wrote: "O you, who paved the way to thinking about the good of the people, of society, of the state—Plato and Montesquieu"; and in another instance: "a rural inhabitant loves the fatherland more than other co-members of the Russian state."[69]

Catherine the Great took an important step toward institutionalizing such usage. In 1783 she published *The Book on the Duties of Man and Citizen*, which contained her adapted translation of Pufendorf's treatise of the same title.[70] This book became a compulsory part of secondary education until 1819. Among other things, Catherine supplied the correct definition of the fatherland, obliterating any possible distinction between it and the state, a "misconception" that she lamented and condemned:

In its true meaning the Fatherland is a large society of which one is a fellow citizen, i.e. the state whose subject one is either by place of birth or by resettlement and residence. Such a large society, which sometimes extends over many regions, is called the Fatherland because the well-being of all inhabitants and all fellow citizens is maintained and supported by the same authority and laws, just as the well-being of children in the home is secured by father's care. Therefore all those who are subjects of one supreme power are sons of the Fatherland. *Love for the fatherland* consists in showing esteem and gratitude to the government, in obeying the laws, institutions and just rights of society and using them for the common good. . . .[71]

Several novel features of this excerpt are worth noting. First, Catherine II tries to blur the distinction between government and society (or fatherland). However, given that different words are used to designate these phenomena (rather than one word, *gosudarstvo*, as was frequently the case at the end of the seventeenth and beginning of the eighteenth century), the possibility of distinguishing between them, and even of radically opposing them to each other, is already present. Second, the opportunity to define the state in the narrower sense, as an apparatus of government, is manifest. As the dictionary of the eighteenth-century Russian language tells us, the meaning of the word *gosudarstvo* that came to prevail was "a country, the population of which is subject to a single government,"[72] and we see Catherine employing this sense when she talks about "subjects of one supreme power," by either birth or residence. Yet the new metaphor of the state as mechanism, engendered by translations of foreign political treatises, pushes *gosudarstvo* toward being defined as this supreme power, as a self-sufficient and independent entity. Radishchev almost repeats Hobbes's introduction to *Leviathan* when he writes: "the state is a great machine, whose aim is the citizens' bliss. Two sorts of springs set it into motion, mores and laws."[73]

Examples of the usage of the adjective "state" (*gosudarstvennyi*, that is, pertaining to *gosudarstvo*), which had barely appeared in the middle of the seventeenth century,[74] but enjoyed abundant use in the eighteenth century, demonstrate that the state was very close to being seen as a governing body with specific features of its own. This state, narrowly defined, is then thought of as having certain specific rights, as in the following statement: "whoever transcends our ordinance . . . will be executed as the violator of state rights and as an enemy of authority [*vlasti*]." The state has its own "state ranks" meaning court bureaucrats, as in the sentence: "with timid servility state ranks stood around my throne." More importantly, the state has "state places," offices where the business of government is conducted.[75] The state now has its "state council," a set of governmental collegia and ministers. Last, but not least, it has "state peasants" who populate the crown lands and are directly subject to the central government for taxation.[76]

This plethora of people, activities and institutions merited recognition as a separate entity, a body in its own right. Catherine II stopped short of proclaiming it, even though she carried out a final consolidation of the governmental apparatus in practice, by instituting the hierarchy of bodies of provincial government in 1775 and thus completing the setting up of a uniform state machinery.[77] Her usage, as we have already mentioned, suggested that the state was not identical to its subjects and to the person of the ruler—"The intention of monarchical regimes . . . is the glory of citizens, of the state and of the *gosudar*"[78]—but this triple distinction was consistently asserted only by critics of the regime.

Thus Fonvizin wrote: "Where the arbitrary rule of one person is a supreme law, there a firm social tie cannot exist; there is the state, but no fatherland, there are subjects but no citizens."[79] The republican ideal is implied here: a government of laws and not of men guarantees freedom. As Radishchev would write, "And even if the *gosudar*' himself ordered you to violate the law, do not obey him, because he errs, harming himself and society."[80] Particularly interesting in both passages is the affirmation of the need for a vigorous independent society opposed to the state that would preserve freedom. Radishchev, in a famous verse, formulates it in the following terms:

> The czar's authority defends faith
> The czar's authority affirms faith
> Together they oppress society
> One intends to enchain reason,
> Another tries to wipe out the will,
> And both say this is for the common good.[81]

The "society" that Radishchev mentions is not the civil society of modern liberalism, nor is it the unity of all people inhabiting Russia. Rather, in accordance with eighteenth-century usage, it is either the aristocratic "good society" of the Russian capitals, or perhaps *la république des lettres* of thinkers of the Russian Enlightenment.[82] Nevertheless, the opposition between the state and society is drawn radically and resolutely. The modern triplet ruler/state/ruled is finally being formed. If Peter the Great separated the person of the czar from the realm he ruled, then radical Enlightenment thought split this realm into society as a body of private citizens and the state as the machinery of legal power.

The equation of the state with the government apparatus and the separation of the state from society became a commonplace in nineteenth-century Russian works.[83] However, this perception was shared only by the literate part of the Russian population. Kavtaradze's study of nineteenth-century peasant perceptions of the political universe shows that they hardly understood *gosudarstvo* in the modern sense or even used the term. For a typical peasant, the czar was an ideal figure who embodied divine justice and served as a source of distant hope in people's daily hardships, while the state clerks and representatives (for example, provincial governors or tax collectors) were treated as private persons whose abusive actions the czar could at some point curtail. The state as an independent and autonomously regulated machine of power did not exist in their perception; rather, they still regarded officials as the czar's personal servants who abused his orders.

Furthermore, peasants did not have a notion of the common good of the state or an established notion of fatherland. For example, when Napoleon invaded Russia in 1812, this was initially viewed in the villages as a conflict between sovereigns rather than peoples. In the first months of the war peasants resisted the French army only if it menaced their local communities. Only after ravages of some of these communities did the famous "bludgeon of the people's war," vividly poeticized by Tolstoy, appear. The primary allegiance of a peasant was to the *mir*, the local commune, and building extra-communal allegiance to a bigger entity called the fatherland was extremely difficult. Even in the Crimean war of 1855 peasants entered the Russian army without patriotic feelings but possibly expecting a reciprocal favor from the czar. Rumors circulated that the French had entered the war to liberate the serfs, which made enlisting the peasants' "service to the fatherland" in the czar's army even more difficult. Hence, if they did defend the official "fatherland," they could still think that they were thereby earning their freedom, to be granted by the czar. Once again, the military conflict was perceived as a war between princes, not a war between peoples.[84]

It was only the Bolsheviks who brought the state into the everyday life of each citizen of post-revolutionary Russia, and made the modern meaning of the term obvious to everybody. The construction of what Skinner calls "the doubly impersonal character of the state" was finished when, for the majority of Soviet citizens, the state as an independent machine of power intruded into their lives, but became distinctly separate both from the life of the rulers and from the people's own existence. No matter what heights the adulation of Stalin reached, and notwithstanding the fact that almost everybody was employed in state enterprises and offices, Soviet citizens knew that their state, at least in theory, was not the personal property of any ruler, but an independent entity, which—as everyday practice constantly reminded them—also had interests that did not coincide with theirs and which was ready to sacrifice the citizenry for these interests.

IV. COMPARISONS AND CRITIQUE

Comparison of the conceptual development of the term "state" in the English and Russian languages shows different strategies for arriving at the triple distinction that lies at the foundation of the modern concept of the state—ruler/state/ruled—and different forces at play. In English, a distinction between the ruler and the state was achieved by republican thought, while a distinction between the state apparatus and the ruled was carried out by absolutist thinkers. In Russian, it seems, the same result was achieved, but developments happened as if reflected in a mirror: a distinction between the person of the ruler and the state was carried out by absolutist thinkers (frequently the monarchs themselves), while the entity called the state was distinguished from the ruled by the nascent republican tradition.

This mirror-image relationship between conceptual development in English and Russian disappears, however, if we pay close attention to the categories employed in both transformations. Then we can see that in the western

European case a transformation of the initial notion of *lo stato* or "the state" generally conceived as *il suo stato* involved a radical differentiation of this concept—carried out by republicans—into two others. Thus, the state in the sense of *status regis* became interpreted as an estate or duty of princehood, while the state in the sense of *status rei publicae* was interpreted as the optimal condition of things in a republic, as ensured by the rule of laws rather than by the discretion of a princely estate. Later, *res publica* itself was split by absolutists into *res gubernans* and *publica*. The term "state" proved very useful for articulating this later distinction between the state and the people. In the end a triple distinction appeared—*rex/res gubernans/publica*.

In Russia, the core initial problem was drawing a distinction between *dominus* and his *dominatio* or *dominum*. This was similar to splitting the undifferentiated *il suo stato* of western European princes into distinct *rex* and *stato*. However, since the Russian language did not offer linguistic possibilities similar to those of the Germanic or Romance languages—Russian words close to the Latin *status* hardly existed and the vocabulary of Roman law was all but ignored—conceptual development happened by means of interpreting *gosudarstvo* as "fatherland"—that is, *dominum* was interpreted as *patria*—thus separating it from the person of the czar. Furthermore, both czar and people were supposed to serve this *patria* until indignant republicans had split this *patria* into one part to which they returned the derogatory title of *gosudarstvo* (which linguistically implies domination of the *dominus*) and a second part—a body of oppressed *compatrioti*—that could jointly oppose this apparatus of domination.

In both cases of conceptual development, however, one finds a crucial point of asserting a commonality beyond the figure of the common ruler, be it the *respublica* or commonwealth of western European thinkers, or the Russian equivalent of the Latin *patria*. But if this commonality beyond the figure of the prince was obviously suggested by many republican thinkers in Europe, why was the same commonality demanded and imposed by Russian autocrats? Was it out of altruistic motives and by virtuous self-limitation as befits an enlightened monarch? Or did the autocrats have sound reasons to advance a theory of the common good—reasons that, if explored, might shed light on European developments as well? Indeed, the Russian case, because of its stark absurdity—with monarchs using their considerable power to impose from above the conception of *res publica* on a recalcitrant populace—may reveal what was at stake in this idea of the common good, which modern states are now so obviously taken to represent.

My hypothesis is simple. Appeal to the idea of the common good was necessary to regulate and control people more thoroughly than ever before, both in western and eastern Europe. In Russia this increase in control had to happen faster and in a very limited period of time—since the czars had to catch up with the rest of Europe, which had moved farther along the road of technical progress and population management. So the czars had to rely on autocratic means to hammer this idea of the common good into the heads of their subjects. Those European countries which first set out to control their populations through the fiction of the common good (handily offered by the republican tradition), could initially afford gentler measures. They did not have to face fierce military competition from technically advanced adversaries that had already learned to enlist mass support.

Let's take a closer look at the instance of Peter's dramatic appeal to the common good before the Poltava battle. He exhorts soldiers to treat this battle as their own, rather than their sovereign's, as a battle for their kin, for the land of their fathers. Heretofore the czar's subjects could volunteer (or not) to engage in the czar's service and even if dragooned into the czar's army against their will, could dissimulate obedience and compliance. Now, with the erection of a new deity called *patria* or fatherland, when they sabotaged the czar's orders they were not simply opposing the dominating sovereign, but betraying their own fathers and ancestors, the whole community. Since *patria* is a common concern, all must participate in serving it, with no exceptions.

The same appeal to common necessity during hostilities between feudal lords justified the imposition of additional burdens on a reluctant populace in western Europe as well. Of course, republican treatises on the common good stressed the other side of this imposition, on the ruler, rather than on the ruled. *Optimus status rei publicae* could be achieved if individual advantage is subordinated to "the common good of the city as a whole" as Campano wrote in 1502, or when the ruler "remains oblivious to his own good, and ensures that he acts in everything he does in such a way as to promote the public benefit" as Beroaldo asserted in 1508.[85] Such passages reveal the intellectual origins of the medieval proliferation of common-good theories that had sprung from Latin translations of Aristotle's *Politics*, which described the regime of justice in the city as upholding the common good. However, another source of their popularity were the frequent situations when princes had to appeal to conditions of dire necessity to justify their taxation of each (corporate) subject of their principality. "When for the public welfare, the defense of the realm, a king asked for an extraordinary tax to meet this necessity, special privileges, immunities and liberties . . . all of which amounted to private contracts between king and individuals and corporations, were not valid."[86]

In 1179 and 1215 the Third and Fourth Lateran Councils decided that Italian communes could tax even the clergy if common necessity was evident and if the Pope was first consulted and gave his consent. Lawyers quickly extended this to apply to kingdoms. Hence, in 1295–1296 Pope Boniface VIII discovered "that he had to consent to extraordinary taxation of English and French clergy by Edward I and Philip IV. Ironically, each of the monarchs claimed that his necessity was a just war of defense against the other."[87] Kings effectively resorted to the fiction of common necessity to tax and pool the scarce resources of their subjects in order to win in this war. Given the Norman conquest of the Anglo-Saxon kingdom, the disputed status of some provinces in what now is France and the absence of the "nation" in the modern sense of the word, this was hardly a war between the nations of England and France (as contemporary anachronisms would have us believe), but a turf war between two gangs of competing landlords of similar origins.

The populace seems to have always reacted to these "pleas of necessity" and rhetoric of common good with obvious suspicion. For example, in England, this was a subject of constant dispute between the king and the Parliament. As late as 1610, the Parliament claimed that, except in times of dire necessity, kings should be able to "live off their own," meaning on the income from crown possessions rather than from taxing each subject.[88] What constituted dire necessity was also up for discussion in many European general estates and representative assemblies, and the most renowned discussion signaled the start of the French Revolution. As we remember, this was not a problem of western Europe alone; Russian peasants in 1812 and 1855 were hard to persuade that a situation of dire necessity was on their agenda and that they should contribute their efforts and revenues to the war of their sovereign. As we see, Peter's propaganda may have been successful at Poltava but hardly penetrated the minds of the masses of his subjects elsewhere. The majority of the population remained unaware of the common good of the fatherland even a century later.

This imposition of the fiction of the common good that effectively serves the interests of the dominant classes (who thus manage to represent their concerns as universal) is a classic point of the Marxist critique of the state.[89] A newer version of such a critique has been proposed by Pierre Bourdieu, who is more interested in demonstrating the "how" of the imposition of the fiction of the common good rather than answering why it was imposed. Bourdieu discerns many pragmatic changes that this imposition entailed.[90]

For example, Peter the Great understood very well that requesting universal service to the fatherland helped in the extraction of taxes and accumulation of scarce resources. A standing army constantly needs provisions, which—as Peter's father was quick to discover—required either procuring supplies through a special apparatus (hence the development of the resources of the Secret Chancery in seventeenth-century Russia) or tax contributions from all. Peter chose the second path, stopped taxing the recalcitrant and elusive unit called the household and instead collected the famous soul tax, imposing the tax yoke on

each individual, now obliged to serve the fatherland. Contributing to the fatherland's welfare seemed more justified than merely financing the czar's military
entertainment.[91] In western Europe also the first centralized tax collection de-
vices looked rather unfounded to the populace until the imposition of the fiction
of the common good. Bourdieu writes: "it is only progressively that we come to
conceive of the taxes as a necessary tribute to the needs of a recipient that transcends the king, that is, the 'fictive body' that is the state."[92] Concomitant to the
imposition of the fiction of the common good, king's levies and patrimonial re-
distribution in the form of gifts and sovereign largesse (which partly legitimated
the levying of patrimonial taxes) were reformed to conform to the newly professed image of a bureaucratic spending of "public expenditures" that made universal taxes tolerable and even "natural."

Creating a feeling of commonality among the subjects of the same sovereign was another matter. Wars and joint taxation fuse populations, of course,
but only to a certain extent. Imposing uniform classifications, developing a
common literary language and teaching "national culture," particularly in the
form of common literature, after the installation of a universal secondary
school system is most decisive for the naturalization of the idea of the state
as a representative and servant of the common good.

Holding that "the state" is a fictitious agent and that only individuals act,
Bourdieu posits a question about what groups of individuals in particular
might be interested in advancing this fiction of the acting state that provided
foundations for our puzzling but most widespread contemporary use of the
word "state." In the case of France, his conclusion is quite straightforward: in
the early modern era, the juridical profession profited most from advancing
the fiction of the common good and public service.[93] The centralization of
courts in early modern France through the royal appeal procedure created the
permanent local bodies of lawyers, Parlements. Their jurists, by explaining
the rule of French monarchs in terms of the common good, also justified their
own special position in the system of upholding justice for the common good.
This appearance of "state nobility" in France is likely to have coincided with
the appearance of the academic title that allowed its holders to present themselves as objective experts, examples of "disinterested devotion to the general
interest."[94] Altogether, the jurists had an interest in giving a universal form to
the expression of their vested interests, in elaborating a theory of public service and of public order, and thus in working to autonomize the *reason of
state* from dynastic reason, from "the house of the king," and to invent
thereby the "res publica" and later the republic as an instance transcendent to
the agents (the king included) who are its temporary incarnations.[95]

The appearance of the doctrine of the reason of state concomitantly with
the advent of the fiction of the common good may explain some other uses of

this fiction. This doctrine tells us that actions in the interest of the state are not subject to standard human morality used in private interactions—the Judeo-Christian Ten Commandments, for example—and princes are sometimes obliged in the interest of their states to commit what would be considered heinous crimes in private life. Machiavelli is generally taken to epitomize this doctrine, though the term *ragione dello stato* appeared before his writings; it became the subject of the special treatise by Botero in 1584, well after Machiavelli's death. By advising a prince to use all measures to *mantenere lo stato*, if one understands *lo stato* as the modern state, as a suprapersonal entity established for the common good of all, Machiavelli is said to have ushered us into the world of specifically political rationality.[96]

Clearly, acts justified by the doctrine of reason of state would be considered inhuman if they were done to attain private goals. By instituting a fiction of the common good, however, the servants of the state might commit atrocities (now made acceptable) while serving this fiction. Furthermore, some of them would decry the reminders of the moral unacceptability of such behavior heretofore, justifying their actions now by the "morality of responsibility," to use a Weberian term. Indeed, Weber in his famous lecture "Politics as a Vocation" juxtaposed the "morality of responsibility"—that without much ado completely absolves the statesman from all guilt for the use of his or her discretion in employing violence and other dubious means in attaining state goals—with the "morality of ultimate ends," this reminder from the old days when reprehensible means, even if used, were deemed reprehensible.[97] Modern statesmen frequently come to rely on the first morality only, forgetting about the second and the fact that Weber called for the necessity of the combination of both in political life. The eclipse of the morality of ultimate ends and the rise of the morality of responsibility was not an easy task to accomplish, however. Meinecke noted that on the subject of reason of state there are unstudied "catacombs . . . of forgotten literature by mediocrities."[98] Indeed, it required a constant drill of repeating the same doctrine over and over again (and with such a prolonged effort that even flocks of the most mediocre authors could manage to jump on the bandwagon) to finally make early modern Europe abandon the heretofore predominant discourse of "thou shalt not kill" and sanction some people to kill others freely and easily in the rationally defined "interests of all."

Bourdieu is frequently criticized for having universalized a French experience that makes his theories hardly applicable to other cultures. For example, the US obviously did not have the same *noblesse de robe* or centralized administration of justice. But the Russian case fits his theory rather well. The first antecedents of the modern bureaucratic apparatus formed under Czar Alexei Mikhailovich coincide with the first timid attempts at assertions of working for the common good, as in the aforementioned Ordyn-Nashchokin case.[99] The decisive installation of the fiction of the common good happens against the background of unprecedented growth and rationalization of the czar's bureaucracy. Peter replaced the chaotic system of overlapping chanceries that he inherited with a clearly delineated structure of eleven collegia (ministries) to supervise all of the affairs of the state. His first main innovation, however, was the creation of the Senate in 1711—initially an ad hoc body that supervised the czar's affairs in his absence during yet another military campaign. In 1717 the Senate was reformed to become a standing high government, in 1718–1722 collegia were established and attached to it. People recruited to staff these new bodies rarely came from the old ranks of patrimonial chanceries, but were newcomers from all estates, frequently sent by Peter to be educated abroad. Peter examined the returning students himself before appointing them to posts in his governmental apparatus. As if according to Bourdieu's theory, in 1724 an Academy of Sciences was established, which started providing scholars with titles that certified the disinterested pursuit of truth, and thus allowed them to be servants of the state. Many of these new state officials and certified experts became ardent proponents of the idea of the common good.[100]

Thus, the state officials and objective scientists, certified in their objectivity by this state, form a happy symbiosis. Only a few political and social scientists manage to escape the alluring charm of the fiction of the common good. But this charm does not seduce all. A long tradition of disputing the right of some to define the common good for all may be drawn from at least the anti-Federalists' responses to *The Federalist Papers* in the US to different versions of nineteenth- and twentieth-century critiques of liberal democracy that tried to reveal vested group interests behind the facade of the state allegedly serving the common good.

Let me give some recent examples of similar criticisms that have eschewed surrendering to state mystique, but also added something more to a rather hackneyed search for the hidden vested group interest. In his famous article on state formation as organized crime, which succinctly summarized the thesis of a series of his works, sociologist Charles Tilly speaks of the state as a centralized and differentiated organization of officials that more or less effectively controls the production of a protection racket in a given territory.[101] However, he remarks that these officials do not offer their commodity in a free market of protection services—a mistaken idea, entertained by Frederick Lane, Tilly's predecessor in thinking along these lines—rather, the imposition or maintenance of the state has the character of a forced sale. In the language of institutional economics, this means that following this sale, protection acquires the character of a "public good," that is, a shared utility like clear water or clean air. Tilly, however, stops short of examining how organized officials first managed to force this sale of protection services on all people in a given realm, and how they then managed to maintain the smooth functioning of this forced sale through a specific claim—that, first, "safety" was a common good, and second, that the violence of some was waged in the interest of all—which finally was accepted by the whole population of this realm.

In another piece of recent sociological research, Edward Laumann and David Knoke were surprised by the existence of specific independent interests of modern US state bureaucracy.[102] They have closely followed the formation of state policy in the 1970s and early 1980s in two departments of the US federal government—food administration and energy. The authors have come to the conclusion that in the majority of studied cases of policy formation, governmental offices are not neutral umpires, but active promoters of their own agenda. They do not necessarily serve some external interests, rather they have interests of their own such as survival, adaptation, growth, and control of the environment. This makes governmental officials depend on this environment which consists of a multitude of other actors, public and private—other offices of the US government, major private corporations, trade unions, professional associations, well-entrenched interest groups, and so on. Hence when a certain new policy is adopted or the old one amended— say, on the level of carbon dioxide in exhaust fumes—a complex set of negotiations with all of these actors occurs, because in any case many of them have the resources to press their viewpoint.

Given the frequent transfer of officers between the public and private organizations involved, it is the network of well-acquainted individuals representing relevant organizations that is the primary battlefield for adopting governmental decisions. The authors conclude: "the state is not a unitary actor, but a complex entity spanning multiple policy domains, comprising both governmental organizations and those core private sector participants whose interests must be taken into account. . . . Intimate consulting and lobbying relationships, frequent employment interchanges and open communication channels between government and interest groups creates the inseparably intertwined institutions that constitute the modern state." Of course, it is a certain governmental official who ultimately has to proclaim a decision, binding for all, but this decision is formed in myriad exchanges within the network, split into shifting coalitions forged by cleavages following contingent particular events.[103]

Bourdieu's research team has discovered similar processes at play in state policy formation in contemporary France. At least, in the case of state policy in the housing sector, researchers did not find the state "a well-defined, clearly bounded and unitary reality which stands in a relation of externality with outside forces that are themselves clearly identified and defined."[104] As a rule, certain state commissions or bureaus entrusted to adopt a policy become a field for the clash of public (i.e., of state ministries, their sections, *grand corps*—the professional association of French civil servants—and so on) and private actors (banks, construction firms, architectural bureaus, and the like). The summary influence of this configuration of interests is far from clear in the beginning of the process of formulating any given "state policy." Conclusions of Bourdieu's research team are: "the notion of 'the state' makes sense only as a convenient stenographic label—but for that matter, a very dangerous one—for these spaces of objective relations of power . . . that can take the form of more or less stable networks (of alliance, cooperation, clientelism, mutual service, etc.) and which manifest themselves in phenomenally diverse interactions ranging from open conflict to more or less hidden collusion."[105] One should note that this picture is not a vision of established interest groups clashing for control of the state machinery, but rather a complex alignment and realignment of shifting forces, produced by mobilization aimed to address particular issues and then disbanded after the event, that together establish and transgress the boundaries of the state.

Another recent theorization of the state, which also depicts it as a convenient but misleading shorthand given to a complex situation, as "no more than a composite reality and a mythicized abstraction"[106] of polyvalent and diverse relations of force comes in the work of Timothy Mitchell. He analyzed the obvious difficulty of the proponents of two main schools of studying the state—the "political system" theorists such as David Easton and Gabriel Almond and those such as Theda Skocpol who assert relative state autonomy—in delineating the boundary between the state and society. The failure to do so, in Mitchell's opinion, is not a small lamentable obstacle to the final success of empirically studying the state, rather it is an indicator that "the state-society divide is not a simple border between two free-standing objects or domains, but a complex distinction internal to these realms of practice," a boundary constantly subject to change depending on the political situation.[107]

As an example, he cites the Aramco case, when the 1940s royalty increase for the exploration of oil resources of Saudi Arabia from 12 to 50% of profits could not be accommodated by the US oil companies that were part of the Aramco consortium. Instead of raising the price of oil on the US market or cutting down their profits, the corporations managed to persuade the federal government to consider their increased payment to the sheiks a sort of direct foreign tax and thus were exempted from the equivalent amount of taxes paid to the US federal budget. Drawing a distinction between allegedly private oil companies (who were nevertheless powerful enough to be able to directly influence the federal government's decisions) and "the state" allowed a political decision to support conservative regimes in the Middle East at taxpayers' expense to be cast as a matter of private corporate policy not subject to public discussion. Mitchell concludes: "We must take such distinctions not as a boundary between two discrete entities but as a line drawn internally, within the network of institutional mechanisms through which a social and political order is maintained."[108] The task then would be to study the political processes through which this uncertain yet powerful distinction between state and society is produced.

The overall picture presented by these sociologists who do not uphold the fiction of the state as striving for the common good is rather disheartening. Networks of individuals fight over or negotiate access to a general power to rule others by means of legislation or administrative regulation. The outcome of this clash or collusion is then dubbed "public policy to further the common good." Of course, civil servants who finally announce and then enact these policies, far from being representatives of any vested interest (as primitive Marxism would have us believe), might have their own interest in furthering their position as rulers and announcers of state policy. Among people staffing governmental offices, there is even a specific interest in appearing disinterested, a behavior that is highly rewarded not by economic gains but by symbolic capital—the high esteem of a given official among other officials and the public.[109] This symbolic capital may eventually be converted into economic capital or, if reconversion of capital is not what an individual official is looking for, it may eventually allow him or her to gain an even higher office with more power to rule the lives of other individuals.

Why then do the ruled, who clearly perceive the individual interests of given bureaucrats in everyday interaction with them—including an interest in being disinterested—accept their rule when it appears as a rule of some entity called "the state"? There are two sorts of responses to this question, best exemplified by the positions of Mitchell and Bourdieu. First, Mitchell would tell us that in ordinary life people refer to many examples of uniform, regular, and orderly conduct of people designated as state or civil servants as obvious instances of state action. We encounter many individuals in the same uniforms staffing similarly named offices, soldiers who march in a recognizable standard manner, bureaucrats who are supposed to act uniformly in processing incoming requests as if they were automatons of a paragraph, in Weber's phrase, and so on. These sequences of disciplined and orderly action create a shared perception of the existence of some abstract entity that stands outside all of these instances and guides them. "Order and precision of such processes created the effect of an apparatus apart from the men themselves, whose 'structure' orders, contains and controls them."[110] The ordered quality of the modern world makes one habitually look for an agent, for the source of this order, which is then found in the abstraction of the state. This sounds plausible as an explanation, but how did this shared perception come about? How do certain people get designated and accepted as soldiers, state officials, or civil servants and thus get endowed with the capacity to rule the behavior of others?

Here Bourdeiu might help us with the answer. He thinks that mass acceptance of the rulers happens at the level beyond intentional agreement, at the level of "doxic submission." This acceptance is not a consent, open or tacit, given by a citizen to a legitimate government in a situation of original social contract. Rather, it is an acceptance of our everyday life and, with it, of those state-produced categories that structure our everyday life, like descriptions of professions and skills, academic titles and names of scientific disciplines, judicial classifications of actions and the classification of memorable historical events. People overlook the constructed character of the social universe, since they are born into a world already structured, say, according to the principle of the legal and symbolic importance of a nuclear family (rather than of extended kin), and they ignore the fact that at a certain point in time there was a government decision to take the nuclear family rather than extended kin as a basis for legal classifications. A contingent historical choice, certified by "the state," provided a category with the help of which we now construct our normal everyday reality.[111]

Of course, people who create these state classifications, adopted as universal in the name of the common good, only impose their individual decisions (or the preference of a decision-making network) on the entire population. But their action is seen as the work of universal importance, since once imposed on all subjects of the state, these categories are used by all subjects to interpret their everyday reality. In short, these categories become universal, because everybody willy-nilly uses them, and not because these categories reflect the interest of all people concerned. Individuals who produce these categories imposed on all are then seen as servicing a reality common for all—and become intuitively treated as representatives of a thus conceived, and hence misconceived, universal interest. We uncritically assume that in the final account state officials work for the common good, since we are commonly obliged to inhabit the symbolic universe of goods produced by them.[112]

Bourdieu traces this state power to define what is real back to the power of authoritative nomination that belonged to a medieval sovereign.[113] Initially, kings could issue definitions of statutory honor and invent new nobility titles. They also possessed the power of judicial verdict—the ultimate definition of social reality that is hardly contestable in many societies. With the proliferation of an army of state experts these functions were diversified and delegated by the sovereign. We now have special individuals who in the name of the common good register our births and marital status, bestow and confirm honors and educational degrees, issue legitimate medical and professional definitions of specialized statuses (for example, recognizing people as invalids, veterans, plumbers, doctors), and so on. At the foundation of all of these acts of classification, certification, or definition of legitimate reality lies the power to institute, the power of performative naming.[114] "The real source of the magic of performative utterances," according to Bourdieu, "lies in the mystery of the ministry, i.e. the delegation, by virtue of which an individual— king, priest or spokesperson—is mandated to speak and act on behalf of the group, thus constituted in him and by him."[115] The scepter of kings and czars came as a symbol of speech that gives a definition of reality; it developed from the *skeptron* of ancient Greeks who passed it from one to another during group discussions to mark authoritative speech.

V. MYSTERIOUS DELEGATION

Here we finally approach the mystery at the core of contemporary usage: why do we speak about the state as acting when we know that only individuals act? This usage, as it turns out, is linked to the residues of mystical doctrines that underlie the process that institutes public authority.

Historians have shown that the modern concept of political delegation— which rests on a conception of a group as a fictive entity that can be represented by one physical person or a number of them—has its origins in two medieval sources, scholastic interpretations of Roman law and the medieval concept of kingship. After the blending of the theory of corporate representation coming from the Roman law with the Christian conception of a mystical union in the body of Jesus, a notion of the "mysteries of the state" became possible, as Kantorowicz shows, quoting James I on this matter.[116] Hanna Pitkin tried to sum up the main thesis of mystical embodiment theories thus: "the king is not merely the head of the national body, not merely the owner of the entire realm, but he *is* the crown, the realm, the nation." This idea, however, "goes beyond either representation or symbolization as we now conceive them and involves a mystic unity which 'theoretical analysis can hardly divide'."[117] English lawyers of the Tudor era thus restated it for political purposes: the king has two bodies, one natural and subject to illnesses and eventual death, another political and immortal. As Plowden wrote: "But his Body politic is a body that cannot be seen or handled, consisting of Policy and Government, and constituted for the direction of People and Management of Public Weal."[118] Initially the lawyers used the metaphor of the phoenix which was very convenient: with every death of the natural body of yet another king, the same body politic was reborn again. Later the usage habituated, and Henry the VIII could say: "At no time do we stand so highly in our estate royal as in the times of Parliament, wherein we as head and you as members are conjoined and knit together in one body politic."[119]

Christian mysticism lying at the foundation of the medieval and early modern concept of kingship allows one to understand what invisible essences might have been available to the mind's eye of a faithful king's subject when she or he was looking at the gathering of King and Parliament. Perhaps, indeed, in this regime of truth that established true statements through exegesis from the testimony of a few authoritative texts, an individual could perceive with inner vision the mystical body of the nation that expressed itself through the mouth of the King and acted through his sovereign orders.[120] Altogether, speaking of "the state" as an active agent immanently made sense—it was an immediate reality, the *ens realissimum* for inner vision trained on direct perception of the mysteries of the sacred texts.

It was Hobbes who secularized this vision:

> A Common-wealth is said to be Instituted, when a Multitude of men do Agree, and Covenant, every one, with every one, that to whatsoever Man, or Assembly of Men, shall be given by the major part, the Right to Present the Person of them all, (that is to say, to be their Representative;) every one . . . shall Authorize all the Actions and Judgments of that Man, or Assembly of men, in the same manner, as if they were his own.[121]

The mystical body is reinterpreted in this formulation as being a result of free covenant, which makes it susceptible to future puzzling difficulties. Hobbes still retains elements of the doctrine of mystical embodiment, that is, those stemming from Christian mysticism—even if these elements are preserved in a secularized form. For example, describing Leviathan, Hobbes implies that Sovereignty is not in the famous picture on the title page of the book, it is unseen, since it is "an Artificiall Soul, as giving life and motion to the whole body."[122] This is yet another restatement of medieval platitudes—for example, as Post has noted, in the doctrine of the king's two bodies "prince was the soul, the *lex animata* and the *vigor instituiae* and *pater legum*."[123] However, this restatement of medieval images allows Hobbes to formulate the doctrine of the state as distinct from both the rulers and the ruled. The essence of the state—sovereignty—resides in the invisible soul, distinct from the figure of the ruler or the body of the ruled.

This invisibility to empirical vision, but openness to an inner sight, enlightened by religious insight, provides specific difficulties for an atheist like Hobbes. In the picture that adorns the title page of *Leviathan* we indeed see an Artificiall Man constructed of many minuscule subjects. Leviathan's head does not consist of men, only his body. This, of course, is reminiscent of the words of Henry VIII: "you as members and we as head are knit together in one body politic." The head in the picture is bigger than any other individual, thus perhaps pictorially representing the majesty of the king's natural person; the mouth also belongs to him: only through the king does the body politic speak. Our contemporary can thus see the natural head of the king, the natural bodies of his subjects, and see the body politic that is the head attached to the body that is formed of subjects. However, this contemporary reader cannot see what animates this artificial man (which is the State, as Hobbes says): it is the invisible soul. Mystical unity cannot be registered by the empirical gaze of our contemporary.

Looking at the picture, one can only say that Leviathan is a nice metaphor: people united in the state can be perceived as the most powerful creature. However, even in the picture, they are all singular individuals. Thus, the real problem of a modern state, in Bourdieu's words, is that it functions not as a metaphor, but rather as a metonymy: one person (or a selected group) from the multitude takes the function of speaking for all and acting for the good of all.[124] A part is assigned a function to represent the whole multitude—in order to make the universal interest, allegedly common to all, manifest. As we have seen, this frequently leads to the imposition of the particular interest in the guise of universal interpretations of the common good. And this universalization mechanism seems to be built into the mechanism of representation or delegation as such.

However, this is not inescapable: it only seems that next to particulars there should exist a universal, embodied as a separate entity. As medieval nominalists asserted, the universal concepts exist as *universalia in re*, as combinations or configurations of particulars; it is a mistake to grant them separate existence *next to* particulars. For nominalists, the body of Christ is one such example: Christians are joined in it directly, and do not need a specific separate entity to represent this unity in Christ. Thus, this vision of universals was alien to a conception of the Christian church as embodied in the visible Pope and the kingdom as embodied in the figure of the Prince. Accordingly, William of Ockham insisted that each Christian had to be consulted on matters of faith in the general council of the church.[125] No one could assume to represent the universal interest of the Church, only the gathering of all of its members could do so.

Interestingly enough, in solving today's similar problems, such nominalism could lead us away from the pitfalls of the fiction of the common good that is imposed by those who allegedly represent the common interest on others who are left with scarcely anything else than to ignore it rather than to accept it.

NOTES

1. Joseph R. Strayer, *On the Medieval Origins of the Modern State* (Princeton: Princeton University Press, 1970), 5.

2. Max Weber, *Gesammelte Aufsätze zur Wissenschaftslehre* (Tübingen: Mohr, 1968), 200.

3. Alf Ross, "On the Concepts 'State' and 'State Organs' in Constitutional Law," *Scandinavian Studies in Law* 5 (1960), 123–24.

4. Ross, "On the Concepts 'State' and 'State Organs'," 124–25.

5. This nice summary of Hexter's thesis occurs in Hanna Pitkin, *Wittgenstein and Justice: On the Significance of Ludwig Wittgenstein for Social and Political Thought* (Berkeley: University of California Press, 1972), 311.

6. Jack H. Hexter, *The Vision of Politics on the Eve of the Reformation: More, Machiavelli, and Seyssel* (New York: Basic Books, 1973), 156, 159.

7. Machiavelli, *The Prince*, trans. Harvey C. Mansfield, Jr. (Chicago: University of Chicago Press, 1985), 5.

8. Also see Harvey Mansfield, "On the Impersonality of the Modern State: A Comment on Machiavelli's Use of *Stato*," *American Political Science Review* 77 (1983), 849–57. Quentin Skinner disagrees with Hexter: some instances of ambiguous usage in Machiavelli provided an opportunity to later think of *lo stato* as an apparatus of government that may initiate actions. By the middle of the seventeenth century almost all western European authors shared this vision. Of course, the conceptual slide is just beginning in Machiavelli's time, insists Skinner, but it would be wrong to overlook the first leanings in this direction. (Skinner, "The State," in *Political Innovation and Conceptual Change*, ed. T. Ball, J. Farr, and R. Hanson [Cambridge, Eng.: Cambridge University Press, 1989], esp. 164–67.)

9. Skinner, "The State." This article belongs to a tradition of thought exemplified also by writings of Dowdall and Hexter—people who closely examine the conditions of appearance of the concept, which, in their opinion, are closely tied to the appearance of the designated phenomenon itself. The debate on whether the phenomenon of the (political) state existed even before the concept appeared is for readers to adjudicate themselves. For example, Ernst Kantorowicz and Gaines Post have ruled in favor of this phenomenon's existence in medieval Europe. Kantorowicz thus found the antecedents of the modern concept of the state in Aquinas (Kantorowicz, *The King's Two Bodies* [Princeton: Princeton University Press, 1957], 271). In another version of the argument, Post asserts that even if the Latin term *status* did not apply to what we could consider to be "states" in medieval Europe, the term *regnum* (which was frequently defined as a corporate body) did, and thus was used to designate these states *avant la lettre* (Post, *Studies in Medieval Legal Thought* [Princeton: Princeton University Press, 1964], viii). Andrew Vincent in his overview supports the Dowdall-Hexter-Skinner vision (Vincent, *Theories of the State* [Oxford: Blackwell, 1987], 17).

10. Harold C. Dowdall, *The Word "State"* (London: Stevens and Sons, 1923), 4.

11. Skinner, "The State," 91.

12. Dowdall, *The Word "State,"* 5.

13. Quoted in Skinner, "The State," 92.

14. Post, *Studies in Medieval Legal Thought*, 12–13.

15. *Oxford English Dictionary*, s.v. "state," section #28.

16. Advice books are "popular" literature only in relation to the glosses and treatises of medieval legists that had a very circumscribed circulation. Thus, Latin expressions that Post and Kantorowicz found in sparse medieval juridical treatises which may have tried to first articulate the modern concept of the state were hardly consequential—they are ignored in the abundant mirror-of-princes literature, which is almost exclusively concerned with the domination of the prince and the condition of his domain. See Skinner, "The State," 96.

17. Skinner, "The State," 99. Dowdall, *The Word "State,"* 28, even tried to define this regime, based on varied sources, but tracing it ultimately to the definition contained in the first sentence: *lo stato* is a *dominio* that exercises *imperio* over people.

18. Skinner, "The State," 100.

19. Skinner, "The State," 101.

20. Skinner, "The State," 102, 104. Skinner's best case for the thesis that the new meaning of state machinery, independent from the person of the ruler, is already present in Machiavelli refers to an excerpt in *Discorsi,* book I, ch. 18: "In Rome there was a constitution regulating government, or rather its form of government (*e ordine del governo or vero dello stato)*, and then laws enabling the magistrates to keep the citizens in order." Machiavelli, *The Discourses*, ed. B. Crick (London: Penguin, 1983), 160; Italian original quoted in Skinner, "The State," 110.

21. Skinner, "The State," 106, 109.

22. Skinner, "The State," 119.

23. *Oxford English Dictionary*, s.v. "state," section #29a.

24. *De Cive*, quoted in Skinner, "The State," 119.

25. Hobbes, *Leviathan*, ed. C. B. Macpherson (London: Penguin, 1985), 81.

26. Hobbes, *Leviathan*, 75.

27. I am greatly indebted to Claudio Ingerflom who first brought my attention to the topic and whose remarkable article (Ingerflom, "Oublier l'état pour comprendre la Russie?" *Revue des études slaves* 66 [1993], 125–134) provides the only systematic (if brief) account of the development of the Russian equivalents of the English term "state." In his analysis of Russian usage in the fourteenth to seventeenth centuries he primarily relies on Andras Zoltan, *Iz istorii russkoi leksiki* [From the History of Russian Lexics] (Budapest: Eotvos Lorand University, 1987), a text in Russian but printed in Hungary, thus making it now largely unavailable to both English and Russian-speaking audiences. This text is based on Zoltan's dissertation defended in Moscow in 1984, the findings of which were also published in an abridged form as Andras Zoltan, "K predistorii russkogo *gosudar'"* [Towards the Prehistory of the Russian Term *Gosudar'*] *Studia Slavica Academiae Scientarum Hungaricae* 29 (1983), 71–109. I use the 1983 text more extensively since other readers can consult it, and refer to Zoltan's 1987 text, courteously supplied to me by the author, for details omitted in 1983. For earlier attempts at lexicographical description see G. Stoeckl, "Die Begriffe Reich, Herrschaft und Staat bei den orthodoxen Slaven," *Saeculum* 5 (1954), 104–118, and Wladimir Vodoff, "Remarques sur la valeur du terme 'tsar' appliqué au princes russes avant le milieu du XV siecle," *Oxford Slavonic Papers* 11 (1978), 1–41.

My general argument on eighteenth-century usage closely follows the study of Liudmila Chernaia, "Ot idei 'sluzheniia gosudariu' k idee 'sluzheniia otechestvu' v russkoi obshchestvennoi mysli vtoroi poloviny XVII—nachala XVIII v." [From the Idea of Serving the Czar to the Idea of Serving the Fatherland in Russian Social Thought of the Second Half of the Seventeenth—Beginning of the Eighteenth Centuries], in *Obshchestvennaia mysl': issledovaniia i publikatsii, vypusk 1*, ed. A. L. Andreev and K. Kh. Delokarov (Moscow: Nauka, 1989).

28. Richard Pipes, *Russia under the Old Regime* (New York: Scribner, 1974), 78.

29. In this family of words, Pipes stresses the Indo-European root **ghes*, meaning "to strike" that has led to such Latin term as *hostis* (enemy), and become part of the household vocabulary of many European languages through such words as "guest" and "host" in English (Pipes, *Russia*, 77). Etymological dictionaries of the Russian language note two ancient Slavonic roots in the word *gospod'*, *gost'* and *pod'*, with the first one meaning "hospitable owner" and the second stemming from Indo-European **potis*—"master, head of the household, male spouse." Russian *gospod'* may be related to Latin *hospes*, in genitive—*hospitis*, "hospitable master, hosting foreigners," coming from the blend of the same two Indo-European roots, with an original form **hostipotis*. (Pavel Chernykh, *Istoriko-etimologicheskii slovar' sovremennnogo russkogo iazyka* [Moscow: Russkii iazyk, 1994], I, 209; and Max Fasmer, *Etimologicheskii slovar' russkogo iazyka* [Moscow: Progress, 1986], I, 446.)

30. Zoltan, "K predistorii russkogo *gosudar'*," 72.

31. Zoltan, "K predistorii russkogo *gosudar'*," 76.

32. Zoltan, "K predistorii russkogo *gosudar'*," 78.

33. Ingerflom, "Oublier l'état?" 127. Zoltan disputes the authenticity of the 1427 epistle and dates the first Muscovite document using *gospodar'* as of 1434 (Zoltan, "K predistorii russkogo *gosudar'*," 93). The most exhaustive, though not the most accurate, dictionary of ancient Russian, however, gives the first example in 1461 only: *Gospodin i gospodar' velikii kniaz' Vasilii Vasilievich* (Stepan Barkhudarov, ed., *Slovar' russkogo iazyka XI–XVII vv.* [Moscow: Nauka, 1975–1992], article on *gospodar'*).

34. See the overview of reasons in Zoltan, "K predistorii russkogo *gosudar'*," 71. Many scholars think this happened purely for phonetic reasons. Others attribute it to the fact that *gosudar'* could be related in popular consciousness to *sud*, "court," with the princely title correspondingly interpreted as "the supreme judge." Given the fact that both terms were frequently written with an overword tilde, in the approximate form of *g~sdr'*, it is hard to establish the exact date of *gosudar'* becoming the dominant form—perhaps not earlier than the sixteenth century. (Chernykh, *Istoriko-etimologicheskii slovar'*, I, 210.) The first registered full spelling of *gosudar'* in a written source dates from 1645 only (Zoltan, "K predistorii russkogo *gosudar'*," 105.) *Gospodar'* was in use until the nineteenth century, with three meanings in the eighteenth, according to the latest dictionary of that time: 1) *gosudar'*; 2) owner of the household used in Southern Russia; 3) official title of a king of Moldavia. (Iurii Sorokin, ed., *Slovar' russkogo iazyka XVIII veka* [Leningrad: Nauka, 1987], V, 190.)

35. See. e.g., Anna Khoroshkevich, "Iz istorii velikokniazheskoi titulatury v kontse XIV–kontse XV vv." [From the History of the Titles of Great Princes in the

End of the Fourteenth—Beginning of the Fifteenth Centuries] in *Russkoe tsentralizovannoe gosudarstvo: obrazovanie i evoliutsiia, XV–XVIII vv.*, ed. V. T. Pashuto (Moscow: AN SSSR, 1980), 29. Pipes (*Russia*, 65), however, holds that the main distinction is between *gospodin*, a term of public law in the fifteenth century meaning "ruler over free people," and *gosudar'*, a term of private law, meaning at that time "owner of land and serfs, *dominus*." Then it seems very significant that the feudal republic of Novgorod called itself "Gospodin velikii Novgorod" which implied rule of the free people, while Muscovite princes adopted the title *gosudar'* in order to describe their subjects as serfs. This account overlooks many difficulties with fitting details into this neat distinction. For example, Novgorod also called itself by both titles—*Gospodin gosudar'*—in 1469 (see Barkhudarov, *Slovar' russkogo iazyka XI–XVII vv*, article on *gospodin*). Also, the word *gospodin* itself, as we know, came from the word *gospoda*—a feudal household with land and serfs—while *gospoda* was also a term used in public life of the republic of Novgorod, and so on.

36. The title of "czar" is an abbreviated and Russified "Caesar," a Byzantine title which was first officially adopted by Ivan IV with all the appropriate theological connotations. *Gosudar'* and czar coexisted since then as parts of the official title of the sovereign. Also, the Russian empire appeared officially only when Peter the Great was proclaimed emperor—in Russian, *imperator*—in 1721.

37. Chernaia, "Ot idei 'sluzheniia gosudariu'," 30.

38. Original chronicle text quoted in Lev Cherepnin, *Obrazovanie russkogo tsentralizovannogo gosudarstva v XIV–XV v.* [Formation of the Russian Centralized State in the Fourteenth–Fifteenth Centuries] (Moscow: Sotsekgiz, 1960), 872, my translation. Cf. also Pipes, *Russia*, 82, for his version.

39. See this point, central for his argument, elaborated in Pipes, *Russia*, 77–78.

40. In theory, this rule was never completely unbridled and monarchs were subject to God's sanction. The vocation of the czar was conceived not as a right, but as a duty, service to God that was limited by canon law and custom. As the famous Russian historian Kliuchevsky asserted, the czar had extensive power over individuals, but not over the way of life. (*Razvitie russkogo prava v XV—pervoi polovine XVII vv.*, ed. Vladik Nersesiants [Development of Russian Law, Fifteenth–First Half of the Sixteenth Centuries] [Moscow: Nauka, 1986], 85–87.) Cf. also: "the people, renouncing its will, transfers power not to the monarch but entrusts itself to the divine will, with the czar just being God's chosen one. The czar, for his part, renounces his personal will as well and conducts his service as a work of divine obedience." (Vladimir Karpets, "Nekotorye cherty gosudarstvennosti i gosudarstvennoi ideologii Moskovskoi Rusi: Ideia verkhovnoi vlasti" [Some Aspects of Statehood and State Ideology in Muscovy: The Idea of the Supreme Authority] in *Razvitie prava i politiko-pravovoi mysli v Moskovskom gosudarstve*, ed. Z. M. Chernilovskii [Moscow: VIuZI, 1985], 21.)

41. The dictionary of ancient Russian gives the earliest meaning of *gosudarstvo* as territory in 1431, supported by a mistaken interpretation of Photii's epistle. Pavel Chernykh in his *Ocherk russkoi istoricheskoi leksikologii: drevnerusskii period* [An Outline of Russian Historical Lexicology: Ancient Rus'] (Moscow: MGU, 1956) has shown that this quotation—"bless the prince . . . with his sons and grandsons and *gosudarstvo*"—clearly means regime of domination rather than territory (216). However,

the same epistle of Photii has another relevant passage—"and from other lands, g~sdr'stv, grand duchies, and from Lithuanian land." (Zoltan, *Iz istorii russkoi leksiki,* 38).

42. A west-Slavonic source from Vilno mentioned "the borders of *gosudarstvo*" in 1494, the first time that the connotation of territory unambiguously appeared. Also, Russian transliteration of the Polish term, *panstvo*, was used as a synonym of the Russian word *otchina* (patrimonium) in Russian sources from 1490 on, which implies that Russians were well aware of the Polish usage. (Andras Zoltan, "Polskie 'panstwo' a rosyjskie 'gosudarstvo'," *Zeszyty Naukowe Wydzialu Humanistycznego Uniwersytetu Gdanskiego, Filologia rosyjska* 10 [1982], 112.)

43. Mikhail Krom, "Nauchnaia terminologiia, iazyk epokhi i politicheskie realii XVI v." [Scientific Terminology, Language of the Epoch and Political Reality of the Fifteenth Century] in *Politicheskie instituty i sotsial'nye straty Rossii (XVI—XVIII vv.),* ed. E.A. Antonova *et al.* (Moscow: RGGU, 1998), 66.

44. Zoltan, *Iz istorii russkoi leksiki,* 42.

45. Pipes, *Russia,* 77.

46. Chernaia, "Ot idei 'sluzheniia gosudariu'," 32.

47. Pipes, *Russia,* 67. Exact dates of establishment of certain offices or description of their structure are hard to find, since internal documentation in scrolls was not kept with care and also suffered from frequent fires. Thus from witnesses we know for example that deacon Viskovatyi was ordered to start "ambassadorial service" sometime in 1548–1549, but do not have the written order *prikaz* or *ukaz* founding it, nor are we aware of its early regulations, if there were any. (Sigurd Shmidt, *U istokov rossiiskogo absolutizma* [Origins of Russian Absolutism] [Moscow: Progress, 1996], 448.)

48. Alexander Zaozerskii, *Tsarskaia votchina XVII veka* [Czar's Patrimonium in the Seventeenth Century] (Moscow: Sotsekgiz, 1937), 43.

49. In an ordinance on merchants from 1681 (Marc Raeff, *The Well-ordered Police State: Social and Institutional Change through Law in the Germanies and Russia, 1600–1800* [New Haven: Yale University Press, 1983], 207), though this still might be taken to mean the personal rule of the *gosudar'.*

50. Mikhail Krom, "Politicheskii krizis 30–40kh godov XVI veka" [The Political Crisis of 1530–1540s], *Otechestvennaia Istoriia* 41, no. 5 (1998), 3.

51. Chernaia, "Ot idei 'sluzheniia gosudariu'," 32.

52. Chernaia, "Ot idei 'sluzheniia gosudariu'," 43.

53. Chernaia, "Ot idei 'sluzheniia gosudariu'," 36.

54. Nikolai Pavlenko, *Petr Velikii* [Peter the Great] (Moscow: Mysl', 1990), 485.

55. Feofan Prokopovich, *Istoriia imperatora Petra Velikago* [History of Emperor Peter the Great] (St. Petersburg, 1773), 212. The whole speech might have been invented by Prokopovich for political purposes, but given the fact that he served as a mouthpiece for many Petrine reforms, his usage is representative of the sovereign rhetoric.

56. Vladimir Kolesov, *Mir cheloveka v slove drevnei Rusi* [Human World in the Literature of Ancient Rus'] (Leningrad: LGU, 1986), 246.

57. Mikhail Krom, "Christian Tradition and the Birth of the Concept of Patriotism in Russia," in *The Emancipation of Russian Christianity*, ed. Natalia Pecherskaya (Lewiston: Edwin Mellen Press, 1995), 29–31.

58. Ernst Kantorowicz, *"Pro Patria Mori,"* in his *Selected Studies* (Locust Valley, NY: J. J. Augustin, 1965), 310–13.

59. Krom, "Christian Tradition," 24.

60. Gary Marker, *Soloviev's Peter: Otets otechestva, otsovstva i muzhestva* [Peter in Soloviev's Description: Father of Fatherland, Fatherness and Manliness], Unpublished manuscript, Dept. of History, SUNY Stony Brook, 1999.

61. Pavlenko, *Petr Velikii,* 482.

62. Pavlenko, *Petr Velikii,* 484; *Khrestomatiia po istorii SSSR XVIII v.* [A Collection of Documents on the History of Eighteenth Century Russia], ed. Mikhail Beliavskii and Nikolai Pavlenko (Moscow: Sotsekgiz, 1963), 126, 132.

63. Texts of eighteen popular soldiers' songs from the early eighteenth century most frequently mention "service to the czar" and describe it as a series of daily routines and burdens. *Gosudarstvo* is not mentioned at all, and the officially proclaimed separation between the person of the czar and the body of the state is impossible to find in the texts of these songs. (Olga Ageeva, "K voprosu o patrioticheskom soznanii v Rossii pervoi chetverti XVIII v." [Patriotic Consciousness in Russia in the First Quarter of the Eighteenth Century] in *Mirovospriiatie i samosoznanie russkogo obschestva (XI–XX vv.),* ed. L. N. Pushkarev [Moscow: IRI RAN, 1994], 47.)

64. See Ingerflom, "Oublier l'état?", 129–130, on this general thesis spelled out in detail by the Tartu school. Many readers might have noticed by now that my presentation as a rule ignores the political theology of the Russian czardom. This is done in order to limit the exposition to only exploring parallels with Skinner's thesis. A separate study on how the term *gosudarstvo* fared in theological usage and quasi-religious political doctrines after the seventeenth century is undoubtedly necessary.

65. A theme appearing most distinctly in Beroaldo. See Skinner, "The State," 97.

66. All quotations are from *Panegiricheskaia literatura petrovskogo vremeni* [Panegyrical Literature of the Petrine Epoch], ed. Vladimir Grebeniuk (Moscow: Nauka, 1979), 281, 289, 292.

67. Feofan Prokopovich, *O pravde voli monarshei* (St. Petersburg, 1726), 27.

68. V. Surin, "Lichnost' i gosudarstvo v russkoi literature vtoroi poloviny XVIII v." [The Individual and the State in Russian Literature of the Second Half of the Eighteenth Century], *Sbornik Kharkovskogo istoriko-filologicheskogo obshchestva* XIX (1913), 114.

69. Sorokin, *Slovar' russkogo iazyka XVIII veka,* article on *gosudarstvennyi,* 197, 199.

70. See a detailed analysis and a chapter by chapter comparison between Pufendorf's original and Catherine's adaptation in Vadim Volkov, *The Forms of Public Life,* unpublished revised version of chapter 1 (European University at St. Petersburg, 1997).

71. Joseph L. Black, *Citizens for the Fatherland: Education, Educators, and Pedagogical Ideas in Eighteenth Century Russia.* With a translation of *Book on the Duties of Man and Citizen,* 1783 (New York: Columbia University Press, 1979), 246–247.

72. Sorokin, *Slovar' russkogo iazyka XVIII veka,* article on *gosudarstvo,* 198.

73. Sorokin, *Slovar' russkogo iazyka XVIII veka,* 199.

74. First usage registered in 1649: Barkhudarov, *Slovar' russkogo iazyka XI–XVII vv.*, article on *gosudarstvennyi*.

75. Peter I is usually credited with establishing these and arranging their internal layouts, having clearly separated the governors and the governed in space. See e.g., Raeff, *The Well-ordered Police State*, 203.

76. All examples in this paragraph are from Sorokin, *Slovar' russkogo iazyka XVIII veka,* article on *gosudarstvennyi*, 197–98.

77. Raeff, The *Well-ordered Police State*, 229.

78. A. A. Alekseev, "Istoriia slova *grazhdanin* v XVIII v." [History of the Word "Citizen" in the Eighteenth Century], *Izvestiia AN SSSR, seriia literatury i iazyka* 31, no. 1 (1972), 69.

79. Alekseev, "Istoriia slova *grazhdanin*," 69.

80. Sorokin, *Slovar' russkogo iazyka XVIII veka,* article on *gosudar'*, 200.

81. Quoted in Chernaia, "Ot idei 'sluzheniia gosudariu'," 42–43.

82. For conceptual adventures of Russian terms for society see Vadim Volkov, *The Forms of Public Life*, Ph.D. thesis, Cambridge University, UK, 1995.

83. See Ingerflom, "Oublier l'état?" 132, for relevant examples.

84. Ingerflom, "Oublier l'état?" 132–33.

85. Skinner, "The State," 95.

86. Post, *Studies in Medieval Legal Thought*, 18.

87. Post, *Studies in Medieval Legal Thought*, 19.

88. Skinner, "The State," 103.

89. See a Marxist version of such analysis in Pavlenko, *Petr Velikii,* 497: " 'common good' is a fiction of the eighteenth century that justified the necessity of each subject to fulfill duties imposed on him by the state, according to the estate to which he belonged."

90. Pierre Bourdieu, "Rethinking the State: Genesis and Structure of the Bureaucratic Field," in his book *Practical Reason* (Cambridge: Polity Press, 1998).

91. In his young days, well before setting up the regular Russian army, Peter already formed two "fun regiments" that entertained him by staging mock battles. See e.g. Pavlenko, *Petr Velikii,* 34.

92. Bourdieu, "Rethinking the State," 43.

93. Bourdieu, "Rethinking the State," 48.

94. Pierre Bourdieu, *The State Nobility: Elite Schools in the Field of Power* (Stanford: Stanford University Press, 1996) 377, 380.

95. Bourdieu, "Rethinking the State," 58.

96. This point is best known in Friedrich Meinecke's formulation. See his *Machiavellism* (London: Routledge and Kegan Paul, 1957). As Hexter shows, however, since there is no notion of the body politic in Machiavelli one can hardly find traces of the reason of the state doctrine. *Lo stato* is about tenancy of command over men, and even if Machiavelli immorally supplies advice on the laws of this command he does not justify slaughter in the interest of some higher entity called the state. The closest he comes to stating something like the reason of the state doctrine is his description of the founding of Rome in *Discorsi*, when the assassination of Remus by Romulus is justified by the fact that this had allowed for the institution of a lasting *vivere civile*. Hexter, *The Vision of Politics*, 167.

97. According to Gaines Post (*Studies in Medieval Legal Thought*, 10), a medieval corporation called "the state" could cease being a corporation and become the state—a political union that overpowers all other unions—only if it rejected the preponderance of Christian morality and of the laws of the empire, to which each other corporation was subject at that time. Also see Carl Schmitt's critique of Gierke: the state is a decisive political unity and thus is not subject to *Genossenschaftsrecht* of the Holy Roman empire (Schmitt, *The Concept of the Political* [New Brunswick, N.J.: Rutgers University Press, 1976]).

98. Meinecke, *Machiavellism*, 67.

99. Generally, historians now view Peter's revolution in bureaucracy as having been well prepared by the previously overlooked Western leanings of the bureaucrats during his father's rule. See Natalia Demidova, *Sluzhilaia biurokratiia v Rossii XVII v. i ee rol' v formirovanii absoliutizma* [Servitor Bureaucracy in Seventeenth-Century Russia and Its Role in the Formation of Absolutism] (Moscow: Nauka, 1987).

100. Pavlenko, *Petr Velikii,* 434–474; Evgenii Anisimov, *Gosudarstvennye preobrazovaiia i samoderzhavie Petra Velikogo v pervoi chetverti XVIII veka* [State Reforms and Autocracy of Peter the Great in the First Quarter of the Eighteenth Century] (St. Petersburg: Bulanin, 1997).

101. Charles Tilly, "War Making and State Making as Organized Crime," in *Bringing the State Back In*, ed. P. Evans, D. Rueschemeyer, T. Skocpol (Cambridge: Cambridge University Press, 1976).

102. Edward O. Laumann and David Knoke, *The Organizational State: Social Choice in National Policy Domains* (Madison: University of Wisconsin Press, 1987).

103. Laumann and Knoke, *Organizational State*, 381–86.

104. Pierre Bourdieu and Loic Wacquant, *An Invitation to Reflexive Sociology* (Chicago: University of Chicago Press, 1992), 111.

105. Bourdieu and Wacquant, *Reflexive Sociology*, 112.

106. Michel Foucault, quoted from *The Foucault Effect: Studies in Governmentality*, ed. G. Burchell *et al.* (Chicago: University of Chicago Press, 1991), 103.

107. Timothy Mitchell, "Society, Economy, and the State Effect," in *State/Culture: State Formation after the Cultural Turn*, ed. G. Steinmetz (Ithaca: Cornell University Press, 1999), 83.

108. Mitchell, "Society, Economy, and the State Effect," 77.

109. Pierre Bourdieu, "Is a Disinterested Act Possible?" in his *Practical Reason* (Cambridge: Polity Press, 1998).

110. Mitchell, "Society, Economy, and the State Effect," 89.

111. Bourdieu, "Rethinking the State," 64–74.

112. Only symbolic universes that crumble reveal the contingent character of their construction. The USSR's classification of crimes related to property engendered a category of everyday life known as a "speculator," a person who would buy scarce consumer goods under the counter at one price in a state market, and resell them on the street for a profit. Adoption of this classification of human behavior as "natural" and given—although historically first imposed by the Soviet authorities in the 1930s—did not entail an open consent to Marxist teaching on property, but just involved growing up in a society filled with speculators, "honest laborers" who do not

resell commodities for profit, "shadow dealers" and so on, and habitually using these categories to interpret the events of everyday life. The claim to universality and the illusion that Soviet authorities were serving the common good were gone when the Soviet state lost its monopoly of classification during *perestroika*. The newly visible followers of Friedrich von Hayek would call speculators the best agents of the market who quickly conveyed information on bottlenecks in the economy; imprisoning people for reselling goods at a markup now seemed an absurd if not an absolutely evil act. The legitimacy of state officials as upholders of the common good was shaken in that they were shown to serve one truth among many, rather than serving the only possible common one. Doxic submission requires the extermination of alternative sources of claims for universality.

113. Bourdieu, "Rethinking the State," 50.

114. John Searle has analyzed the logical structure of these utterances of institution: "X will count as Y in context C." However, he ascribes these acts to "collective intentionality," a category that uncritically reflects the mythology of an original contract in a community of equals. To support his point he gives predominantly US examples of acts of institution. (Searle, *The Construction of Social Reality* [New York: Free Press, 1995], 114–120.)

115. Pierre Bourdieu, *Language and Symbolic Power* (Cambridge, Mass.: Harvard University Press, 1991), 75.

116. Ernst Kantorowicz, "Mysteries of the State", in his *Selected Studies*, 382.

117. Hanna Pitkin, *The Concept of Representation* (Berkeley: University of California Press, 1967), 246.

118. Kantorowicz, *The King's Two Bodies*, 7, 9.

119. Post, *Studies in Medieval Legal Thought*, 332.

120. The sovereign thus logically held the power of authoritative nomination—only through him did the mystical body of the realm acquire its voice.

121. Hobbes, *Leviathan*, 228–229.

122. Hobbes, *Leviathan*, 81.

123. Post, *Studies in Medieval Legal Thought*, 355.

124. Bourdieu, *Language and Symbolic Power*, 206.

125. Pitkin, *The Concept of Representation*, 243.

Chapter Two

Civil Society

Following Charles Taylor, one may distinguish between two main traditions of understanding civil society in the West.[1] What he calls the L-stream is a theoretical tradition, with John Locke as a paradigmatic figure that envisions civil society as a pre-political ethical community that delegates certain limited powers to the minimal state. By contrast, the M-stream, taking its name from Montesquieu, sees civil society as a set of associations, or the association, that mediates relations between an individual and the strong state and defends the former from the encroachments of the latter. Let us first sum up and sharpen this distinction proposed by Taylor so that it could serve as an analytical tool for our further exposition.

According to Taylor, the L-stream comprises many other thinkers of the Anglo-American liberal tradition. The central component of reflection on civil society in this tradition comes from Locke's conception of the state of nature rather than from his exposition on "civil society" as such, since he frequently used this term interchangeably with "political society" or "the state," following the usage of his epoch. For L-stream thinkers, it is important that the state of nature in Locke already possesses many features that will be ascribed to "civil society" by his followers when they redefine the term in the XVIII century, in such books as Adam Ferguson's *Essay on the History of Civil Society*, Adam Smith's *Theory of Moral Sentiments* or Tom Paine's *On the Rights of Man*.

In contrast to the pessimistic conceptions of the state of nature, as for example presented by Thomas Hobbes, Locke's theory stresses the peaceful and rich character of human existence in a pre-political condition. People can develop industry, trade, culture and the arts already in the state of nature, and they choose to unite into a political state largely for the reason of some trifling inconveniences of this condition. As a consequence, the state has a fiduciary character: it is entrusted with carrying out the minimal function of eliminating these few

41

inconveniences of human coexistence. If the state expands its powers beyond those functions that were entrusted to it and unjustifiably penetrates the pre-political spheres of life of the community that had founded it, then this trust is revoked and the state is "dissolved," in the famous term of Locke.

Introducing the term "civil society" in its modern understanding, Ferguson and Smith also base themselves on this Lockean vision of peaceful and multi-faceted pre-political life of the community. First, they oppose "civil society" to a "military society" as a non-belligerent community that prefers to use civil rather than military means in attaining its aims and clearly values peaceful trade over armed conquest. Second, in their conception civil society is opposed to bar-baric society that does not know fine manners and is ignorant of the industrial and cultural achievements of contemporary civilization. In short, civil society is the one that partakes in the fruits of civilization. Civilized manners, civil rather than military methods of solving the few existing disputes, and a common pride in the achievements of civilization tie people into a community that exists according to laws of civil life outside the political sphere. The minimal political state emerges only when this civil society calls it into life.

By contrast with this vision of the L-stream, the implicit starting point of the M-stream is the pre-existence of a strong centralized state. Montesquieu, Benjamin Constant and Alexis de Tocqueville centered their concerns on the problem of defending individual liberties against the despotic leanings of the modern state. Accordingly, suggests Taylor, the core concept of the M-stream is *corps intermediaires* that mediate the relations between the individual and the state. For example, Montesquieu envisions traditional privileges of the aristocracy and the clergy, and recognized liberties of cities, guilds and cor-porations as the "mediating bodies" that curtail the despotism of European monarchies. Indeed, the functioning of justice, collection of taxes, even the formation of armies were frequently delegated to the powerful aristocratic families, provincial assemblies and parliaments, city corporations and munic-ipalities. Thus the crown was divested of some of these powers by these bod-ies, the members of which the king frequently could not nominate. Therefore, the relative independence and ancient privileges of these mediating bodies served as a bulwark against the despotism of centralized power.

Tocqueville, who lived after the elimination of many of these intermediary corporate institutions in the wake of the French Revolution, acutely perceived the threat to individual liberties coming from the direction of the centralized state. He thus proposes that the function of defense of individual liberties, that is, the role played by the old *corps intermediaires*, may be assigned to the new associations of free citizens. Apart from defending the individual from the encroachments of the state, these associations are also to become a kind of school of freedom where citizens would learn the civic virtues necessary for the preservation of liberties in an age of what he calls the threat of a democratic despotism.[2]

Hegel finally supplies the first formulation of the opposition of the civil society and the state as such, when he synthesizes the L- and M-streams in his conception. In his understanding, civil society is just a stage in the unfolding of the ethical Idea, a lamentable condition where private interests prevail, and the contradictions of which are finally resolved only with the appearance of the universal state that pursues the general interest. Still, the "corporations" that form part of Hegel's vision of the civil society are pictured rather positively, and may remind the reader of *corps intermediaires*. This ambivalence of Hegel's theory is very important to stress since Antonio Gramsci, whom one might include among renowned thinkers of the M-stream also, revives attention to Hegel's corporations in the XX century. Curiously, he does so within the Marxist tradition of aspiring for the annihilation of the difference between the civil society and the state. Marx himself, of course, considers the presence of association-like corporations in Hegelian theory a residue of the feudal past and thus reduces civil society to economic life as the main sphere of realization of private interest.[3]

The vision of civil life inherent among the M-stream thinkers, who represent civil society as a set of independent associations that mediate relations between the individual and the state, came to dominate contemporary Russian debates on civil society also. Historically, this may be explained by the fact that the most popular version of the civil society thesis came to Russia in the 1980s through the East European interpretations, particularly by means of interesting attempts to interpret the experience of the Polish Solidarity movement through the lens of Gramscian analysis.[4] The clash of the authoritarian state of the Soviet type and the semi-or quasi-independent associations of what was called "civil society" in Eastern Europe at that time seemed to be the fundamental political dynamic of the epoch. Accordingly, creating and maintaining similar free associations still seems to be the decisive guarantee of the consolidation of the democratic regime in contemporary Russia. However, careful consideration of the religious roots of different conceptions of civil society suggests that this is not the only and, perhaps, not the main avenue of its consolidation and development in Russia.

RELIGIOUS BACKGROUNDS
OF CIVIL SOCIETY CONCEPTIONS

Adam Seligman has already pointed to the implicit religious background of the "classic" understanding of civil society as an ethical pre-political community (what Taylor would call the L-stream): it is a Protestant vision of ethical life within a religious community, characterized by "natural benevolence" and minimal coercion.[5] Seligman's study of such early theorists of civil society in the Anglo-American tradition as Locke's disciple Lord Shaftesbury, Smith, Ferguson and Hutcheson has revealed that all of them base themselves to a certain extent on the idea of something like an innate human capacity for benevolence and mutual sympathy that ensures the existence of peaceful and civilized life. This optimistic perception of human nature seemed strange, if not ridiculous, to David Hume, and many contemporary readers perhaps still take Hume's sneer at this perception of an innate goodness as well-founded. However, as Seligman has suggested, this shared perception of human benevolence was not a product of some historical naiveté, but was rather a consequence of Lockean representation of the state of nature in accordance with the basic precepts of Calvinist theology.

The state of nature in Locke is not a hypothetical construct or a description of some really existing society or some stage of its development; rather, it is part of the common and unquestioned Calvinist world-view. Seligman relies here on the famous thesis of John Dunn, who has indicated this Calvinist background of Locke's thought: "The state of nature, then, is a jural condition and the law which covers it is the theologically based law of nature . . . That is to say: men confront each other in their shared status as creatures of God without intrinsic authority over each other and without the right to restrict the (natural) law-abiding behavior of others. But though it is a state of liberty it is not a state of license; though apolitical it is not amoral."[6] Predominantly peaceful life in the state of nature is explained by the fact that an attack on the life or property of a fellow Christian is interfering with God's providence and thus is impossible for a good Protestant.

Having described these transcendental roots of the vision of civil society as a rich, peaceful and civilized pre-political coexistence, Seligman then points out some elements in the way of life of early Protestant communities in America that corresponded to that vision. If one simplifies and radicalizes his account, one may claim that the life of the first Protestant congregations could serve as an empirical referent for the state of nature in Locke's conception, so that in this case later English and Scottish ideas about natural benevolence of a human being in a civil society were not far off the mark. Indeed, in a tight Puritan congregation of the New World attacking a fellow lay saint was almost inconceivable. Furthermore, many New England settlers could possibly agree with a proposition that secular political power was created as if following the Lockean doctrine, as a body of government arising from the life of a pre-political religious community. Thus, one of the founders of the Massachusetts Bay colony, John Winthrop, wrote in 1637: "Whereas the way of

God hath always been to gather his churches out of the world: now the world, or civil state, must be raised out of the churches."[7]

Seligman's convincing hypothesis on the religious roots of the "classic" theory of civil society—of the L-stream, in Taylor's designation, or what one might also call the Anglo-American, or the Calvinist, tradition of thinking on civil society—may be extended to comprise the M-stream as well. This theoretical tradition may accordingly be re-described as offering the Franco-Italian, South European or—more generally—a Catholic vision of civil society. Here we find a different perception of the ethical foundations of social life: for example, in contrast to the Protestant congregations of the New World, Catholic congregations of France, Italy and Spain always encountered a problem of facing more or less strong secular powers. In theory, Catholic theology decreed this problem solved in Pope Gelasius's doctrine of the two swords: the Church took care of the matters of salvation, while secular power sustained law and order in this world. However, in practice, when their interests clashed in this world, the Catholic Church could act as a supreme association that defended its members against the encroachments of the secular state. One may suggest that theorists belonging to the M-stream based their conceptions of civil society to a greater or lesser extent on this vision of the ethical role of the Christian congregation in this world.

Of course, the Catholic Church is not the sole example of *corps intermediaires* in Montesquieu or Tocqueville; still, both grant it a rather central position in their descriptions of the intermediary bodies of the Ancien Regime. For instance, in his famous consideration of the principle of monarchy, Montesquieu first mentions aristocracy as the most "natural" of the *pouvoirs secondaires*, but then immediately switches to a consideration of common issues in the jurisdiction of the aristocracy and the clergy, which surprisingly ends with the thesis on the decisive role of the Church as the last barrier against absolutism: "Though the ecclesiastic power is so dangerous in a republic, yet it is extremely proper in a monarchy, especially of the absolute kind. What would become of Spain and Portugal since the subversion of their laws, were it not for this only barrier against the torrent of arbitrary power?"[8] Also, he repeatedly notes that in despotic regimes no defense is available to the individual but religion, which may oppose the will of the sovereign.[9]

In his discussion of the role of the intermediary bodies before the French Revolution, Tocqueville dedicates to a consideration of the clergy as much space as he assigns to all the other three *corps* he mentions together (aristocracy, bourgeoisie and independent courts). The clergy was ". . . one of the most independent bodies in the land and the only one to enjoy a freedom none dared call in question."[10] On the verge of the revolution the provinces had lost their liberties, the cities kept only a shadow of their previous ones, a dozen aristocrats could not get together to discuss some important questions without prior permission from the king, while, Tocqueville writes, the French church preserved its periodic assemblies. In the new democratic age Tocqueville also asserts the place for associations, similar to church congregations. For example, enumerating the spheres of activity with which the *corps intermediaires* that disappeared after the French revolution had been traditionally concerned, but are now taken care of by the centralized state, Tocqueville names charity, education and religion itself, that is, spheres traditionally entrusted to the Catholic Church.[11] Consequently, he thought that entrusting these spheres to the new civic associations, i.e. modern equivalents of obsolete *corps intermediaires*, would help thwart the new threat of democratic despotism.

At first sight, the internal hierarchy of the Catholic Church seems hardly compatible with the principles of functioning of the free citizens' associations. But, as Tocqueville stressed in *L'Ancien Regime*, one of the factors that contributed to the preservation of the spirit of liberty among the Catholic clergy was a system of internal checks on the power of a bishop, which was duly respected: the Church did not prepare its members for political slavery.[12] Also, Tocqueville's conception may have had another implicit empirical referent rather than a centralized Catholic hierarchy—religious confraternities that played a very important role in Catholicism. For example, looking at the bustling associational life of America, and conceiving of American associations as a model for potential re-creation of the French *corps secondaires*, but on a more democratic basis, he gave—in one startling excerpt—a most extensive list of associational activities: "Americans combine to give fetes, found seminaries, build churches, distribute books and send missionaries to the antipodes. Hospitals, prisons and schools take shape in that way." Save for perhaps the prison, this description of American civil associations stresses activities that in a different cultural setting properly pertained to a Catholic confraternity.[13]

Robert Putnam stressed the connection of these associations of laymen with the formation of the civic tradition in Northern Italy.[14] In theory, the Pope's authority in matters of salvation was never put into question, but starting from the Renaissance, religious feelings and aspirations were frequently channeled through these semi-secular brotherhoods. Indeed, in Northern and Central Italy no less than 80 confraternities were founded in the XIII century, 202—in the XIV and 218—in the XV century.[15] Usually, parishioners of a certain local church would join a confraternity to perform pious works and devotional exercises together. The list of their activities is reminiscent of the American civil associations described by Tocqueville. Confraternities prepared and conducted religious festivals, staged periodical pious processions, sang hymns and engaged in charity. Members of confraternities visited others who fell ill, and attended their funerals. Starting from the XV century, however, works of charity became targeted not only to the membership of the confraternity: members visited prisoners, collected dowries for poor brides, founded hospitals and asylums. In the opinion of contemporary historians, this testified to the formation of a new understanding of faith as a "social Christianity."[16]

Putnam traced the development of these quasi-religious associations until the XX century, which may put Tocqueville's conception of civil society into an interesting context. In the XIX century many Catholic associations were abolished, while creating new ones was prohibited in both France and Italy. However, confraternities and mutual help societies, similar to them in structure and aims, formed the foundation for future civic associations. In Italy, for example, the place of prohibited pious confraternities was taken at the end of the XIX century by other associations of parishioners—groups of "social Catholicism," which soon became the core of the Popular Party. Simultaneously, "chambers of labor" gave rise to the Socialist Party, and, according to a widespread opinion, the subsequent competition between the white (Catholics) and red (Communists) traditions defined the character of political life in Italy in the XX century. Still, according to Putnam, this red-and-white picture should not obscure the fact that both mass parties had common sociological roots in the ancient traditions of collective solidarity and horizontal collaboration.[17] Another claim may be equally plausible: the common sociological roots that Putnam mentions were in fact linked to an implicit Catholic model of a civic association.

Perhaps Gramsci was aware of this commonality as no one else. His conception of civil society, a direct heir to the Hegelian synthesis, also has some typically Italian origins. According to Cohen and Arato, for example, his idea of gaining hegemony in the civil society in order to curtail the power of "political society" (this term is most frequently used by Gramsci to designate the apparatus of violence, i.e. the state) came, among other sources, from successful resistance by the Catholic Church to the assault of the liberal state on the traditional bonds of Italian society.[18] Gramsci wished to repeat this success of the Church, which at the end of the XIX and in the early XX centuries managed to maintain its cultural hegemony through the system of all-penetrating church functions, festivals in neighborhoods, church education and church press, and thus thwarted liberalism from becoming a dominant ideology in Italy. Similarly, if the Communist Party could gain hegemony in the associations of civil society, it would gradually eliminate the domination of the capitalist state. In the authoritative opinion of Norberto Bobbio, "Gramsci translates another great historical antithesis, between the Church (broadly speaking, the modern church is the [Communist] party) and the state into the antithesis between civil society and political society."[19]

A Catholic vision of the civil society may also be found in the works of the Polish Solidarity authors who used Gramscian concepts to describe their opposition to the repressive state. Jadwiga Staniszkis has suggested that behind the high rhetoric of Kuron and Michnik was a simple idea of resistance to the state imposed from abroad.[20] Solidarity spoke about the conflict between the civil society and the state, while in practice it followed the example of the Catholic church—a most serious stronghold of Polish national liberation in the XIX and XX centuries and the only real bulwark of resistance after the imposition of Communist rule. Thus, together with Staniszkis, one may say that the rhetoric of civil society just covered the reality of the struggle for national liberation. But another interpretation is possible also: the vision of civil society that was formed by the Solidarity authors was primarily conditioned by the Catholic roots of Polish culture.

Let us sum up some provisional results of this exposition. Anglo-American theories of civil society rest on the vision of ethical life in a Protestant congregation,[21] while Franco-Italian conceptions are closely linked to the vision of the ethical role of a Catholic congregation in this world. But if these theories were formulated against the background of their corresponding religious visions of the ethically founded life, then, perhaps, other religious traditions with differing background perceptions may offer their own visions of civil life as well.[22] Thus, Orthodox Christianity may harbor its own vision of ethical life of a Christian congregation, functionally equivalent to those that underlie the Catholic and Protestant conceptions, but contributing to a very specific conception of civil society, different from those outlined above.

DOSTOEVSKY ON THE MISSION OF THE CHURCH

Ivan Karamazov first appears in the Dostoevsky novel in an episode discussing the fate of ecclesiastical courts that may seem either strange or archaic to a contemporary reader. But this discussion was very important at the time of the novel's appearance when the Russian reformers intended to clearly segregate the jurisdiction of the church and secular courts, and to rationalize the procedures of both. In the novel, Ivan has just published an article rejecting the liberal opinion that all the secular affairs still remaining under the church court jurisdiction (as was the case with some matters pertaining to marriage and divorce, for example) should be transferred to secular courts, and proposing instead that the scope of affairs under the ecclesiastical jurisdiction should be radically expanded. In Ivan's opinion, the church court should come to regulate all aspects of secular life, so that the merciful authority of the Church would be substituted for the bloody state punishment handed down by secular courts. If this happened, states Karamazov, the Christian Church would finally fulfill its mission in this world. He says:

> When the pagan Roman Empire desired to become Christian . . . it included the Church but remained a pagan State in very many of its departments . . . The Christian Church entering into the State could, of course . . . pursue no other aims than those which have been ordained and revealed by God Himself, and among them that of drawing the whole world, and therefore the ancient pagan State itself, into the Church. In that way . . . every earthly State should be, in the end, completely transformed into the Church and should become nothing else but a Church, rejecting every purpose incongruous with the aims of the Church . . . If everything became the Church, the Church would exclude all the criminal and disobedient, and would not cut off their heads.[23]

Ivan stresses that the Church should in no way take over the state functions of repression of crime and sustaining political life (Dostoevsky, like many other Orthodox authors of that time, ascribed this yearning to Catholicism). In his project, the Church would not punish, it would not become the state: rather, all social relations would be recast in accord with the New Testament. The elder Zossima, who participates in the conversation, supports Ivan:

> If anything does preserve society, even in our time, and does regenerate and trans- form the criminal, it is only the law of Christ speaking in his conscience . . . If the jurisdiction of the Church were introduced in practice in its full force, that is, if the whole of the society were changed into the Church, not only the judgment of the Church would have influence on the reformation of the criminal such as it never has now, but possibly also the crimes themselves would be incredibly diminished. And there can be no doubt that the Church would look upon the criminal and the crime of the future in many cases quite differently and would succeed in restoring the excluded, in restraining those who plan evil, and in regenerating the fallen.[24]

Father Paissy, present at the conversation, sums up the shared prophecy: ". . . the Church is not to be transformed into the State. That is Rome and its dream. That is the third temptation of the devil. On the contrary, the State is transformed into the Church, will ascend and become a Church over the whole world—which is . . . the glorious destiny ordained for the Orthodox Church. This star will arise in the east!"[25]

Obviously, this vision of the ethical mission of the Christian congregation[26] is very different from those already discussed. This vision does not imply an au- tonomous pre-political congregation that later creates the minimal state, as in Calvinist conceptions, neither is it based on the vision of the congregation which has to coexist with the powerful secular state, as in Catholic conceptions. Rather, the Christian congregation attempts to supplant the state altogether. From the point of view of the characters in the Dostoevsky novel, this Orthodox vision still reflects the true, "right" (the meaning of *orthos* in Greek) project of the Christian church: not to coexist with the violent state as a necessary evil (a point on which both Catholics and Protestants seem to agree) but to strive with the radical denial of this evil through the deification of man (a famous Orthodox *theosis*)[27] and through the reconstruction of the world on church principles.

Let us tentatively call this project of the conversion of the world into the Church and of supplanting the state "the project of Dostoevsky," keeping in mind that the space of this article does not allow us to consider to what extent the words of the characters in the novel corresponded to the views of Dostoevsky himself, whether the early Christian communities really strove to supplant the state, what was or could be the opinion of the guardians of the official dogmatic theology of the Russian Orthodox Church on Dostoevsky's pronouncements, and so on. What is important is that Dostoevsky articulated a vision of ethical life shared by many of his contemporaries, who thought that this project captured the essence of the Russian Idea. For example, Semyon Frank also wrote: "The highest mission of human life is . . . to let the beneficial spiritual forces pervade human nature to a fuller extent and saturate it up to the end, and, consequently, to let the 'world' dissolve in the church without residue."[28]

Many Russian authors stressed the non-violent foundations of Church life. Standard Church apologetics affirmed, for example, that Russia did not have an Inquisition in the strict sense of the word, since the Orthodox Church never practiced bloody retribution.[29] Of course, princes could execute heretics in accordance with the code of Justinian, following their wish to eschew the corruption of the mores and the disturbance of law and order, but this act of the secular arm did not belong to church affairs. The Church jurisdiction proper did not exceed the words of Jesus (Matthew XVIII: 15–17):

> . . . if thy brother shall trespass against thee, go and tell him his fault between thee and him alone: if he shall hear thee, thou hast gained thy brother. But if he will not hear thee, then take with thee one or two more, that in the mouth of two or three witnesses every word may be established. And if he shall neglect to hear them, tell it unto the church: but if he neglect to hear the church, let him be unto thee as an heathen man and a publican.

In other words, the Church influence in principle could be reduced to three correctional practices: to denounce sin, to admonish into righteousness, and—if the sinner does not listen to admonitions—to excommunicate. Almost all Russian pre-revolutionary introductions to canon law cited this standard description of the three central practices of Church discipline.

We are now in a position to outline what kind of civil society corresponds to this Orthodox vision of the ethical mission of a Christian congregation, or at least, to the "Dostoevsky project." First, the Orthodox version of civil society may be seen as advocating non-militaristic and civilized life (as it appears in the Protestant conceptions). Second, it may defend individuals from state encroachments on their liberties and educate them in virtue (as in Catholic conceptions). However, and this is its main feature, the Orthodox version of civil society would strive to completely supplant the secular state and its use of the means of violence by bringing church means of influence to regulate all terrains of human life.

SOVIET COLLECTIVES AS ORTHODOX CONGREGATIONS

Paradoxically, the Russian Revolution may have tried translating the Dostoevsky project into reality. Nikolai Berdiaev was perhaps the first to forcefully state this thesis, expressed, however, in semi-mystical formulations that annoy so many contemporary readers who are used to the language of positivist science: Soviet Communism won and consolidated so easily because it fed on the deep religious energy of the Russian people. An atheist facade should not deceive an astute observer, implied Berdiaev: it only covered the essentially religious mechanisms at work in the Russian revolution.[30]

However, the change brought about by the Russian revolution did not mean only the seizure of state power or the subsequent predominance of the "religious asceticism turned inside out," in the apt characterization of Berdiaev. In my book I suggested that one of the most fundamental changes elicited in the everyday life of millions of Soviet citizens concerned the radical transformation of the structure of a small contact group.[31] A group of workers on a given factory shop floor, a group of colleagues in a given Soviet office, a group of servicemen in a given army regiment, a group of inmates in a given cell, even a group of Soviet people on holiday in a given resort hotel—all were supposed to be transformed to become a "collective."

This word is used in contemporary common Russian parlance to designate any contact group. However, at the beginning of the century the term "collective" in Russian applied not to any human group as such but only to those that were structured in a very specific way, with Soviet social psychology stressing this important difference until the very end of its existence. Only after all major types of contact groups were transformed to become collectives did groups that were structured not as collectives become almost unnoticeable, and the term "group" almost became synonymous with the term "collective." Furthermore, by the end of the Brezhnev era a pyramid of Soviet collectives formed the skeleton of Soviet society, with each individual belonging to this or that official collective. Only a small amount of external violence was needed to maintain the assigned system of ties between these collectives and to punish the deviants who chose or happened not to fit into them. That is, after a huge amount of violence was applied in the initial creation of the new system of collectivized life, a radically reduced amount of it was needed to maintain the stable functioning of the system. The secret of this stability and restricted use of physical violence in normal Soviet life consisted in the fact that each Soviet collective functioned as a quasi-religious congregation, employing the principles of the New Testament to maintain the powerful system of circular social control within each collective.

Anton Makarenko described the stages for the introduction of this circular control in his numerous works on the construction of the collective.[32] The first stage in collective building involves imposition of a collective goal for a group of more or less randomly assembled individuals and introduction of collective responsibility for attaining this goal. The second stage is the stage of formation of the core of the group, called the *aktiv*, which would first fulfill the tasks of in-group surveillance and regulation of the behavior of its members in accordance with group goals and norms. The *aktiv* disciplines those who are the reason for failure to attain the group goals. At the third stage of building the collective the *aktiv* itself should be subjected to the same norms, so that the group becomes self-regulating. Circular horizontal surveillance unites all; each suffers from it as a victim but willingly imposes its demands on others.

The immediate roots for Makarenko's pedagogy lie perhaps in various doctrines of progressive education of the XIX and XX centuries and in his personal experience of military discipline, but the wide spread of his methods for constructing a collective and their easy adoption in so many different Soviet milieus—in schools, factories, sports teams, army regiments and prison cells, to name but a few—point to the fact that the methods advocated captured something fundamentally important for Russian life. Many would say that Makarenko's techniques concisely summed up the principles of organization of the Russian peasant land commune after 1861. While not denying the validity of this familiar thesis, I would like to stress also another parallel: the Russian Church used similar methods in organizing a model Christian congregation. This assertion may sound strange for those who are used to seeing the Soviet collective and the Orthodox congregation as two essentially different and opposed phenomena. However, from the perspective of sociology of everyday life, that is, in analyzing their habitual functioning and the practices they employ, one finds that the structures of these two seemingly opposed phenomena coincide in a spectacular way.

Let us consider the cenobite statute of St Joseph Volotsky that was written at the beginning of the XVI century and then taken as a model statute for many Russian monasteries. Circular surveillance presented as brotherly help forms the background for efficient implementation of the statute's precepts:

As St Ephraim says, it is appropriate to us, brethren [to act as follows] — the strong should raise the infirm, the industrious should console the exhausted, the vigilant should rouse those falling asleep, the orderly should punish the disorderly, the reverend should teach the outrageous, the abstinent should remonstrate with the non-hesitant [to sin], the healthy should show compassion to the sick — and holding ourselves in such manner, teaching good to one another, we will unanimously defeat our enemy, and glorify our God.[33]

In order to transform the cloister into a "single body," Joseph proposes to create the corps of special brothers that he calls "bigger" (*bolshie* or *preimushchie*) brothers. This disciplinary core of the monastery is recruited from those "who are first in virtue and reason, willing and able to help the abbot in his care for pious order." This monastery *aktiv* fulfils all the immense work of enforcing collective discipline. For example, during the liturgy bigger brothers stand in different parts of the temple, and, if need be, "reprimand with humility." In the refectory they seat themselves so as to break impious conversations, discipline those who are late and those who steal food. One of the bigger brothers makes an hourly walk on the territory of the monastery, searching for the idle and assigning them work. The bigger brothers also police the monastery at night, capturing those who try to leave without the abbot's permission. They check material possessions of monks in their cells, allowing not more than two shirts, trousers, mantles and so on. They search for the drunk and destroy the potion, accompany visitors on the monastery's territory, women and boys in particular, so that the devil would not tempt the brethren, and so on.[34]

A transgressor is disciplined in accordance with the evangelical writings: at first, the brothers "humbly denounce" a sinner in private; if he does not listen to them, they denounce him in the face of the monastic community; if he is still resilient, then the abbot expels him from the cloister. This outcome, however, is an ultimate threat seldom invoked in practice. The preferred disciplinary means advocated by the Church is mutual corrective surveillance: ". . . let the sinner fear you more than he fears the abbot. If he fears only the teacher he may sin again soon; if he fears many fathers and many lips, he will shrivel in many ways."[35]

Of course, this list of disciplinary arrangements is not so different from those advocated by many other, both Eastern and Western, monastery statutes. What is important, though, is that the principles of setting up a pious cloister became a feature of the everyday life of almost every Soviet citizen after small contact groups were restructured as collectives. Joseph's rhetoric allows an insight into the secret of the Soviet regime: the power of the collective is not the power of one Big Brother; rather, it is the tyranny of a whole multitude of sanctimonious "bigger brothers." The great achievement of Makarenko was a certain democratization of this power: in his children's labor colonies, and later in Soviet schools, factories and offices, each could become a "bigger brother" from time to time, and could always help the cause of discipline by word and deed. The Soviet system might have based itself not so much on the hierarchical surveillance and despotism of the boss as on humiliating peer surveillance and on the tyranny of righteous admonition, presented as friendly help.

One can thus define the Soviet collective as a small human group restructured on the model of a saintly Christian congregation. All the terrifying aspects of the horizontal disciplining of the individual are shared by both this congregation and the collective. Paradoxically, this proximity also means that the life of the collective reminds one of elements of the visions of civil society contained in different religious traditions of its conceptualization. First, the collective does not inflict violence on its members; all of its measures are of the admonitory-educative type. That is, instead of uncivilized brutality civil methods are employed, which recalls the Protestant vision of civil life. Second, the spread of the system of collectives — i.e. transformation of each contact group into a collective—decreases the need for state violence to control deviant behavior. This corresponds to the Orthodox project as proposed by Dostoevsky's characters. Third, the collective defends its members from the arbitrary rule of supreme rulers or immediate bosses, a condition that is reminiscent of the Catholic conceptions of civil life.

It is rather interesting to consider the third aspect of the Soviet collective's activities in a more detailed way, because this is important for the following discussion of the fate of civil society in post-Soviet Russia. Of course, the collective could hardly defend its members against the encroachments of the KGB, but in many everyday situations it could counterbalance the powers of the centralized state. This statement would hardly be novel for those who still remember, for example, how the comrades' courts were transformed in the 1970s and 1980s from being part of the system of Communist training into a ritualized ordeal of individual public penance that supplied cheap means of escaping more serious charges; how "public defense" during a trial or "taking on mutual guarantee" (*vziatie na poruki*) after it by the representatives of the work collective could save the accused from a term in a corrective institution, and so on.

The collective could also curtail the tyranny of immediate bosses. Alexander Zinoviev—at his best in his early descriptions of the mundane realities of

Soviet life that are drastically superior in power of analysis and insight to his latter-day polemicizing and biased rhetoric—was the first to notice an interesting function of hierarchical violence that mediated relations between the upper and lower-level cells in the pyramid of Soviet collectives. Gosplan, and the state punitive bodies that united all Soviet collectives into a single system, embodied the constant threat of vertical violence and thus could curtail the arbitrary rule of the *aktiv* of each collective. Periodic inspections from the top made the leadership of a given collective support and maintain its outward image of the community of equal builders of Communism. The rank and file members of the collective could use these inspections to thwart the boss and the *aktiv* who—in the absence of such inspections—were likely to transform the collective into a group where the powerful openly oppressed and brutalized the weak. Zinoviev calls the final stage to which the collective may devolve "a closed shop" (*chastnaia lavochka*) or a gang, a mafia: "The mafia becomes the sovereign ruler and rules according to its own communal laws, virtually ignoring the limitations imposed by formal laws."[36]

Still, these two functions of the Soviet collective—maintaining civil means of interaction and defending an individual against the encroachments of immediate bosses or the state punitive bodies—do not make it worth calling it the most important element of civil society in Russia. The collective was unfree in two fundamental aspects: first, official collectives were created by regime decision rather than spontaneously; second, inside the collective individual freedom was almost non-existent, and the individual was hardly ever defended from the terror of collective denunciation. This unfreedom prohibits us from taking the collective as an element of civil society, even if it corresponds to the realization of religious projects of developing ethical life in many respects. Notwithstanding which conception of civil society-Catholic, Protestant or Orthodox—one espouses, contemporary reflections on civil society make sense only as part of the discourse on freedom. Theories of civil society implicitly rely on visions of ethical life inherent in each religion, but they are not to be reduced to these visions. Indeed, these visions simply constitute the background (usually unreflected) for the discourse on individual freedom, and thus cannot force us to adopt those of its corollaries that constrain individual liberties.

For example, Tocqueville could not directly import in his conception of democratic liberty those elements of monarchical liberty that were pointed out by Montesquieu—*corps intermediaires* that curtailed the power of the centralized state—because they did not guarantee individual liberties and thus were not suitable for the democratic age. He instead found the acceptable analogue of these *corps* in the free associations of American citizens that played the role of "intermediate powers" in the new democratic society but also supported individual liberties. Similarly, one may look for the post-Soviet equivalent of the Soviet collectives that would fulfill their main functions but would also ensure the freedom of the individual. Luckily, one need not spend time in long searches: even the old Soviet regime witnessed the origination of groups, similar to the collective in their structure, but formed spontaneously and not practicing the terror of collective denunciation. These were non-official groups of friends or, as I shall call them in the remaining exposition, "friendly networks."

Ksenia Kasianova has dubbed these non-official networks of friends "diffuse groups." Basing herself on Kingsley Davis's analysis of stratification, she has proposed distinguishing between diffuse and concrete types of interaction. If concrete interaction is concerned with instrumental gains for an actor who pursues it, then a person enters diffuse interaction not because his or her partners may be useful in attaining this person's goals but because of some deep interest in the personalities of these partners. One may say that this classification restates the familiar Kantian opposition of treating another human being as a means or as an aim in itself.

A diffuse group forms itself over an extended period of time, in the course of many mutual perspicuous tests, and has a certain degree of reticence. Having been formed, it has two main features. First, a member of a diffuse group allows it to interfere in his or her personal affairs, even "to form himself as a persona," according to Kasianova, because this friendly network guarantees the unquestioned support and defense of the individual: "No social welfare system, never and nowhere, could guarantee a man such confidence and freedom as that given by the support of a group of a diffuse type." Second, the diffuse group is tolerant toward individuals constituting it, and ensures authentic communication without any need to dissimulate, serving as the arena for the formation of the image of a given individual self: "In this group a man can be himself: playing a role or impersonating some intended other is simply impossible. Consequently, only one variant of behavior is possible—they should accept you as you are, such as you have become to this very moment, with your drawbacks, sins and weaknesses."[37]

Therefore, a friendly network functions similarly to Makarenko's collectives, because it employs all the same evangelical methods of influencing people, but differs from it in that it does not enserf its members (entering the network and abandoning it are free) and is not an institutionalized social unit, collectively responsible for achieving the unit goals imposed from the outside. Collective surveillance in this case does not result in periodic assemblies to discuss who is to blame (for loss or punishment imposed on the group as a whole), which constitute the rhythm of work of any official collective and which unleash the terror of group denunciation of an individual.

UNCIVIL SOCIETY IN CONTEMPORARY RUSSIA

Contemporary Russian society comprises a rather complicated set of transformed elements of Soviet society and new bodies. First, old Soviet collectives are either destroyed or have devolved into a condition that I designate,
for lack of a better term, as "the post-collective": ties that kept the small
contact group functioning as a collective became radically loosened. The goal
of group activity, heretofore imposed by the bodies of state governance, has
now to be set up by the group itself. Consequently, throughout the 1990s the
collective-building mechanisms were frequently reoriented to pursuing a new
group goal—survival of the collective as such.[38] There are ample grounds to
suspect, however, that in the absence of hierarchical surveillance over the
aktiv—if Zinoviev's hypothesis still holds—collectives habitually devolved
into "closed shops." The *aktiv* from the old days found it more profitable to
directly manipulate the opinion of their colleagues or bully them into compliance, perhaps even to seek recourse to primitive violence, than to support
the fiction of the collective as a group of equal colleagues. The first stages of
privatization may have simply helped to legalize this overt violence of the
strong.

Second, many new groups that emerged in the business sphere—for example, groups of employees of new commercial firms, banks and so on—do not
even care to present themselves as collectives, openly proclaiming the indi-
vidualistic principles of their formation and functioning. The regular Friday
tea or cocktail parties, set up according to the recommendations of human relations consultants in order to create some kind of team spirit, do not hide a
fact obvious to everybody involved—someone is an owner or a boss and
someone else is just a hired employee.

Third, bodies of state regulation and repression that had mediated relations
between the Soviet collectives were either dissolved or were gradually losing
this function in the 1990s. The need for coordinating business relations between
small groups in post-Soviet society has been met by the phenomenal proliferation of businesses providing protection and security services.[39] Protection services are now provided by a whole spectrum of suppliers starting from the
transformed or privatized parts of the old Soviet repressive apparatus to new
semi- and fully criminal structures. The selective enforcement of law makes
even the official judiciary and power ministries subject to widespread criticism
that they are frequently nothing but an instrument in a forceful resolution of
economic conflicts. Furthermore, it is becoming increasingly difficult to draw
a line separating these "public" and "private" suppliers of protection, given the
multiplication of semi-public and semi-private firms producing security, and
given a constant turnover of businessmen in governmental positions and the

outflow of government officials into business or attempts at controlling key companies even while in office.

Fourth, friendly networks that formerly existed as if on the obverse side of social life have emerged into the open. On the one hand, they have become an obvious part of the post-Soviet business world and of what some observers call clan politics. Although networks of patron-client relations seem to be more important for the formation of political cliques and the establishment of business ties in contemporary Russia, one may suspect that friendly networks also play a role in their formation. At least, some friends' networks, transformed and institutionalized to a certain extent in assigning related government or business positions, lie at the core of many power groups.[40] On the other hand, those friendly networks that withstood the temptations of jointly pursuing wealth or power, and thus have eschewed the fate of testing their cohesion under those pressures, seem to retain the functions they inherited from the old days. They provide the most fundamental means of social welfare and defense for the individual, and ensure the maintenance of the arenas of existentially important communication contributing to personality formation among their members.

Overviewing this terrain of diverse groupings and ties, one notes two curious features. On the one hand, the post-collectives and the new business groups are tied into a post-Soviet society by means of semi-private and semi-public protection providers that use the threat of physical violence to maintain predictable behavior of civil bodies. The weak state calls into existence a whole plethora of entities that use violent non-civil methods to ensure the smooth functioning of businesses. On the other hand, all of these bodies, civil and militant, are penetrated by the networks of friendly concern, mutual help and non-violent influence. The central problem of contemporary Russian civil society thus may consist in transforming the relations of uncivil violence according to the principles of friendly networks.

Building a civil society in Russia is perhaps directly linked to introducing civil—meaning non-military and non-violent—means of tying post-collectives and new business groups into a single society. Of course, creation of free associations that would mediate relations between the individual and the state—a project of building civil society that is now usually taken as the only possible one—is also very important and necessary. But in a country that has witnessed the collapse of the monopoly of state violence—that is, where the "state" is the name assigned to the powerful provider of protection services (but not the most powerful now once you are outside Moscow)—defense of the individual against the encroachments of this entity can hardly be central to the task of ensuring individual liberties. If the "state" is just a linguistic marker attached to a firm for production of violence that has its office in the Kremlin and by tradition claims to represent the rest of the country in international negotiations, then the relations between the individual and this "state" are not very different from relations between the individual and other firms manufacturing violence. Defending oneself from uncivil means of interaction as such, rather than defending oneself from the "state" as one of the providers of such means, is the task that a post-Soviet citizen encounters on a daily basis.

Concentration of attention on the creation of free citizens' associations that (potentially) oppose the state and educate the citizenry is, as I have tried to show in this article, a result of the theoretical vogue for Catholic conceptions of civil society. The Russian state, however, is severely limited in its capacity to attain its goals; its traditional competencies, especially in the realm of production of protection services, are diffused among many firms and corporations. This diffusion of violence has attained menacing proportions, hence the current attempts of "strengthening of the power vertical." In order to make a Catholic model of civil society make sense in these conditions, one has therefore first to re-create the absent monopoly of legitimate violence, a task pursued by many in the current Russian government.[41] And only after that think about building effective civic associations that would oppose those actions of a newly reborn state that could threaten individual liberties. This task is formidable, and requires a two-pronged strategy of rebuilding the state, on the one hand, and developing civil society associations, on the other. But logic suggests that a simpler development is also at hand.

Russia is paradoxically close to the realization of the Dostoevsky project, a project of building civil society on the Orthodox model. That is, instead of strengthening the weak state, one may help to finish the transformation of a vast contemporary terrain of uncivil life according to evangelical principles. Indeed, Russia has a very weak state and uncivil society, which employs military rather than civil methods in solving the problem of its integration. And instead of trying to re-concentrate violence—that is now diffused among many actors—in the single hands of the state once again, one may counteract this diffusion of violence by the diffusion of a civil way of life. To play on Kasianova's terms, the main task of creating civil society in Russia would then be a reconstruction of the bodies of diffuse violence on the principles of diffuse communication.

PROBLEMS

In closing, one should mention that this conception of civil society based on the Orthodox Christian tradition has two serious drawbacks. On the one hand, it seems to be highly idealistic; on the other, its realization harbors many dangers. However, one may try to eliminate both of these disadvantages.

Let us start from the first one. A proposal to transform violent, gangster-like methods of social integration according to the principles practiced in friendly networks will not seem as unrealistic if one reminds oneself of a troubling partial coincidence between the ideologies of St. Joseph's brethren and the contemporary Russian criminal "brotherhood"; it is not for nothing that the self-designation of Russian gangsters is *bratva* rather than *la famiglia*, as is the case in the Sicilian mafia. One may also recollect that one of the central problems that concerned Kasianova in her studies of friendship networks was the emergence of *avtoritet*, the Russian word for both "moral authority" and "an informal leader of a criminal world."[42] Zinoviev's hypothesis about an unavoidable devolution of the collective into "a gang" or "a mafia group" in the conditions of decreasing hierarchical surveillance also points to some proximity of the evangelical practices and the main mechanisms of group formation among gangs or other brothers-in-arms supplying violence in Russia.

Problems of small group development and interaction between them have been neglected after the virtual collapse of the Soviet "science of the collective" in the late 1980s. Hence it is very hard to evaluate the prominence of the parallels suggested; this is a subject for future research. One thing is obvious, however: sermons on brotherly love in the face of thugs, no matter what their provenance is, is the shortest route to discrediting the Orthodox project of building civil society, of transforming centers of diffuse violence according to peaceful and civil principles. One would need stern but attractive political and economic mechanisms that would steer the former virtuosos of violence in the direction of employing civil means of interaction.

A second drawback of the Orthodox vision of civil society concerns the danger inherent in the practical implementation of this vision. Frank, whom I have already cited, first formulated this threat. In his opinion, the transformation of the world on church principles, but carried out by worldly means, can only lead to the debasement of the church, its entrapment in worldliness and mundanity, rather than to a deification of the world. Frank asserted that the total dissolution of the world in the church would only happen "beyond the empirical being of man"; any attempts to dissolve the world in the church by this-worldly means leads to all the atrocities inherent in the projects of building the Holy Commonwealth on earth. Thus, the transfiguration of the world into the church should be carried out by holy rather than worldly means, by mysterious Divine Providence rather than by rational human projects of transforming the world. Before this holy transfiguration happens, the fundamental irreconcilable duality of the world and the church should be maintained, wrote Frank; a border between the two realms passes through each human heart.[43]

Translating this emotional warning of Frank into the language of contemporary social sciences, we may get the following: an individual heart should be transfigured on the basis of transcendental rather than this-worldly yearnings; civil principles of life should spread and take root not as a result of rational plans of eradicating diffuse violence but as a result of the mysterious descent of a deep intense personal faith in them on each human being. While this condition is not achieved, a radical duality of the repressive-violent methods espoused by state-like organizations and the mores of Orthodox civil society should be carefully observed and supported.

But what is faith from the standpoint of studies of everyday life? As sociologists are prone to mention, common people—that is, religious virtuosos aside—tend to believe in what is profitable to believe.[44] Of course, everyday observance of certain moral or religious norms, advantageous for the individual in question, may be suddenly highlighted by an acute and extraordinary experience, as a result of which this individual will obstinately insist that he or she really believes now, a sign that some may take as indicating "real internal belief."[45] Until this happens, however, until strong transcendental faith in the unconditional observance of the principles of civilized and civil life does descend on each individual soul, we may be satisfied by the uncomplicated external observance of the rules of this civil life. Attainment of individual faith in the unconditional ideal of civil life by each citizen may be a goal hardly achievable in this world, but we may gradually broaden the terrain of peaceful civil and civilized existence where this descent of faith may happen, while also in the meantime cautiously maintaining the duality between the shrinking state-like bodies and expanding civil society.

NOTES

1. Charles Taylor, "Modes of Civil Society," *Public Culture* 3, no. 1 (Fall 1990). Later this article was reprinted in his *Philosophical Arguments* (Cambridge: Cambridge University Press, 1996).

2. See the best short exposition of this argument in Jeff Weintraub, "Democracy and the Market: A Marriage of Inconvenience," in *From Leninism to Freedom. The Challenges of Democratization*, ed. M. Latus Nugent (Boulder, CO: Westview Press, 1992), 57–61.

3. Jean Cohen and Andrew Arato, *Civil Society and Political Theory* (Cambridge, MA: MIT Press, 1992), 115.

4. See an interesting discussion of limitations on a Gramscian reinterpretation of the Polish experience in Z. A. Pelczynski, "Solidarity and "The Rebirth of Civil Society"," in *Civil Society and the State*, ed. John Keane (London: Verso, 1988).

5. Adam Seligman, *The Idea of Civil Society* (New York: Free Press, 1992), 10.

6. John Dunn, *The Political Thought of John Locke* (Cambridge: Cambridge University Press, 1969), 106.

7. Quoted in Seligman, *The Idea of Civil Society*, p. 72

8. Montesquieu, *The Spirit of Laws, A Compendium of the First English Edition*, ed. David Wallace Carrithers (Berkeley and Los Angeles, University of California Press, 1977), book 2, ch. 4, 113.

9. *The Spirit of Laws*, 115 (book 2, ch. 4): "hence it is that religion has generally so much influence in those [despotic] countries, because it forms a kind of permanent depositary; and if this cannot be said of religion, it may be of the customs that are respected instead of laws"; and 125 (book 3, ch. 10): in despotic Persia "there is one thing that may be opposed to the prince's will; namely religion."

10. Alexis de Tocqueville, *The Old Regime and the French Revolution*, trans. Stuart Gilbert (Garden City, NY: Doubleday, 1955), 111.

11. Alexis de Tocqueville, *Democracy in America*, trans. George Lawrence (New York: Anchor Books, 1969), 680–81.

12. Tocqueville, *Old Regime*, 111: "Within the Church the powers of the high ecclesiastical authority had well-recognized limits; even the lowest orders of the hierarchy had effective means of defending themselves against would-be tyrannical superiors. Thus they had not been tamed by all-powerful bishops to a habit of blind obedience, which as a result they might have practiced likewise toward the temporal power."

13. Tocqueville, *Democracy in America*, 513. Tocqueville mentions "religious, moral, serious, futile, very general, and very limited, immensely large and very minute" associations right before the quoted passage, and cites associations that would like to "proclaim some truth, or propagate some feeling by the encouragement of the great example" immediately after it. These words also support the claim for religious roots of associational life, since all examples come from spheres of some higher religious or moral concern. He also eliminates in this excerpt, first, political and, second, industrial and commercial associations from consideration; hence only religious and moral ones are left. Still, claiming that Tocqueville viewed American associations solely on the model of the religious confraternity is unwarranted. Although the quoted excerpt gives some grounds for this radical claim, others may easily disprove it. For example, in another famous description in vol. 1, part 2, ch. 4, (*Democracy in America*, 189), he gives the following examples of civil associations: an assembly to eliminate the object blocking the road; an association "to make festivities grander and more orderly," and finally, moral associations. Thus, it seems more appropriate to speak of the special role of moral and intellectual associations (closely linked to a religious model) in Tocqueville's vision of civil life, or about contradictory evidence. Whether commercial corporations and political associations (bodies of local self-government, such as townships and counties, or juries and political parties) should be included in Tocquevillean "civil society" strictly defined is a subject for discussion. Of course, their role is very important since political associations, for instance, defend citizens "against the encroachments of royal power" or "despotic action of the majority" (513). It would seem logical to suggest that those associations

rather than "intellectual and moral associations" are the closest candidates to replacing the *corps secondaires* in terms of defence of the individual. However, moral associations are the closest to replacing the "powerful private persons" of the past as sources of public emulation and of the spread of moral ideas. Hence "the latter are as necessary as the former to the American people; perhaps more so" (515–516). In any case, too much of Tocqueville's discussion of civil associations depends on examples of quasi-religious activities, a fact not to be ignored.

14. Robert Putnam, *Making Democracy Work. Civic Traditions in Modern Italy* (Princeton: Princeton University Press, 1993), 127.

15. Peter Burke, *Culture and Society in Renaissance Italy* (New York: Scribner's, 1972), 215.

16. Burke, *Renaissance Italy*, 216. Historians also note the prominent role of the confraternities in financing the development of Renaissance art. They collected money for paintings and statues for the churches under their patronage, placing orders with such masters as Leonardo and Carpaccio. Brothers also ordered new hymns and compositions of church music. Some confraternities were based on common membership in a guild rather than in a parish. Hence, confraternities may be considered an epiphenomenon of a growth of civic virtue rather than its driving force, in the manner in which Putnam usually describes them. I would like to stress what Putnam usually omits from consideration: the religious background of much associational activity in what is usually taken to be a secular republican tradition.

17. Putnam, *Making Democracy Work*, 142.

18. Cohen and Arato, *Civil Society and Political Theory*, 144.

19. Norberto Bobbio, "Gramsci and the Concept of Civil Society," in *Civil Society and the State*, ed. John Keane, 95.

20. Jadwiga Staniszkis, *Poland's Self-Limiting Revolution* (Princeton: Princeton University Press, 1984).

21. I equate here Protestantism and Calvinism to make the argument more succinct. Lutheranism, however, poses special problems: its radical religious individualism, on the one hand, and advocated obedience to secular authority, on the other, are perhaps best captured in Hegel's synthesis that depicts clashing individual interests subsumed in the universal state. For an argument that considers Lutheran roots of a Scandinavian understanding of civil society see Henrik Stenius, "The Good Life is a Life of Conformity: The Impact of Lutheran Tradition on Nordic Political Culture," in *The Cultural Construction of Norden*, ed. Oysteln Sorensen and Bo Stråth (Oslo: Scandinavian University Press, 1997).

22. This argument should not be understood as introducing some type of "religious determinism." I am just assembling some facts that would reveal a coherent background setting, following a lead proposed by Seligman. Two methodological points are in order here. First, those other sources of civil society in the West that are frequently invoked—such as independent cities and guilds, republicanism, civic rather than religious virtue, and the like—are paid little attention here in order to highlight a different common denominator for cross-cultural comparison. Second, showing what presuppositions (and/or practices) constituted the shared background against which different conceptions of civil society were formulated is not akin to causal

analysis. Religious perceptions of ethical life constrain the limits of what is thinkable or sayable in the theories of civil society to be shaped in a given religious tradition, though they do not define or cause what will be said about civil society in this tradition.

23. Fyodor Dostoyevsky, *The Brothers Karamazov*, trans. Constance Garnett (New York: Modern Library, 1960), 61, 63.

24. Dostoyevsky, *The Brothers Karamazov*, 65.

25. Dostoyevsky, *The Brothers Karamazov*, 66.

26. I use the term "congregation" here in a broad Weberian sense of "an association dedicated to exclusively religious purposes" (Max Weber, *Economy and Society*, ed. Guenther Roth and Claus Wittich [Berkeley and Los Angeles, University of California Press, 1978], vol. 1, 454). Of course, this ignores his distinction between incompletely and fully congregational religions, and may also seem inappropriate to the Orthodox clergy who would claim that the term *kongregatsiia* pertains to Protestantism only.

27. On this category of Orthodox theology see, e.g., Timothy Ware, *The Orthodox Church*, revised ed. (London: Penguin, 1993), 231.

28. Semyon Frank, *Dukhovnye osnovy obshchestva. Vvedenie v sotsialnuiu filosofiiu* [Spiritual Foundations of Society. Introduction to Social Philosophy, orig. 1930] (Moscow: Respublika, 1992), 97.

29. N. I. Barsov, *Sushchestvovala li v Rossii inkvizitsiia?* [Did the Inquisition Exist in Russia?] (St. Petersburg, 1892), 6.

30. Nikolai Berdiaev, *Istoki i smysl russkogo kommunizma* [Origins and Meaning of Russian Communism] (Paris: YMCA-Press, 1955).

31. Oleg Kharkhordin, *The Collective and the Individual in Russia: A Study of Practices* (Berkeley and Los Angeles: University of California Press, 1999), esp. chapter 3.

32. A thorough treatment of his methods may be found in James Bowen, *Soviet Education. Anton Makarenko and the Years of Experiment* (Madison: University of Wisconsin Press, 1962).

33. St. Joseph (Volotsky), "Dukhovnaia gramota prepodobnogo Iosifa," in *Velikie Chetii Minei* (St Petersburg, 1868), book of readings for 1–13 September, 576.

34. St. Joseph, "Dukhovnaia gramota," 588–607.

35. St. Joseph, "Dukhovnaia gramota," 574.

36. Alexander Zinoviev, *The Reality of Communism*, trans. Charles Janson (London: Gollancz, 1984), 200.

37. Ksenia Kasianova, *O russkom natsionalnom kharaktere* [On Russian National Character] (Moscow: INME, 1994), 254. Here one may suspect a certain contradiction: how may one be oneself when the group forms your persona? Perhaps the answer lies in a very Russian mechanism of self-formation (partly captured, however, by Erving Goffman also): I know who I am only as a result of a relevant group judgment on myself; without this judgement "being oneself" is impossible since one does not know who one is without appropriate peer review. On the mechanism of self-revelation in public review, and its religious roots, see Kharkhordin, *The Collective and the Individual in Russia*.

38. On the post-Soviet managers' stated priority to help the collective survive see Oleg Kharkhordin and Theodore P. Gerber, "Russian Directors' Business Ethic: A Study of Industrial Enterprises in St. Petersburg, 1993," *Europe-Asia Studies* 46, no.7 (November 1994), 1075–1107.

39. See Vadim Volkov, *Violent Entrepreneurs. The Use of Force in the Making of Russian Capitalism* (Ithaca, NY: Cornell University Press, 2002) and Federico Varese, *The Russian Mafia. Private Protection in a New Market Economy* (Oxford: Oxford University Press, 2001).

40. On networks of friends around Chubais see Janine Wedel, *Collision and Collusion: The Strange Case of Western Aid to Eastern Europe, 1989–1998* (New York: St. Martin's Press, 1998). On the role of personal ties in Putin's administration see Andrew Jack, *Inside Putin's Russia* (London: Granta, 2004).

41. Most people remember only the ending of the Weberian definition of the state and forget that Weber fully defines it as "a human community that (sucessfully) claims" the monopoly of the use of legitimate violence within a given territory (*From Max Weber: Essays in Sociology*, ed. H. H. Gerth and C. Wright Mills [New York: Oxford University Press, 1946], 78). This implies that the only indisputable recent success in state-building was achieved during the crackdown on non-Kremlin-controlled media, when the Kremlin managed to succesfully suppress all major discursive challenges to its claim to possess the monopoly of legitimate violence. However, hardly many would agree that it managed to either reestablish the crumbled monopoly in reality or to make the Kremlin violence legitimate.

42. Kasianova, *O russkom natsionalnom kharaktere*, 264, 327.

43. Frank, *Dukhovnye osnovy*, 97–98.

44. See e.g. Pierre Bourdieu, "Genesis and Structure of the Religious Field," in *Comparative Social Research*, vol. 13, ed. C. Calhoun (Greenwich, Conn.: JAI Press, 1991), 15.

45. Compare Michel de Certeau, *The Practice of Everyday Life*, trans. Steven Rendall (Berkeley and Los Angeles: University of California Press, 1984), 178: "As a first approximation, I define 'belief' . . . as a subject's investment in a proposition, the act of saying it and considering it as true—in other words, a 'modality' of assertion and not its content."

Chapter Three

Private Life

In the summer of 1926 a student of the Leningrad Mining Academy named Davidson committed suicide. There was enough evidence to suppose that her partner in civil marriage, Konstantin Korenkov, also a student of the same academy, was the reason for her suicide. Over the preceding year he had continuously humiliated her, calling her names like "rabble" and "Jewish creep," discussed with his friends his sexual relations with other women in her presence, and locked her up in their dorm room when she was a nuisance (such as when she was bleeding after one of three consecutive abortions). The day she committed suicide, Korenkov told Davidson that he was leaving for the Crimea to spend a summer vacation alone: why did he need her there when he had other women to meet? He left a loaded revolver in the top drawer of the desk and went down into the dorm's backyard to play soccer. Said a witness:

> I have known Korenkov and Davidson since 1925. . . . I am not aware of the details of their family life, but I heard from others that they did not do very well together. On the day Davidson died, before the shot sounded, we were playing ball, and Korenkov was among the players. When we finished, we parted, and in half an hour I was told that Davidson had shot herself. Initially I did not believe it, and as they live upstairs and I live downstairs, I did not even go to check it out.[1]

Korenkov could not be put on trial for murder. However, the local Komsomol cell, of which he was a member, excluded him from both Komsomol and the Party on the grounds of "moral responsibility for the suicide of a comrade." The district Party Control Commission overruled this decision as too harsh a punishment, and substituted a "severe reprimand and warning" for it.

Shortly thereafter, in June 1926, Korenkov and his younger brother staged a holdup of the cashier's office of the Mining Academy. They stabbed the cashier to death and heavily wounded his wife. The brothers needed money for a vacation in the Crimea.

These two related episodes did not surprise many readers of newspapers at the time: 1926 was a year filled with press reports of such crimes as dismemberment and group rape. However, Sofia Smidovich, a former chairwoman of Zhenotdel, the section of the Party's Central Committee that was specifically set up to deal with problems of women's liberation, chose this story as representative of the most serious illness that was corrupting the body social in 1926. Of course, she was appalled by the way Korenkov had treated his wife; of course, she linked his gangster behavior to this treatment. But the peculiar thing about her article was that these aspects were not its central concern: Smidovich wanted to expose a specific type of social illness she called "Korenkovism." The most dangerous feature of Korenkovism, she wrote, was that young people who encounter him [Korenkov] every day and watch his relations with poor Davidson, who perceive his unbelievable rudeness, cynicism and humiliation of her, do not react to this fact at all and ostracize him only after the commission twice rules him guilty of Davidson's death.

Smidovich finds the essence of Korenkovism in this nonchalant reaction of the dormitory inhabitants to their neighbors' private lives, the sphere where dark and ominous forces lurk:

> The private life [*lichnaia zhizn'*] of my comrade is not of my concern. The students' collective watches how Korenkov locks up his sick, literally bleeding wife—well, this is his private life. He addresses her only with curse words and humiliating remarks—nobody interferes. What's more: in Korenkov's room a shot resounds, and a student whose room is one floor beneath does not even think it necessary to check out what's going on. He considers it a private affair [*lichnoe delo*] of Korenkov and Davidson.[2]

What is interesting here is that Smidovich, the Bolshevik Feminist par excellence, chooses to focus not so much on the case's manifest misogyny as on the parlous condition of the collective that does not interfere in private lives. What is most serious is that the collective is tainted: it watches everything, as all the drama takes place in public sight, but it does not react. Consequently, what Smidovich is trying to cure is not the way men treat women, but the way individual lives are to be handled by the collective.

One should not simply denounce Smidovich, bringing in the judgment of a different epoch and a different society. My task in this chapter is to understand the intertwining of public and private life in Soviet Russia as it is represented, for instance, in Smidovich's fears and Korenkov's actions. And, as the later exposition will show, the Korenkov case is important because it not only exemplified, but was also instrumental in, the formation of the specifically Soviet configuration of public and private life.

To understand the long-term process by which this configuration emerged, however, we need to reconstruct the cultural practices that constituted the background for the episode just described. Bolshevism aimed not merely to change institutions, but to radically transform everyday life and to create a new, morally redeemed individual—the much-celebrated "New Soviet Man." In fact, Soviet society did succeed in creating a new individual, though not precisely the one intended. The goal was to construct a new society that would make saintly zeal its central organizing principle; the result, the unfolding of which this chapter will trace, was a society whose key constitutive practice was a pervasive and, in the long run, increasingly cynical dissimulation. In order to grasp the logic of both this curious project and its denouement, we must begin at the root—which means, ultimately, with the religious background of the Russian Revolution of 1917.

THE BOLSHEVIK REFORMATION

Conceiving Bolshevism as a religion is hardly novel for Russian studies. Nikolai Berdiaev gave a classic rendition of the thesis. According to him, Bolsheviks channeled the religious energy of the Russian people to suit Bolshevik aims, and in so doing became the malignant outcome of the benign millennial development of the Russian Orthodox Church. The Bolsheviks' facade of atheism should not deceive an astute observer, for it covers up the essentially religious mechanisms that explain the advent and dynamics of Communism in Russia.[3]

Berdiaev was pointing at the bedrock of Soviet civilization, but he did not concentrate on the change in Orthodox religious practices that the Bolsheviks inaugurated. This change, however, lies at the heart of Bolshevik successes and is similar to what another renowned Russian thinker, Pavel Miliukov, described as a transition from "ritualized piety towards the religion of the soul."[4] In his study of religious sectarianism in Russia during the eighteenth and nineteenth centuries, Miliukov outlined what he saw as a central feature of "spiritual progress" at this time: the change from mass ritual worship (the essence of traditional Orthodoxy) towards a deep individual belief, which was characteristic of the sectarians. One could suggest that the same transformation occurred in Bolshevik conversions: a fervent individual belief might have replaced the stale sacramental piety of Orthodoxy.

Therefore, it would seem quite plausible to compare the Bolshevik revolution in Russia with the Puritan Reformation in England. Michael Walzer was first to outline the similarities in the radical politics presented by the two cases, and my argument will be greatly indebted to his study.[5] However, I will specifically concentrate on one aspect in which they seem analogous that is marginal to Walzer's brilliant analysis.

Both "revolutions of the saints" involved the transformation of collective belief in sacramental rituals into deep individual faith in a professed discursive doctrine. Although the discursive articulations employed in the Puritan and Bolshevik Reformations seem to be radically opposite, the former being formulated in religious and the latter in starkly atheistic terms, the changes in practice that the majority of the "reformed" experienced might have been similar. First, a believer was expected to renounce any mediation between himself or herself and higher truth. This truth was contained in a special body of texts, available to everybody for interpretation. Second, the acute individualization of belief was based on individual revelation and conversion. Third, neither Puritan nor Bolshevik "individualism" of belief led to respect for privacy.

The last similarity is most important for the present argument. The "sacred" character of the private space, which originated in what Steven Lukes calls the "mystical individualism" of Augustine and Luther, was alien to both Puritans and Bolsheviks. For Lutherans, privacy was sacred because this was the realm where communion with God took place.[6] On the contrary, writes Michael Walzer,

> Puritan individualism never led to a respect for privacy. . . . Puritan zeal was not a private passion; it was instead a highly collective emotion and it imposed upon the saints a new and impersonal discipline. . . . Tender conscience had its rights, but it was protected only against the interference of worldlings, and not against "brotherly admonition."[7]

Almost the same obtains for Bolshevism. To understand how individualism —of a certain kind—and total disrespect for privacy coexisted in Bolshevism, one should take a closer look at the origins of the Bolshevik individual. The paradigmatic process in the formation of a Bolshevik individual could be described as conversion to fanatical faith in the revealed Doctrine. And the central practice of this conversion is captured by the Russian word *oblichenie.*

BOLSHEVIKS REVEALING AND REVEALED

Oblichenie is the central term of *What Is to Be Done?* Usually translated as "exposure" by interpreters who assume that the secular meaning of the word was primary for Lenin, this word can also be translated as "revelation." The word is crucial for the third chapter of this Bolshevik manifesto, which discusses the differences between Bolshevik and traditional trade-unionist politics. The word *oblichenie* is repeated so often that it provides the chapter with a certain rhythm. The refrain is the same: the objective of the Bolshevik party of the new type is "to organize political revelation."

First of all, Lenin opposes *oblichenie* to mere discussion and explanation. Explanations do not suit Bolshevik aims, according to Lenin; rather "agitation," which will arouse workers' passions on the basis of the revealed truth of exploitation, is needed.[8] A little later, in a characteristic excerpt, imaginary workers demand from revolutionary intellectuals that the truth of the crimes of government be *revealed* to them in a "vivid" way, not simply communicated:

> You intellectuals can acquire this [political] knowledge and it is your duty to bring it to us in a hundred- and thousand-fold greater measure than you have done up to now; and you must bring it to us not only in the form of discussions, pamphlets and articles (which very often—pardon our frankness—are rather dull), but precisely in the form of vivid *revelations* of what our government and our governing classes are doing at this very moment in all spheres of life. *Devote more zeal to* carrying out this duty and talk less about "raising the activity of the working masses."[9]

Second, the mechanism *of oblichenie is* very simple. A Bolshevik propagandist reveals the crimes of the governing classes to the workers by positing a certain Truth beyond appearances; she or he reveals the vile intentions of the powers that be and the reality of class domination, which are presented according to Marxist doctrine. The reality revealed is not the apparent, everyday, proximate reality of the given factory that the worker experiences; rather, this is Reality as it functions in the world religions, the *ens realissimum.*[10] This Reality, which is not and cannot be directly perceived by the senses, becomes the Higher and Indisputable Reality which is available to the mind's eye in the inner light of Revelation. The Reality revealed in accordance with the Word—this is what a worker should receive from a Bolshevik. But, laments Lenin, an average worker still does not get it in 1902:

> Why do the Russian workers still manifest little revolutionary activity? . . . We must blame ourselves, our lagging behind the mass movement, for still being unable to organize sufficiently wide, striking, and rapid revelations of all the shameful outrages. When we do that (and we must and can do it), the most backward worker will understand, or will feel, that the students and religious sects, the peasants and the authors are being abused and outraged by those same dark forces that are oppressing and crushing him at every step of his life. Feeling that, he himself will be filled with an irresistible desire to react, and he will know how to hoot the censors one day, on another day to demonstrate outside the house of the governor who brutally suppressed a peasant uprising, on still another day to teach a lesson to the gendarmes in surplices who are doing the work of the Holy Inquisition,

etc. As yet we have done very little, almost nothing, to bring before the working masses prompt revelations on all possible issues.[11]

Third, workers are capable of local "revelations" that will uncover the injustices of a given factory manager or a shopfloor supervisor, but they arc unable to link these local injustices to the Doctrine, which would recast them as local appearances of a single profound injustice. This link is to be revealed by a Marxist propagandist. His or her role, then, is akin to the role of the "seditious ministers" whom Hobbes held to be among the causes of the Civil War in England. William Perkins, the father of Calvinist "covenant theology" in England, wrote in the 1580s, in his book *The Whole Treatise of the Cases of Conscience,* that the duty of the preacher was "to apply . . . the doctrines rightly collected [out of the text] to the life and manners of men in simple and plain speech."[12]

According to Robert C. Tucker, Stalin was drawn to Lenin precisely by this project of linking the everyday experiences of workers to the Marxist Word. The chief stock-in-trade of Stalin as revolutionary, writes Tucker, was an impressive knowledge of the fundamentals of Marxism and an ability to explain them very simply to ordinary workers. "[His] seminary experience gave him a catechistic approach to teaching and a facility for finding homely examples which must have been effective in his worker classes."[13] This "catechistic" style was frequently found in Stalin's later writings, too, which often consisted of short lists of concise dogmatic answers to explicitly posed basic questions.

Other parallels between Puritan ministers and Bolshevik propagandists immediately come to mind here. Both acquired the knowledge of the Doctrine by the "self-taught Word," which was then to be disseminated among the laity. Sermons were the most popular type of literature in sixteenth-century England;[14] the newspaper *Iskra* became the tribune for the clear and simple sermons emanating from Bolshevik ministers. Lenin explicitly uses the word *propoved´,* meaning "sermon" in Russian; translators secularize it into "speech" and "propaganda" in the English-language edition.[15] The activities of the Puritan laity—taking copious notes on the sermons and participating in Bible study groups—were replicated in the workers' Marxist study circles in Russia. But the primary importance of individual reading for conversion was indisputable for both: hence, the program to teach everybody to read (no matter what it cost) was essential to the so-called Cultural Revolution in Russia. Russian "seditious ministers" were to stop at nothing in the project of giving everybody the opportunity to become a "lay saint."

The title of Perkins's book suggests another overlooked parallel. The objective of Puritan and Bolshevik revelations was the acquisition of godly Conscience, a direct knowledge *(conscientia)* of Higher Truth. Bearing this in mind, one can see that the familiar "spontaneity/consciousness" dialectic constituting the basic argument of *What Is to Be Done?* may be reinterpreted as progress from the state of the unenlightened chaotic soul to Higher Conscience, that is, as a process of conversion. By responding to revelations, a worker-Bolshevik overcomes the spontaneous, profane movements of his soul.

Later the narrative of the ascent to Bolshevik Conscience became what Katerina Clark calls the "masterplot of Socialist Realism."[16] This masterplot was repeated in almost every Socialist Realist novel: a disciple, under the guidance of the wise teacher, overcomes enormous difficulties, learns to control passions by doctrinal insight, and thus rises to Conscience. Clark notes that literary techniques employed in these novels were virtually identical to the techniques of nineteenth-century Russian hagiography. What she does not say is that the plot itself was a narrative of conversion, the endlessly reiterated narrative of Protestant literature.

The model of conversion and acquisition of Higher Conscience, as formulated by Lenin and later epitomized in Socialist Realism, had to be linked to mundane life; sacred Reality had to be grounded in profane reality. How was an individual to prove to him or herself that she or he had achieved Higher Conscience (and was not still responding to spontaneous instincts)? In other words, how was a Bolshevik individual to be sure of acquired grace?

Here another meaning of the word *oblichenie* comes to the fore, different from the one discussed so far—that is from *oblichenie* as an activity of Bolshevik propagandists. The classic dictionary of the nineteenth-century Russian language captures this meaning with the following example: "Deeds, and not words, reveal *[ob-lichaiut]* the man, demonstrate his real face [*litso*] and his self [*lichnost'*]."[17] In a sense, human beings are endowed with a personality, or a self, by this self-revealing *oblichenie*. Of course, having established his or her own *lichnost'* (literally meaning "personality," but also a word for "self" in Russian), the individual may become capable of revealing the crimes of others according to the true doctrine—the currently predominant meaning of *oblichenie,* illustrated in the dictionary by examples such as the following: "Good Conscience likes revelations."

Thus, fundamentally, the self of a Bolshevik is revealed by his deeds. The way to arrive at the knowledge of one's true self, then, is not through inner light or meditation. One acquires one's self through public deeds which might be said to literally en-person *(ob-lichaiut),* to endow a body with a true self or personality *(lichnost').* This insistence on the knowledge of oneself through public deeds, on the reception of one's self in these deeds (actually, on being endowed with one's self through one's deeds, because you cannot actively obtain it), is not uniquely Bolshevik. It seems likely that the Bolsheviks took it over from the Orthodox practice of *oblichenie* through penance.

Michel Foucault opposed penance and confession as two possible ways of knowing oneself in Christianity. In his sketch of the origins of the Western individual (which was to be developed in the unpublished volume 4 of the *History of Sexuality*), Foucault claimed that in the West confession eclipsed penance as the practical way to know oneself. Confession, introduced by Cassian, came to predominate in the West after a lengthy period of historical development. Once confessional practices merged with the fictional object called "sex" in the eighteenth century, Western individuals were produced as "deep subjects" who posit their secrets by confessions on matters of sex.[18]

However, the practice of penance, outlined by Tertullian and described by Foucault as one of the abandoned ways of knowing oneself in the West, seems to have survived as central in Orthodox Russia. Tertullian uses the phrase *publicatio sui* to designate the way a penitent knows him or herself. Only in going public, in publicizing one's self in public penance, can one know it: the self is constituted by this special kind of deed. Thus, Foucault said:

> The acts by which [a penitent] knows himself must be indissociable from the acts by which he reveals himself. . . . Penance in the first Christian century is a way of life acted out at all times by an obligation to show oneself. . . . The Tertullian expression, *publicatio sui,* is not a way to say the sinner has to expose his sins. The expression means that he has to present himself as a sinner in his reality of being a sinner. [Why?] The showing forth of the sinner should be efficient to efface the sins.[19]

A penitent in a public ritual revealed his or her true self to the community, and in so doing liberated himself or herself from the sins and, in a sense, acquired a new true self, imbued with Conscience. Later, says Foucault, this practice of showing one's self by public penance contributed to the model of knowing oneself through public martyrdom.

I would suggest that this model constituted the bedrock of Russian civilization for ages. The examples are numerous and range from "holy fools in the glory of God" to revolutionary martyrs. All make a specific claim to know truth about themselves and the world. One could say that the Christian hero of Russian Orthodoxy, a saint who knows himself not through private confession but through public penance, was taken over by the Bolsheviks, who remolded the religious practices of *publicatio sui* to suit the new aim, that is, to reveal a Bolshevik atheist individual.

This individual may now know himself or herself through revolutionary martyrdom, or—in less heroic situations—through public display of deeds that reveal Higher Conscience. The emphasis on deeds and not words to judge a person is common to both Lenin and Stalin. Lenin stated it clearly in his first major work, *Who Are the "Friends of the People," and How Do They*

Fight against Social Democrats? Stalin reinforced it, by casting it as the only correct way to know one's self, in his letter to the editors of the journal *Proletarskaia Revoliutsiia* at the beginning of the 1930s. In discussing the disputed Bolshevism of Lenin, Stalin retorted to critics that no matter what personal documents might be found indicating that Lenin was a vacillating Bolshevik, he proved by his revolutionary deeds that he was not. And this proof by deeds was the ultimate truth, ruled Stalin.[20]

Two features of the Bolshevik constitution of *lichnost'* through *oblichenie*, that is, of constitution of the self through revealing deeds—are extremely important here. First, a Bolshevik may know himself or herself only through the eyes of the relevant public, which is primarily the Parry. Thus, she or he may get an assurance of righteous behavior, which is indicative of the Higher Conscience, only from the Party. Therefore, disciplined obedience to the Party's will becomes essential to a given Bolshevik's assurance of grace. This obedience may or may not reveal the Conscience to the public, but discipline is an essential condition of entry into the realm of virtuous and saintly living. Thus, one of the most saintly of Bolsheviks, Soltz, asserted that voluntary submission to Party discipline was the primary virtue of a Bolshevik:

> What is the difference between our discipline and the discipline of a military barracks . . . which kills every initiative and lively creative thought? Our discipline is voluntary, as the Party is also a voluntary union of persons, who may leave it at any time. We are a voluntary army which pursues a certain objective and wages war by common effort. The consciousness of this gives us moral satisfaction when we obey the Party, even while disagreeing with this or that decision.[21]

Second, if a Bolshevik self is constituted in and by the public gaze, then by definition it cannot be secret. It is all and always on display, because only by means of this display, in *publicatio sui,* can a Bolshevik self exist at all. This condition has far-reaching consequences. The Bolshevik self, contrary to the liberal self, cannot be meaningfully defended "against the encroachments of the public," because it exists only in the eyes of this public. *Lichnost'* is formed by *oblichenie,* and this *lichnost' is* what is always seen to be revealed to the public.

Consequently, *lichnaia zhizn'* (which is usually translated as "private life") is subject to constant public gaze also: only in the whole totality of one's deeds is the true *lichnost'* manifested. Hence one cannot close *lichnaia zhizn'* off; for a Bolshevik self closing off is absurd, because obstacles to a public (that is, Parry) gaze would lead exactly to the inability of a Bolshevik self to emerge. A translation of *lichnaia zhizn'* as "private life" is thus misleading in important respects, and can give rise to serious confusions. The underlying meaning of *lichnaia zhizn'* helps explain the Bolshevik insistence—which seems both absurd and unacceptable from the liberal perspective—on the need for the "public" to keep "private" life under constant surveillance (and for the "private" to be exposed to the public gaze).

After the revolutionary public became institutionalized in the revolutionary state, this state had the complete right to interfere in the "private" lives of Bolsheviks; indeed, it was obliged to interfere in order to let the most minute deeds be registered—so that all deeds representative of the Higher Conscience or its lack would contribute to the revelation of a Bolshevik individual.

LICHNAIA ZHIZN' AND CHASTNAIA ZHIZN'

However, the Russian language has a second term, *chastnaia zhizn'*, which is also usually translated as "private life." This phrase bears the connotation of partiality, as *chast'* means "a part of something" and *chastnyi interes* means "partial interest." If *lichnaia zhizn'* is subject to an ever-present public gaze, then *chastnaia zhizn'* is not necessarily so and may possibly be closed off from the public or even counterpoised to it. These two types of "private life" experienced different fates in Soviet Russia. If *lichnaia zhizn'* was continuously fostered by the regime and was subject to its unending care, then *chastnaia zhizn'* was fought and almost discursively assassinated. The largest Russian dictionary, published in the 1950s and 1960s, registered this near death.

All the examples of usage of *chastnaia* are connected with the pre-revolutionary life that was swept away after 1917. "Private household," "private stipend," "private service," and "private philanthropy" all fell out of usage once the core of this sphere, private property (*chastnaia sobstvennost'*), was abolished by the Bolsheviks. In the section on *chastnaia* one finds only one example of a post-1917 usage, which, not surprisingly, pertains primarily to life abroad: "He had a salary of a head physician in the cantonal sanatorium. He had a private practice."[22]

The dictionary's examples of *lichnaia* cover a broader range. For example, it quotes the head of the Soviet government, Kalinin, who tells us that the Constitution "obliges us to care for public property, to put common interests ahead of private, individual ones [*stavit' obshchie interesy vyshe lichnykh*]." Then an example from the years of the Second World War states that "the private became public *(lichnoe stalo gosudarstvennym]*, anxiety for the fate of the motherland entered the hearts of Soviet people, and fused their ranks." The final example of usage belongs to the postwar years: "Perhaps, because Rudakov always hid his private life [*svoe lichnoe*] so thoroughly, it was strange to see him in the role of a caring husband and a loving father."[23]

The very complicated entanglement of *obshchaia—obshchestvennaia—gosudarstvennaia—lichnaia—chastnaia—individualnaia* (these are often translated into English as either "public" or "private," though they originally mean, respectively: common—social—state—personal—partial—individual) still awaits an avid and careful student. For the time being I will concentrate only on the distinction between *lichnaia* and *chastnaia*.

For the sake of conceptual clarity, I will translate *lichnaia* as "personal" and *chastnaia* as "private" in the following exposition. *Lichnaia zhizn'* will be translated as "personal life" to signify the specifically Bolshevik sense attributed to it after the revolution: that is, life which does not involve official organizations, but is (ideally) as demonstrative of the Bolshevik personality as official life. *Chastnaia zhizn'* will be translated as "private life" to signify the way of life, related to private property, which the Bolsheviks fought and almost vanquished.

One should not forget, nevertheless, that the two together constitute what is commonly referred to as "private life" in everyday English usage—that is, life within a family or with friends, and more generally life outside the realm of public duties and public organizations. I will try to trace the development of "private life" in Soviet Russia, keeping in mind both the public-private distinction in English and the *lichnaia-chastnaia* distinction in Russian.

A DRIVE FOR COMRADELY ADMONITION

In the country where the alleged Bolshevik saints had finally gained power, the majority of the population was not saintly at all. More than that, this majority threatened to contaminate the saintly purity of the Party ranks. A special body, the Party Control Commission, took over the function of estimating what appertained to the saintly conscience of a party member. The question of saintly behavior in mundane situations was the most difficult to resolve: what were the standards representative of higher conscience in such matters as sex, clothes, everyday contacts with neighbors, and the like?

While a "debate on party ethics," aimed at establishing these standards, proceeded in 1923–26, the humble Party members reported their "corrupt" comrades to the Central Control Commission (CCC). Comradely investigations were staged, which resulted in suspensions and exclusions from the Party. However, the leaders of the CCC were completely unsatisfied by the results of the campaign. The very establishment of an internal Parry vice squad, according to them, was something abnormal. How could it be normal for a comrade, asked Soltz, one of the chairmen of the CCC, to bring another comrade before a Party prosecution, instead of influencing the faltering comrade into righteous conduct by comradely advice and admonition)? He asserted:

If, for example, your brother or your wife, your close friend makes a mistake, I am sure that you don't summon him immediately to the C[ontrol] C[ommission], but you try to resolve the problem among yourselves, because it would be strange if a son brought his father to the CC or to judicial prosecution.[24]

Soltz, a professional revolutionary since 1898, had in mind a romantic model to be reestablished: the tight comradely unity of the underground Bolshevik sect, which allegedly existed before the Revolution. Now this unity was diluted by the arrival of many new Party members, who represented "raw material" not tempered by the harsh conditions of underground discipline. But perhaps the reestablishment of this discipline could recreate the lost unity. Now, with the underground conditions gone, this discipline had to be imposed by what Soltz called "public opinion."

This opinion, Soltz clarified further, would be akin to the "aristocratic opinion" which had earlier made impossible the marriage of an aristocrat and a peasant; this opinion would ensure discipline and the conscientious behavior of Party members without any quasi-judicial bodies. Soltz not only advocated it, he tried to create it in fact. Many of his speeches simply recounted the points made in the official resolutions of the CCC. Soltz added nothing new to the content of the resolutions, but he specifically stressed that he was trying to establish "public opinion" on the righteous conduct.

In some sense, Soltz was a good self-conscious Austinian. He consistently repeated that his objective was communicating not simply locutionary meaning, but also illocutionary and perlocutionary effects. The refrain of his speeches is always the same:

Comrades! Before everything else, I would like to tell you that on the question of party ethics we should have discussions instead of listening to reports with corresponding resolutions. . . . This is, comrades, what I wanted to tell you. It is extremely important that we exchange opinions here today, because we should create public opinion and not listen to reports.[25]

One has reasons to think of Soltz's "public opinion" as closer to Locke's "Law of Opinion" than to Habermas's "critical publicity."[26] The mechanism of Soltz's "public opinion" is the mechanism of traditional family mores or of "aristocratic opinion," given and not reflected upon. Emelian Iaroslavskii, another co-chairman of the CCC, summed it up in the following manner: "We must constantly watch such vacillating comrades, and when we see the tiniest signs of danger threatening this comrade, we should warn him, help him get out of this situation."[27]

Mutual surveillance, construed as brotherly help, was not a novel Bolshevik invention. The congregation of Puritan saints, according to Walzer, also preserved the purity of individual conscience by means of the mutual control of its members. Thus, two Puritan theologians, Field and Wilcox, wrote in *The First Admonition to the Parliament* that a congregation was held together by "an order left by God onto his Church, whereby men learn to frame their wills and doings according to the law of God by instructing and admonishing one another, yea, and by correcting and punishing all willful persons and contemners of the same." In another Walzer's telling example, Baxter reported that in his Kidderminster parish the enforcement of the moral discipline was made possible "by the zeal and diligence of the godly people of the place, who thirsted after the salvation of their neighbors, and were in private my assistants."[28]

This combination of mutual surveillance and private consciencewas not such an easy and "natural" achievement in the 1920s in Russia. However, as more and more workers and peasants joined the Party and moved upward, they contributed to the installation of mutual surveillance within the Party, first by bringing into the new milieu their traditional mutual control techniques, and second by providing a solid pretext for its installation. When a worker or a peasant became a Soviet or Party official, certain behaviors and comportments, which were heretofore fully accessible to the gaze of, and tolerated by, his or her peers, suddenly became intolerable for a Party member, and even more so for an official. These behaviors and comportments became a "personal" issue, which was indicative not only of individual corruption, but in some cases of a social illness as well.

The Korenkov case, described in the beginning of this chapter, is representative of this transition. It combines all the essential elements involved in transition to the system of comradely admonition to prevent the corruption of conscience. First, certain comportments are becoming suspect. Mistreating one's wife became highly dubious for a Party member, though such beating up and physical humiliation were accepted in both workers' and peasants' families. As any misdemeanor was revealing of the corruption of the whole Bolshevik *lichnost'*, Korenkov's relation to his wife was an early sign of his corruption. This corruption was amply proved later, by his gangster assault; but the initial signs were demonstrative enough. Second, the means to be employed are implied. Smidovich clearly advocated the introduction of comradely admonition; she pronounced the students' community ill because it failed to provide such admonition. In fact, mutual surveillance already existed as everything happened in the public gaze, but there were no conscientious individuals to warn and admonish Korenkov before it was too late.

In characterizing Korenkovism as a typical social illness, Smidovich provides a second example of it. A certain Morgunov used his official position (as an employment instructor in a trade union) for sexual pleasures. He granted employment assignments to young women only after they agreed to have sex with him. One of the victims refused to have sex, so he raped her. Having been summoned to the preliminary investigation bodies, Morgunov denied the rape, but did not deny that having met her in the district office of the trade union as a teenager for whom he, according to his professional obligations, was supposed to find employment, he engaged in sexual intercourse with her and did not attach "much significance to this fact as one which could produce excessive talk and suspicion; he considered it his personal affair."[29]

The worker Morgunov did not see an issue here. He had presumably tried sexual relations with women before, in workers' dorms in the full sight of his comrades, and it did not produce suspicion. He had behaved according to traditional patriarchal mores which prescribe subjugating a resisting female to an aggressive male, and these mores did not give rise to excessive talk. He did the same in this case, and now honestly could not understand how a workers' state could punish him for such a trifle. Once again, if there had been a comrade to admonish and instruct Morgunov before he slipped from sexual license into criminal rape, corruption would never have occurred.

Until 1926, however, appeals to introduce comradely admonition in the Party and Soviet organizations were largely wishful thinking. Smidovich's articles signified the beginning of the new effort to introduce it seriously. The Chubarov Affair of 1926 marked a watershed. In discussing it I will follow Eric Naiman's book on the Soviet sexual debates of the 1920s. To cut a long story short: twenty-four workers raped one peasant woman in Leningrad. Eight of the rapists were Komsomol members, two were Party candidates. Vivid details of the story filled the pages of newspapers, creating a popular demand that the criminals, who were characterized in biological terms, as a lower species—"loathsome reptiles," and so on—be killed. As there was no adequate punishment for the crime of group rape to satisfy the popular sentiment (eight years of imprisonment was the maximum), prosecutors charged them with banditry, so that their subsequent conviction resulted in a death sentence for eight of the rapists.[30]

The campaign immensely heightened attention to the personal lives of Bolshevik believers. Although "the rural world saw and tolerated for some time violent group rape" in Russia before the 1920s, according to Moshe Lewin,[31] once peasants had moved into the city and become Party members, the Bolshevik congregation could not tolerate it at all. The dangerous transgression of rape testified to a degree of inner corruption in the Party of the saints, in comparison to which the corruption of the students' dorm (of which Smidovich complained) seemed innocent.

One of the most remarkable consequence of the incident was an article by Iaroslavskii, which appeared in *Smena* in October 1926. The article demanded that every communist cell must know what happened in the home lives of the Party and Komsomol members to eliminate dangerous potentialities before they became crimes. Every conscientious Communist should watchfully control the details of the sexual lives of his or her comrades, unless the Party wanted such an affair to happen again. By 1927, according to Naiman, sex had become "a constant topic of non-debate." It was talked about but it was not debated, the party line being clear on these matters. Sex became a dangerous area where the impulses most corrupting to the higher conscience resided.

How did the majority of the Party members react to this dangerous linking of sex with political corruption? This majority, who were not part of the initial sect of the Bolshevik saints, but were only recently recruited, had to respond somehow. Heretofore they could be moderately licentious, and change or combine partners. Irresponsible males could abandon their pregnant females or push them in the direction of suicide. But after 1927 the environment was no longer the same.

Here lies the origin of a second crucial practice constitutive of the Soviet individual. If the initial Bolshevik saint was constituted by conversion based on revelation (*oblichenie*), then the Party members who joined the Bolshevik congregation later were predominantly formed by dissimulation (*litsemerie*). Faced with the installation of an all-pervasive mutual surveillance within the congregation, they had to hide certain comportments from fellow comrades. And since these latecomers were the vast majority, dissimulation became the dominant practice of individualization in Soviet Russia.

Ken Jowitt has grasped this peculiarity of what he calls Leninist regimes, in which, he says, dissimulation ties public and private together.[32] However, for entities to be integrated in a dissimulative structure, they must exist in the first place. Jowitt appears to assume that dissimulation is used to shield a pre-given "private" life from official surveillance and interference. In contrast, my contention would be that this "private" sphere was itself created by Leninist regimes, and dissimulation was the practice that established it. Dissimulation, therefore, would appear not as a derivative of a split between public and private in Leninist regimes, but as a central practice constitutive of this split.

The workers and peasants moving into Party and Soviet offices, which were now filled with comradely vigilance, immediately learned the dubiousness of certain conducts, which they had to conceal both at work and at home. The practice of dissimulation not entirely new, but its form was now radically recast. As Michel Confino has shown, collective dissimulation was practiced by Russian peasants against their feudal masters and the tsar's officials for ages.[33] This dissimulation did not substantially differ from similar "weapons of the weak" as found, for example, in a contemporary Malaysian village: the weak of the peasant world collectively practice dissimulation against the strong.[34] The novel aspect of Bolshevik dissimulation was that it was primarily practiced individually against the members of the peer group, not collectively against superiors. This dissimulation was also different from the dramaturgical presentation of the self in everyday Western life[35] in that it was not secondary to the already existing individual self; on the contrary, Soviet dissimulation was instrumental in constructing the Soviet individual.

The new Bolsheviks now individualized themselves primarily by dissimulation, and this aspect is better captured in the etymology of the word *pritvorstvo* than of the word *litsemerie* (both mean "dissimulation" in English, though *litsemerie* is sometimes translated as "hypocrisy"). The latter literally means "the changing of faces" (a later stage in the genealogy of a dissimulating individual), while the former comes from the Church-Slavonic verb *pritvoriati,* meaning both to dissimulate and to close oneself, as in "to close the door" or in "to close oneself off." Peasants who became workers who became Bolshevik officials had to close themselves off from the comradely congregation; they started to individualize themselves by this practice of closure. They retracted certain parts of their conduct from the public gaze, and these parts constituted the almost completely invisible, most private spheres of their lives. This retraction of dubious conduct into the ultimate and safest privacy could be hardly registered, because of its obvious secrecy. However, this process might have been reflected in what came to be known as the Great Retreat of the 1930s and 1940s.

UNIVERSALIZING SAINTHOOD

In discussing the political entrepreneurship of the Puritan saints, Michael Walzer suggested that godly magistracy was a far better description of the saints' true vocation than either capitalist acquisition or bourgeois freedom. This magistracy centered on secular repression to reform manners, with the rationale that "the men who refused to govern themselves would have to be governed nevertheless—until, in effect, they could be forced to be free."[36] The legislative initiatives of Puritans in the English Parliament included the repression of beggary and usury, and prohibitions on bearbaiting, dancing, swearing, Sunday sports, church ales, and alcoholism. In an overview of all proposed measures to reform manners, Walzer states:

> The "reformation of manners" was, or rather would have been, had it ever taken place on the scale which the ministers intended, the Puritan terror. . . . The revolutionary effort to establish a holy commonwealth in England failed. The rule of the saints was brief; the new forms of repression were never enforced through the decisive activity of a state police. . . . The fearful Puritan demand for total,

state-enforced repression was slowly forgotten . . . . [However,] who can doubt that, had the holy commonwealth ever been firmly established, godly self-discipline and mutual surveillance would have been far more repressive than the corporate system?[37]

Where saintly Puritans failed in England, saintly Bolsheviks succeeded in Russia. One could say that the Holy Commonwealth was established in the USSR after 1929 with all the related consequences. Moshe Lewin describes this development according to a classical scheme of Ernst Troeltsch: the Bolshevik sect was becoming a Church in order to universalize sainthood. The new dogma was represented in *The Short Course of the History of the Communist Party,* edited by Stalin; a laicized version of sins was adopted, and Inquisition (secret police) raged to stamp out the heresies and bring the guilty to confess their sins publicly. After the terror subsided, the quasi-religious civilization was formed: "the sacred borders" separated it from the rest of the profane world; Lenin's Commandments were its guiding light; the outwardly secular demonstrations and public ceremonies took on the role of religious rites.[38]

I would like to add to this account two other elements, often overlooked, which involved a major restructuring of everyday practices. A thrust to universalize sainthood meant that everybody was to become a Bolshevik saint. Thus, everybody had to be able to interpret sacred texts; and everybody was to behave in such a way that their deeds would be revealing of the Bolshevik *lichnost',* imbued with higher conscience. Consequently, the changes in everyday practices included the reinvigorated emphasis on individual reading and the reformation of manners.

Individual reading became the universal way to participate in the affairs of the Bolshevik church-state. Vera Dunham, in her account of the Soviet "middlebrow fiction" of the 1930s and 1940s, notes that it provided a Soviet citizen with "ersatz participation":

> The topical novel of the moment proved one of the few ways of meeting the people's need to understand their society's major workaday problems. . . . Read by parry leaders, by cultural luminaries, and their wives, as well as by high school students and housewives in small towns, and by factory and farm workers throughout the land, fiction, taken as if it were life, turned into a sort of town hall, a platform from which the system justified itself. . . . The novel substituted for the reader's sense of participation in the social processes.[39]

Participation in reading and interpreting sermons was the only initial participation allowed to the layman on the road to becoming a lay saint in Puritanism, and the Bolsheviks did not substantially differ from their counterparts. However, this participation was essential to the quasi-religious civilization. In a special res-

olution of the Central Committee on November 15, 1938, Stalin rebuked everybody who tried to substitute the ritualized public reading of *The Short Course* for
intensive individual study. The didactic Socialist Realist fiction was to play the
role of sermon and additional commentary on the Word.

Another overlooked achievement of Stalinist terror was the imposition of
a new moral order, which bound everybody by a uniform system of norms of
everyday behavior—and which, once imposed, effectively controlled de-
viance without the need for all-pervasive terror. To impose it, however, a profound terror was required; those who pretended to act like the saints, with
their zeal and lack of scruples about the use of violence, were very useful in
the creation of this new moral order.

The Reformation of Manners started once the victory of "socialism in one
country" was proclaimed in 1934. If the Holy Commonwealth had already arrived, how could the Bolsheviks tolerate the unreformed around them? Dunham describes the shift of emphasis from *kultura* to *kulturnost'*, from the deep
spirituality of the intelligentsia to an outward appearance of civilized conduct, which started in the 1930s and culminated in the 1940s. *Kulturnost'*, according to Dunham, meant a "mere program for proper conduct in public"; it
was based on a mechanism of "conforming with prescribed preferences."[40]

The Stalinist regime all of a sudden devoted intensive attention to everyday manners; "impeccable conduct," which meant manageable, predictable,
proper manners, became the center of the propaganda campaign. Obsession
with *kulturnost'*, "a fetish notion of how to be individually civilized," started
with elite attention to personal hygiene, and then spread in admonitory and
educative fashion to the whole society; clean nails, abstinence from cursing
and spitting, and a minimum of good manners now defined the model citizen.

Nicholas Timasheff documents this change in his book *The Great Retreat.*
He argues that after Stalin proclaimed in 1935 that life under socialism should
be "beautiful and joyous," the original Bolshevik ascetic self-abnegation became suspect. *Komsomolskaia Pravda* now wrote:

> We endorse beauty, smart clothes, chic coiffures, manicures. . . . Girls should be
> attractive. Perfume and makeup belong to the "must" of a good Komsomol girl.
> . . . Clean shaving is mandatory for a Komsomol boy.[41]

Manners were constantly discussed and taught. Dancing schools were opened
in 1935. Public carnivals started in 1936, where people could demonstrate the
dancing skills they had learned; these carnivals contributed to a sense of fun
which now seems macabre. A journal *Moda* (Fashion) appeared in 1935 also, to
give guidance about good taste in dress. *The Book of Tasty and Healthy Food*
was quick to follow, with quotations from Politburo member Anastas Mikoyan,
who among many things advocated "moderate civilized drinking." This book

became the bible of *kulturnost'*; possessed by every family, it gave unobtrusive advice not only on cooking, but on civilized manners in consuming food and on the appropriate social setting for this activity.

The inculcation of basic manners was not the sole objective of the "new moral order"; rather, it was concomitant to all the other changes that Timasheff has called the Great Retreat. With Communist experimentation in every realm of life abruptly curtailed, many "traditional" values of prerevolutionary Russia were restored. Thus, the alleged sexual license of the 1920s was replaced by an emphasis on marriage as the most serious affair in life; disrespect towards elders and superiors had to be punished immediately; "cultural revolution" in the schools was reversed to restore the czarist educational system, with its ranks and honors; in literature, art, and theater experimentation had to yield in favor of the popular taste for the understandable and recognizable.

Timasheff explained this radical and sudden "retreat" by the need to strengthen the social basis of dictatorship in the face of the coming war. Stalin was held to have set aside the initial projects of Communist transformation in favor of consolidating the dictatorial system, appeasing substantial groups of the population, and securing the efficiency of national labor.[42] This may be true, but the complementary explanation holds also: all the measures that contributed to the Great Retreat follow the simple logic of a saintly dictatorship becoming a Holy Commonwealth. Thus, we should not take the imagery of "retreat" entirely at face value as Timasheff seems to understand it; for most of the population, the Great Retreat meant adopting profoundly new modes of activity, which marked a new stage in the Bolshevik Reformation.

For example, the reassertion of the "old-fashioned" type of family was completely logical from the standpoint of the saint. Even Calvin, who admonished his followers to break loose from the unclean bondage of Catholic marriage ties and get away from France into Geneva, advised them to marry upon arrival, so each man could become master of a reformed household which was to be structured like a little parish, on godly principles.[43] The same happened with Bolsheviks. They always had the aim of "shaking and restructuring the everyday life,"[44] including breaking down the old marital bondage and building new families that were to become what Lenin's wife Nadezhda Krupskaia called "the union of equal comrades building Communism together." Before 1934 this was an option for conscientious Bolshevik saints; afterwards, when everybody was given the means to become a lay saint, this became a must.

Hence, the novel emphasis on the conscientious *lichnaia zhizn'* of every Soviet person (who was soon to become a lay Bolshevik with the advent of the Holy Commonwealth) emerged. Yet, as sexual transgressions were now held to be indicative of the corruption of saintly conscience, the Great Retreat signified not a radical break with, but a continuation of, the developments of the 1920s: the saintly standards were now imposed on a greater society. And if only Communists initially had to withdraw their sexual behavior from the public gaze, now this was required from every Soviet citizen. All Soviet people had to appear outwardly to be imbued with Stalinist virtue in sexual conduct.

A more radical novelty was contained in the fact that everybody was now supposed to have and foster *lichnaia zhizn'* (about which many Russians did not care before, in the sense that home and family life had not been considered a problematic matter either for them or for the authorities), and simultaneously to abandon *chastnaia zhizn'* (if they ever had one). The two terms, almost synonymous until the 1930s, and virtually indistinguishable for the mass of the population because both were largely a nonissue, parted ways. *Lichnaia zhizn'* (that is, personal life) became one of those lawful terrains where Bolshevik *lichnost'* was to reveal itself; *chastnaia zhizn'* (that is, private life) was increasingly associated with corrupt behavior per se.

Two narratives from 1935 will clarify this pattern. The first one is from the Komsomol journal *Young Guard*. A model collective of young metro construction workers gathers in a dorm to discuss questions of love. In the "cozy room of 14 Komsomol girls" a phonograph is playing and cakes are served on the white tablecloth—signs *of kulturnost'*. (Note, however, that fourteen women living in one room is still considered to be "good living conditions.") At first defenders of the now obsolete Bolshevik "free love" stance and of bourgeois privacy are rebuked; then the central disputation is waged between two model women.

Vera loves a man who consistently overfulfills the plan, but who turns out to be uncultured (*nekulturny*): she cannot talk with him about anything but production plans. Nadezhda makes a rejoinder: this is not the worst case. A *nekulturny* by birth may join a kolkhoz or a factory, get promoted, acquire higher education, and end up as a *kulturny* engineer or manager. The truly "uncultured" person is the one who dissimulates. Nadezhda had been the victim of one of these; he "deceived her, saying that he loved her when in fact he was married." In the end a secretary of the Komsomol organization, pressed to draw a general conclusion, reluctantly sets the "correct line" in family matters: "Our family has serious tasks, because one works well when personal life is organized and rightly adjusted."[45]

This narrative yields some interesting conclusions. The first crucial feature of the debate is that everyone has a specific story from their *lichnaia zhizn'* to tell, which is a novel feature for the genre of the didactic story. Previously, everybody would denounce a single transgressor, who had made his or her *lichnaia zhizn'* an object of specific public attention or an issue of public debate, as Morgunov or Korenkov did, for instance. Now everybody has his or her own *lichnaia zhizn'*, worthy of relating in public. The novelty of this condition is felt by almost everybody present: potential speakers are very nervous, and they keep their life stories, written on little sheets of paper, handy; this may help them overcome the confusion of telling the narrative of their *lichnaia zhizn'* for the first time in their lives. Second, this personal life is righteous only when it is *kulturny* and well organized. The primary corruption of such personal life is represented by the figure of the dissimulator, who certainly should not be part of one's personal life.

Another narrative clearly links *chastnaia zhizn'* to corruption. A corrupting dissimulator has a *chastnaia zhizn'* as opposed to a righteous *lichnaia zhizn'*. In a characteristic article entitled "The Private Life of the Engineer Mirzoev," *Pravda* engages in a campaign against "fluttering scoundrels" of whom Mirzoev is a genuine representative. The narrative is simple. They met at 7 PM in the city park, at 9 they danced, at 11 they decided to marry, and the next day they consummated their marriage. On the morning after—surprise, surprise— the poor girl did not find Mirzoev next to her. He had fled. When she tried to locate him through state agencies, she found out that he was being sought by criminal prosecutors for having married six times already. *Pravda* did not weep over the girl's misfortune, but called for a demonstration trial of such Mirzoevs, who committed such sins in their private lives.[46]

After a gradually mounting campaign, *chastnaia zhizn'* was discursively assassinated in 1938 by no less figure than Zhdanov. The pretext was formidable: top members of the Komsomol Central Committee were dismissed and executed for "lordly neglect" of the everyday life of the rank and file Komsomol members, which allegedly resulted in the infiltration of student dorms by Trotskyites and Bukharinites. Zhdanov specifically underlined that enemies of the people found one of the weakest spots of Komsomol, that is, everyday life, and declared everyday life a "private affair." They tried to corrupt the Komsomol cadres by means of moral degradation: through alcoholism and false drunken camaraderie. . . . The Komsomol leaders [*aktiv*] should not live their lives apart from the masses, as they used to heretofore. . . . They should interfere everywhere where young people spend their time, untiringly enlighten and organize them.[47]

The point was made clear: treating life away from the work site as "private life" was an enemy strategy; "private life" had no right to exist anymore. At the same time the "personal life" of every Soviet youth was to be subject to constant surveillance and organization. Commenting on the results of the recent purge of Komsomol leaders, *Komsomolskaia Pravda* reasserted in the editorial: "Everyday life is not a private affair, it is the most crucial zone of class struggle; everyday life is inseparable from politics; and people who are not honest in everyday life, who are morally depraved, are depraved politically."[48]

THE COMRADELY SOCIETY

By the 1950s mutual surveillance comes to be seen as the primary mechanism of social cohesion. Every collectivity — and not only the party cell — is to be a congregation, based on constant mutual surveillance and the reform or punishment of transgressors. Thus, in 1958, an article in *Kornsomolskaia Pravda* entitled "Is It Necessary to Interfere in Personal Life?" restated the now well-established ideological dictum that

> We live . . . in a socialist society where comradely and friendly relations have been substituted for the lupine laws of capitalism. And we cannot be indifferent to what is called personal life, personal relations, because in the final account these personal relations inevitably become public [*obshchestvennymi*].

But the best means of regulating personal life, as described in the article, consist of "comradely sensitivity" and the "heart-to-heart talk." In the "real story" that constitutes the main body of the article, these means are applied to stop the crumbling of a workers' family. A veteran rank-and-file Communist, a worker from the same factory named Vera Pavlovna (an allusion to Chernyshevsky?), goes to talk with the members of the family, and the problem is fixed in a day. What would have happened, asks *Komsomolskaia Pravda*, "if . . . comrades were to come to a sudden stop in front of the invisible gate bearing the strict inscription 'Personal Life'?"[49]

An important clue to the attitude behind this didactic tale lies in the fact that the Russian word *obschchestvennyi*, translated as "public" in the quotation above, is more literally, and more properly, translated as "social." In fact, contemporary Russian usage barely employs the word *publika* (the most common reference is to the audience in the theater), which has a strong archaic connotation when it is used at all. The English word "public" is usually translated as *obshchestvo*, the same word that is most often used for "society" in Russian. While this might appear to be merely a linguistic accident, it actually points to some deeper conceptual issues, which can be illuminated by drawing on Hannah Arendt's distinction between "the public" and "the social."[50] Arendt's conception of the historical advent of "the social" seems to capture nicely many of the emerging features of Soviet life in the transition to the "benign" society of the period from the 1950s to the 1970s. Thus, one is led to suspect that *Sovetskoe obschestvo* was indeed regulated by mechanisms of a "social" rather than a genuinely "public" character—and that using the word "public" at all in the Soviet context is quite misleading, if not profoundly erroneous.

According to Arendt, the classical form of the public/private divide in the Western tradition marks the separation between a "public realm" of political action and critical discussion about common concerns and a "private realm" of legitimate privacy and particularism centered on the household.[51] These two spheres, while distinct, are also complementary and mutually supportive. A key feature of the modern age, however, is that this borderline has increasingly been effaced by "the rise of the social," a new realm marked by a blend of impersonal administration and mass conformism, whose tendency is to undermine and supersede both "the public" and "the private." The majority of everyday modes of behavior, such as working for large organizations, are neither "public" nor "private," strictly speaking, but are "social" in this sense. On the one hand, "politics" in the sense of "public" action is displaced by command and administration. On the other hand, such formerly "private" tasks as education, welfare, and reproduction become the object of "social concern," while the "private sphere" shrinks to the smallest possible "intimate" sphere, in which obedient individuals engage in leisure activities and culture consumption.

Two features of the social are especially significant for my exposition. First, as Hanna Pitkin notes in her book on Arendt's conception of the social, it is a curiously hybrid realm, neither private nor public, and it looks almost like an enormously overgrown household; members of the social realm are supposed to behave, and be treated, like members of a family. Second, in the words of Arendt herself, "modern privacy in its most relevant function, to shelter the intimate, was discovered as the opposite of . . . the social."[52]

Whatever the value of this account for grasping Western developments, it sheds a great deal of light on the Soviet case. The social expanded in the Soviet Union, stamping out whatever could have been called before its arrival "public" or "private", in Arendt's terms. For example, Soltz called for the Party congregation to be run like a family; later the family-like mechanism of comradely admonition was imposed on all citizens, not only on the Party. And one crucial effect of the imposition of "the social," of *Sovetskoe obshchestvo* —that is, "Soviet society" as opposed to the "revolutionary public"—is the retreat of the private into the intimate. However, this retreat occurred differently from the one in the West. Private life did not shrink to intimacy in the sense of a legitimate and protected sphere of privacy. Both privacy and particularism were completely rejected and stamped out by the social: *chastnaia zhizn'* was discursively assassinated. The social, *Sovetskoe obshchestvo,* was to allocate and regulate both the quasi-public (the world of work) and the quasi-private (the world of personal life, of *lichnaia zhizn'*). There was no recognized sphere left which was not, in principle, part of the social.

The private, however, was reestablished as the secret but pervasive underside of the social, as the invisible sphere of the most intimate comportment, carefully hidden by individual dissimulation. This dissimulation was so thorough that it did not offer even a glimpse of the secret obverse of the social. This was the real Great Retreat. The Soviet people might actually appear to be a monolithic bloc of fighters for Communism, conforming to the official image and providing a referent for the horrifying concepts of some Western theoreticians of totalitarianism. *Chastnaia zhizn'* became invisible; it was hidden not only from the leaders or from foreign observers, but—primarily, and for that reason, more thoroughly—from the pervasive surveillance of surrounding comrades.

EPILOGUE

Michelle Perrot, introducing a volume that deals with the influence of the French Revolution on private life, states that even if the revolution exploded the distinction of public from private in the short run, and denigrated the private in favor of the public, it reasserted this dichotomy in the long run.[53] The exposition of this essay points to the conclusion that something similar happened with the Russian Revolution. Bearing in mind Walzer's convincing argument that Puritan, Jacobin, and Bolshevik politics are simply three different examples of revolutions of the saints, this outcome may seem to have been a foregone conclusion.

However, this chapter has also tried to articulate the differences between the "shaking and restructuring" of public and private in these Western revolutions and the changes that occurred in Russia. The Bolshevik revolution did not explode the distinction between public and private and then reestablish it in a different form. Rather, it swept it away and replaced it, in the long run, with a division between the "social," which consists of transparent "public" *and* "personal" lives, and an unseen, unrecognized private which does not exceed the most intimate. The dissimulation covering this intimate sphere became the most profound practice of Soviet society.

In this comparison another difference comes to the fore. It has been argued that the Marquis de Sade may be considered a logical corollary of the French Revolution. He is said to have put nature and reason in the hands of unrestrained egotism, and he did so in private, thus turning the private into a space of the cruelest enjoyment. He used revolutionary methods to achieve the most private of aims. De Sade is the *reductio ad absurdum* of the French Revolution, Lynn Hunt suggests in her contribution to the Perrot volume.[54]

But de Sade is a singular and visible absurdity, the kind of horrible exception that proves the benign rule, and which the revolution is capable of containing. The Russian Revolution, however, had its own horrible absurdities which it was unable to contain, because it could not see them. Dissimulation just covered them up. Contemporary Russian society may have inherited these along with the dissimulative structure of the Soviet self, which might be perhaps the only stable legacy from the Soviet past.

Andrei Chikatilo, a humble schoolteacher and office worker, raped, killed, and cannibalized fifty-two people between 1978 and 1990.

> Judge Akubzhanov said Mr. Chikatilo succeeded in evading the arrest so long primarily because he was so unremarkable. In everyday life he was a father whose two children paid him little heed, a Communist Party member who always posted pictures of [the] Politburo in his workplace. Yet in his secret life he was an insatiable sadist, always on the prowl for a victim, never leaving home without a knife and rope in the event that he might find one, the judge said.[55]

NOTES

1. Sofia Smidovich, "O Korenkovshchine" [On Korenkovism] in *Partiinaia etika: Dokumenty i materialy diskussii dvadtsatykh godov* [Party Ethics: Documents and Materials of the Party Discussion of the 1920s], ed. A. A. Guseinov *et al.* (Moscow: Politizdat, 1989), 382.

2. Smidovich, "O Korenkovshchine," 383.

3. Nikolai Berdiaev, *Istoki i smysl russkogo kommunizma* [The Origins and Meaning of Russian Communism] (Paris: YMCA-Press, 1955).

4. Pavel Miliukov, *Ocherki po istorii russkoi kultury, vol. 2: Tserkov i shkola* [Sketches of the History of Russian Culture, vol. 2: Church and School] (St. Petersburg, 1897), 93.

5. Michael Walzer, *The Revolution of the Saints: A Study in the Origins of Radical Politics* (New York: Atheneum, 1968).

6. Steven Lukes, *Individualism* (London: Blackwell, 1973), 61.

7. Walzer, *Revolution of the Saints*, 12, 301.

8. Vladimir Lenin, "What Is to Be Done?" in his *Collected Works* (Moscow: Progress Publishers, 1964), vol. 4, 400–401. (All quotations from Lenin follow this translation, except that *oblichenie* is translated as "revelation.")

9. Lenin, "What Is to Be Done?" 417, emphasis added.

10. See Mircea Eliade, *The Sacred and the Profane* (New York: Viking, 1958).

11. Lenin, "What Is to Be Done?" 414.

12. Quoted in Walzer, *Revolution of the Saints,* p. 145.

13. Robert C. Tucker, *Stalin as Revolutionary, 1879—1929: A Study in History and Personality* (New York: Norton, 1973), 116.

14. Walzer, *Revolution of the Saints,* 146.

15. Lenin, "What Is to Be Done?" 430.

16. See Katerina Clark, *The Soviet Novel: History as Ritual* (Chicago: University of Chicago Press, 1981).

17. Vladimir Dal', *Tolkovyi slovar' zhivago velikorusskago iazyka* [Dictionary of the Living Russian Language], 5th ed. (Moscow: Russkii iazyk, 1980), vol. 3, 596.

18. See Michel Foucault, *The History of Sexuality, vol. I: Introduction* (New York: Pantheon, 1978).

19. Michel Foucault, "Truth and Subjectivity" (transcript of the Howison Lectures delivered October 20–21, 1980; kept in the Howison Library of the University of California, Berkeley). An edited version was published as Foucault, "About the Beginning of the Hermeneutic of the Self," *Political Theory* 21, no. 3 (May 1993).

20. Joseph Stalin, "O nekotorykh voprosakh istorii bolshevizma" [Concerning Some Questions of the History of Bolshevism], in his *Voprosy Leninisma* [Problems of Leninism] (Moscow: Gospolitizdat, 1952).

21. Aaron Soltz, "O partiinoi etike" [On Party Ethics, 1924], in *Partiinaia etika*, ed. Guseinov *et al.*, 265.

22. *Slovar' sovremennogo russkogo literaturnogo iazyka* [Dictionary of Contemporary Russian Literary Language] (Moscow: Institut russkogo iazyka, 1955–68), vol. 17, 779.

23. *Slovar' sovremennogo russkogo literaturnogo iazyka*, vol. 6, 298.

24. Aaron Soltz, "O partetike" [On Party Ethics, 1925], in *Partiinaia etika*, ed. Guseinov *et al.*, 278.

25. Soltz, "O partetike," 273, 292.

26. See Jurgen Habermas, *The Structural Transformation of the Public Sphere* (Cambridge, MA: MIT Press, 1989)

27. Emelian Iaroslavskii, "O partetike" [On Party Ethics], in *Partiinaia etika*, ed. Guseinov *et al.*, 175.

28. Walzer, *Revolution of the Saints*, 220, 221.

29. Smidovich, "O Korenkovshchine," 385.

30. Eric Naiman, *Sex in Public: The Incarnation of Early Soviet Ideology* (Princeton: Princeton University Press, 1997), esp. chapter 7.

31. Moshe Lewin, *The Making of the Soviet System* (New York: Pantheon, 1985), 55.

32. Ken Jowitt, *The New World Disorder: Leninist Extinction* (Berkeley: University of California Press, 1992), 72.

33. Michel Confino, *Société et mentalités collectives en Russie sous l'ancien régime* (Paris: Institut d'Etudes Slaves, 1981)

34. James C. Scott, *Weapons of the Weak. Everyday Forms of Peasant Resistance* (New Haven: Yale University Press, 1985)

35. See, for example, Erving Goffman, *The Presentation of Self in Everyday Life* (Garden City, NY: Doubleday, 1959).

36. Walzer, *Revolution of the Saints*, 224.

37. Walzer, *Revolution of the Saints*, 226, 230–31, 305.

38. Lewin, *The Making of the Soviet System*, 305.

39. Vera Dunham, *In Stalin's Time: Middleclass Values in Soviet Fiction* (Cambridge: Cambridge University Press, 1976), 25.

40. Dunham, *In Stalin's Time,* 22.

41. Quoted in Nicholas Timasheff, *The Great Retreat* (New York: Dutton, 1946), 317.

42. Timasheff, *The Great Retreat,* 358.

43. Walzer, *Revolution of the Saints*, 48–49.

44. Lev Trotskii, "Voprosy byta" [Problems of Everyday Life], *Pravda*, 17 August 1923.

45. Galina Ancharova, "Diskussiia u komsomoltsev metro" [Discussion in the Metro Workers' Komsomol Organization], *Molodaia Gvardiia* 14, no. 7 (July 1935), 162–66.

46. "Chastnaia zhizn' inzhenera Mirzoeva," *Pravda,* 19 June 1935.

47. Andrei Zhdanov, "Rech' na Yubileinom Plenume TsK VLKSM" [Speech at the Jubilee Plenum of the Central Committee of Komsomol], *Komsomolskaia pravda,* 4 November 1938.

48. "Bolshe vnimaniia k studencheskim obshchezhitiiam" [More Attention to Student Dorms], *Komsomolskaia pravda,* 15 December 1938.

49. S. Garbuzov, "Nuzhno li vmeshivatsia v lichnuiu zhizn'?" (Is It Necessary to Interfere in Personal Life?), *Komsomolskaia pravda,* 4 January 1958.

50. I rely here on the interpretation advanced in Hanna Pitkin, *The Attack of the Blob: Hannah Arendt's Concept of the Social* (Chicago: University of Chicago Press, 1998).

51. See Hannah Arendt, *The Human Condition* (Chicago: University of Chicago Press, 1958).

52. Arendt, *Human Condition,* 38.

53. Michelle Perrot, ed., *A History of Private Life, vol. 4: From the Fires of Revolution to the Great War,* 9.

54. Lynn Hunt, "The Unstable Boundaries of French Revolution," in *From the Fires of Revolution*, ed. Perrot, 36.

55. Serge Schmemann, "As Shrieks Fill Court, Killer in Russia Is Sentenced to Die," *New York Times,* 16 October 1992.

Chapter Four

Nation and Nature

The thesis of this chapter was suggested by curious etymological parallels in English and Russian: the English words "nation" and "nature" are both related to the Latin word *nasci* (meaning "to be born"); while their Russian equivalents, *narod* (or *rodina*) and *priroda* are both related to the Russian verb *rodit'* (to give birth). If both languages suggest the relationship of concepts of nation and nature to the process of natality, what does this tell us about the contemporary linkage of these concepts? This question seems particularly salient, given the growth of ethno-nationalism in the aftermath of the collapse of the Soviet Union with its civic definition of nationhood, and the recent reemergence of a commonsensical understanding of a nation as a group of common descent or community linked by blood ties. Understanding the complex interrelationships among the concepts of nature, nation and natality may offer some keys to the puzzle of the "naturalness" with which the concept of nation was "re-natalized" recently, if not to suggest ways of challenging the currently predominant ethnic definition of nation in post-Soviet space.

I shall not, however, primarily study the direct links between concepts of "nation" and "nature," contrary to what the title may imply. The role of natural imagery in constructing the idea of the nation, as well as the role of nations in fostering or destroying nature, are not my main concerns. Instead, I shall try to examine the common relationship of these concepts to the concept of natality, and its implications. Thus, I shall first describe the conceptual histories of each term, articulate their links to a currently predominant vision of natality, and then show how these links may be reconceptualized if—following the writings of Hannah Arendt—the underlying concept of natality is recast itself. Briefly, both nature and nation may be now conceived as realms of genuine political action in Arendt's sense of this term.

NATION

Conceptual histories of this term abound. Raymond Williams, in his succinct summary of the development of the English word "nation," states that it was used to designate "a racial group rather than a politically organized grouping" since at least the thirteenth century, and that the new clearly political meaning emerged only in the sixteenth century,[1] although terms like "realm," "kingdom" and "country" were more widespread in usage up until the seventeenth century. Only after that time did "nation" begin to be used to designate all those living in a given country as opposed to some particular subgroup. Liah Greenfeld offered a most detailed historical lexicography of the Latin term *natio* and its equivalents in major European languages, tracing a similar development. In Rome, *natio* indicated a group of foreigners united by a place of origin, non-citizens whose status was lower than that of the Romans. In the Middle Ages, the same meaning—a group of common descent—was applied to describe the famous "nations" of students in medieval universities that were named after the alleged place of origin. Since students engaged in debates, the term came to designate a community of opinion. When similar communities of clerics clashed on ecclesiastical matters, also frequently representing an interest of some secular power at the Church Councils, "nation" became equated to "elite." Even when in English the word "nation" was already employed to describe the whole of the population, writes Greenfeld, Montesquieu, de Maistre, and Schopenhauer still used equivalents of the Latin term *natio* to refer to elites in their countries. Of course, with democratic revolutions, and a concomitant equal status of elite and plebs, "nation" eventually expanded in all European languages to include all of the population of a given country. In the end, with the birth of ethnic and other particularistic nationalisms, the idea of "a particular nation" as distinct from other nations was born.[2]

Hobsbawm's brief *Begriffsgeschichte,* while based on different source material, does not differ much from Greenfeld's story. He, however, puts more emphasis on the French Revolution to demonstrate how particular groups traditionally called "nations"—corporations of students, merchants, or inhabitants of the same region—were stripped of this designation following the introduction of the civic definition of nationhood that applied to the "whole French people," distinguished from particular interests. Altogether, most commentaries on conceptual development stress the double medieval connotation of *natio* that a civic definition of nationhood sought to efface: either birth or descent group, or a "small place of birth," *pays natal.*[3] However, with the spread of modern ethno-nationalism that rejects civic nationhood and also equates nations with communities of descent rooted in common blood ties, these two old connotations reemerged.

This re-emergence is particularly manifest after the recent collapse of those state-socialist countries that previously espoused a civic definition of nationhood (for example, Yugoslavia or the USSR): a natality-based vision of nationhood has returned in everyday interactions. Nowadays, at least in Russia, questions like "what ethnic nationality are your parents?" and "what ethnicity does your family name reveal?" have become the everyday means of defining one's nationhood, now predominantly understood in ethnic rather than in political terms. A usual interpretation of this unproblematic current usage of the "natality test" in everyday interaction—a procedure to which all subscribe habitually and almost unconsciously when thinking on national matters in post-Soviet space—is that it is an indelible mark of the Soviet past, when ancillary categories of ethnic origins were recorded in internal passports.[4] As Rogers Brubaker nicely summed up:

> An . . . elaborate and distinctive system of personal nationality . . . divided the population of the state into an exhaustive and mutually exclusive set of national groups, over a hundred in all, twenty-two with more than a million members . . . Ethnic nationality . . . was . . . an obligatory and mainly ascriptive legal category, a key element of an individual's legal status. As such, it was registered in internal passports and other personal documents, transmitted by descent, and recorded in almost all bureaucratic encounters and official transactions.[5]

Still, given the overarching identity of a Soviet citizen, many people before 1991 defined themselves as "Soviet," rather than "Russian" or "Ukrainian" and so on. With the dissolution of the Soviet Union, these secondary, ethnically defined but state-registered identities came into the foreground, states the usual argument.

In addition to this usual institutional interpretation of the origins of a currently predominant ethnic definition of post-Soviet nationhood, I would like to suggest that it is also rooted in a more fundamental predisposition—in an adherence to an intuitively obvious myth of the nation as stemming from a common process of natality, as a community united by natural evolution and blood ties. Kate Soper, one of the most astute students of the interconnection of nation and nature, writes on this "naturalness" of the ethnic definition of nationhood, so obvious for everyday consciousness:

> . . . the deployment of the idea of the nation as tribe or family, whose members are linked by the blood-tie, is manifestly an attempt to create a piece of "nature": to obscure the artificial, or "fictional" (Ernest Gellner), or "imaginary" (Benedict Anderson) or "fantastical" (Slavoj Zizek) quality of the national entity . . . What is in reality a cultural construction and a quite recent one at that, is massaged into existence by means of a myth of its immemorially archaic origins and "natural" evolution.[6]

Thus, it would seem that this myth of nation as a unity based on common descent and blood ties is rooted in an intuitive appreciation of the process of natality. A vision of an unending process of successive births—a continuous chain of birth labors, one might say—serves to warrant the "self-evidence" of this ethnic mythology.

"Nation," however, is not the only concept whose qualities, self-evident to common sense, derive from its rootedness in natality. The concept of nature is also grounded in a similar appreciation of the process of natality. In particular, the "realist" sense of the term "nature," in Soper's classification,[7] that is, a view of nature as a unity of natural processes independent of man, seems to have been originally modeled on and to be still residually linked to the notion of natality.

NATURE

Raymond Williams starts his exposition on the conceptual history of the term "nature" by claiming that it is perhaps the most complicated word in English. However, he easily distinguishes its three primary meanings. Since the thirteenth century "nature" is used to refer to the essential quality or feature of something, being most frequently used in conjunction with the word designating the object it defines, as in Latin *natura homini,* "the nature of man." Second, from the fourteenth century on the term designates the inherent force which directs either a world or a human being or both (as in examples supplied by the OED: "nature impelled me to that deed" or "a contrast between nature and grace"). Finally, starting from the seventeenth century it comes to designate "the material world itself, taken as including or not including human beings."[8] This third sense will concern us primarily in the following exposition. Indeed, in theoretical constructions nations may be linked to a certain nature of things national (first meaning) or to particular visions of human nature (first meaning, once again), that is, of national character; they may be linked to "natural" urges and forces driving nations to certain ends (the second meaning). Still, ethnonationalism more often depends on the view of nature as a unity of natural things around us or including us, driven by an inexorable evolutionary process, of which the development of nations is just one example.

A study of historical Latin usage shows that this third meaning of *natura* appeared substantially later than its first meaning, which was directly linked to the etymological origin of the term. Being the past participle of *nasci,* *natura* means "the born" of things, whatever is born with them, comes into being with them. *Natura,* of course, was used to translate the Greek word *ph-*

ysis, which meant "something born, engendered, begotten," and which was therefore also frequently linked to the etymological meaning of the root verb, "to give birth."[9] Thus, Sophocles speaks of the *physis* of the sea, meaning its animals as "those born by the sea," *pontou t'einalian physis*.[10] This is an early usage, generally effaced by the later one, in which the inborn qualities developed from being visible external features to be invisible internal characteristics. Thus, Homer implies external features in the single instance of his use of *physis*, in a scene where Hermes tears the herb moly out of the soil "and shows [Odysseus] its nature *(physin)*, that it was black at the root, and its flower was white like milk."[11] By contrast, Parmenides already talks about *physis* as an inner quality of a thing. Yet, etymological connotations of birth are still very much at work: "You will know the nature *(physin) of* ether . . . you will know from where all intimate affairs of the sun are engendered *(exegenonto)* . . . and will know the embracing sky, from where it was born *(ephy,* the root verb for *physis)*."[12]

Eventually the Stoics dislodge this direct link of *physis* or *natura* to natality and birth and develop the second meaning of the term—an inherent driving force of a phenomenon, so that their famous dictum "live according to nature" means living in accordance with the driving force of divine law that moves all things. Later, Lucretius becomes the first to introduce the third meaning of the term *natura*, in the sense of the unity of natural things around us—a usage still absent from the thought of his teacher, Epicurus, and his contemporary, Cicero. Indeed, *natura* is mentioned 234 times in *De Natura Rerum*, mostly in the sense of *natura rei*, a "born" nature of a certain thing (almost two-thirds of the uses). Other uses reflect either the notion of *natura rerum*, a general essence of all existing things, or *natura* as an inherent driving force characteristic of the Stoics. A decisive innovation happens when Lucretius introduces the usage *natura rerum creatrix* (creative) or *natura gubernans* (directing). This third meaning is still a cautious neologism that aims at capturing the role of the world as a unity of active natural forces in the Epicurean philosophy, restated by Lucretius, and is thus mentioned very rarely— *natura creatrix* appears only three times in the poem.[13] Still, this usage introduces a very important vision, so obvious to us nowadays, and reflected in the third meaning of the English word "nature."

Furthermore, an extension of meaning of *natura* that Lucretius offers— envisaging nature as an active creator that gives birth to things without the interference of gods—is very interesting to us in that it stresses the natality inherent in nature. Thus, *rerum natura creatrix* is often used interchangeably with *materia genitalis* (engendering substance, with *materia* related to "mother" in Latin), an expression the etymology of which immediately suggests the motherly quality of nature that gives birth to all existing things.[14]

Conventional representation of Nature as a female goddess or motherly figure is undoubtedly linked to this imagery. Therefore, an initial extension of
the meaning of *natura* by Lucretius—developing from the original Greek
"born quality of the thing" and the Stoics' "inherent force that drives it" to
"everything that exists around us"—is still very much dependent on the concept of natality, on the capacity of Nature to give birth to and create all existing phenomena. Later writers will pick up the three meanings of the Latin
term without necessarily reflecting on the initial link of the concept of nature
to natality. They will employ these meanings to their own aims, or remold
them to create other derivative meanings, seemingly obliterating the links of
the concept to natality. Still, even in contemporary thinking, which frequently
conceives of nature in a realist sense—as a set of processes independent of
human will—there is a residual reminder of the origin of the concept in the
image of natality. There is a striking affinity between the contemporary vision
of natality as an orderly process of natural gestation—a process that two human beings may set into motion, but can scarcely affect thereafter—and the
realist vision of nature.

In many cases, natality even serves as the model for processes carried out
in the "natural way." As Soper notes, one of the main distinctions that structure contemporary thinking on nature opposes what is naturally given to what
is artificially contrived, being a product of culture or convention.[15] Natality
may easily be the best example of naturality in this sense: gestation and birth
long seemed to be least prone to human intervention or convention. What is
important in this perception of the naturalness of natality is the stress on the
inexorable process that progresses in an orderly way through certain stages
independent of the human will. Thus, a conception of natality is still intimately linked to a vision of nature conceived as a set of deep inexorable
processes, independent of humans.

NATURE DENATURALIZED: IMPLICATIONS FOR THE UNDERSTANDING OF A NATION

However, this very independence of natural processes has been recently put
into question by the philosophical and sociological studies of science. It
seems that a nice, clear-cut separation between natural and cultural phenomena, to be studied by radically different types of sciences, is of a recent origin. Before modernity, it would seem, both "nature" and "culture" coexisted
together in an undifferentiated unity. Thus, according to Stephen Toulmin, the
breaking of a single cosmopolis into its constituent natural and political parts
was a result of applying the Cartesian mind-body dualism to this initial unity.

This application and subsequent segregation of the natural from the cultural had clear political underpinnings, since the resulting picture of the world, what he calls the "Modern Framework," helped stabilize Europe after the turmoils of the religious wars of the first half of the seventeenth century, by conferring legitimacy on the system of the newly formed nation-states.[16]

Bruno Latour has offered another version of a critique of the origins of the nature/culture divide. Following a well-known argument of Shapin and Schaffer on the centrality of the debate on vacuum and air-pumps between Thomas Hobbes and Robert Boyle for understanding the character of modernity,[17] Latour picks these scientists as representing the two respective sides of the same modern project. If Hobbes opts for constructing politics without nature, then Boyle constructs nature without politics. Of course, both Boyle and Hobbes paid attention to both natural and political phenomena: Hobbes wrote a lot on the politics of nature, while Boyle had his strong ideas on the nature of politics. These aspects of their works are now conventionally overlooked by contemporary studies, since the followers of Hobbes and Boyle disregarded the discordant elements in their intellectual heritage that did not fit into the clean-cut separation of a career of a political philosopher from that of a natural scientist.

Latour suggests that this separation of nature from politics or culture becomes more and more questionable nowadays. Current multiplication of what he calls "hybrids"—networks of human-technical interaction—make distinguishing their natural from their cultural elements more and more difficult. For example, the problems of ozone layer or AIDS research bring together large collectivities of people and technical artifacts in interdependent networks or chains of interaction, in which a change of one molecule in the formula of an AIDS treatment or aerosol spray may result in the reconfiguration of whole cities affected by layoffs. Maintaining sperm banks, enforcing rights of humans kept in a state of brain death but whose life is artificially supported by elaborate machinery, sales of organs and fetal tissue: are these activities dealing with humans or non-humans? Latour suggests that there is hardly an answer to this question, and that similar questions may indicate our growing awareness that we have always existed in networks of cultural and natural elements. Many cultures have experienced the totem as an undifferentiated unity of human and natural qualities; this "network experience" could apply to modern civilizations as well. Furthermore, theoretical problems appear when we try to conceptually cut the network into two distinct parts, into humans and non-humans: "It is only when we remove the nonhumans churned up by the collective that the residue, which we call society, becomes incomprehensible, because its size, its durability and its solidity no longer have a cause."[18] If each society is just a result of convention, it is hard to understand what gives this convention durability and longevity. By contrast, socio-technical networks possess size, durability and solidity as their obvious qualities: "No one has ever heard of a collective that did not mobilize heaven and earth in its composition, along with bodies and souls, property and law, gods and ancestors, powers and beliefs, beasts and fictional beings."[19]

But if "nature" understood as a result of our habitual subtraction of humans from natural-cultural networks is a dubious construct, then why should "nation" be viewed as a "natural" phenomenon of this kind? Applying Latour's principle of networks or hybrids to nations, one can suggest that "nation" is also just a name of a network of natural-cultural elements, of almost a Heideggerian "fourfold" that unites earth and sky, mortals and gods in one common world.[20] It would seem that this exercise in conceiving a nation as a network may be useful since it challenges the myth of the nation as a unity of people connected by blood ties. Hybrid networks include diverse elements of the natural and cultural kind, and blood ties are not essential to this unity of connections. They are one among possible elements that constitute the network called nation, but are far from being the principal one.

NATALITY AS A HUMAN CONDITION

This attempt to represent the nation as a network of diverse natural and cultural elements, and thus not primarily depending on descent or blood ties, may follow in the steps of other ineffective attempts to criticize ethnonationalism. Perhaps, what does not allow us to debunk decisively the mythic notion of nation as a community of descent that common sense espouses is that we concentrate on criticizing its unnaturalness, its irreality, its contrived quality. Many social scientists would like to challenge the notion that the nation was a "natural" outgrowth of a community of common descent, evolving from the same "natural" origin in archaic time. Thus, Gellner, Anderson and Zizek all concentrate on the fictional, imaginary, fantastic quality of national communities, insisting that they were contrived by specific human efforts. To no avail. They do not effect any tangible change in popular understanding, and people still believe in the naturalness of ethnic nations.

Perhaps this type of theoretical assault on the myth of the nation is doomed to failure for two reasons. First, the concept of nation is rooted in the vision of natality. It is so evidently linked in its etymological origins and its conceptual history to the process of birth—and thus to something immutably "natural"—that it may withstand any criticism of the unnaturalness of the nation. Second, "natality tests" of one's ethnicity in everyday life are simple and efficient. Checking the recorded ethnic nationality of one's parents and the ethnic origins of the family name is what people habitually do to define ethnic identity, and the academic criticism of the nation as an unnatural entity is easily subverted by this widespread habit of testing seemingly natural qualities supplied by birth.

Perhaps, instead of criticizing the unnaturalness of the nation, one should criticize the notion of natality that lies at the foundation of modern ethnic definitions of nationhood and that gives rise to habitual tests of nationhood. If natality could be shown to be not "natural" at all, if it could be revealed as a quality which is either unnatural or is neither natural nor unnatural—a strange hybrid operation—then, perhaps, an intuitive feeling that nations are linked to the processes of successive biological births could be questioned more effectively.

Indeed, natality should not necessarily be seen as a quality of a biological process, and a different view of natality may help us redefine the concepts of nation and nature in a new way. A view of birth as a culmination of an inexorable process that follows scientifically describable stages of gestation, or is just a link in the inexorable life process of a nation or the whole of mankind, is not the only possible one. Nor is it inescapable. Birth may designate something other than the completion of the natural process of gestation. As the word suggests, it may simply designate the moment of appearance of something new in the world.

Hannah Arendt allows us such a reconceptualization of natality.[21] Arendt has provided us with a critique of what, following her, we may call the "process attitude" towards nature and of natality viewed as something less fundamental than a basic human condition of existence. In Arendt's opinion, this process attitude to nature is a sign of modern times that forgot genuine natality inherent in political action, and treats giving birth as part of a purely biological process of sustaining the life of the species mankind. On the contrary, natality as a human condition is the capacity to bring something profoundly new into the world rather than a simple capacity to procreate in an orderly fashion. For example, the glad tidings mentioned in the Gospels—"a child has been born unto us"—signified not only a biological process of birth successfully completed (even if started by supernatural force) but the appearance of a unique person, a newcomer who will eventually reveal his extraordinary "who" in unforgettable deeds that will affect the life stories of many humans.[22] Nation and nature reconceptualized on the basis of this notion of natality would look profoundly different from what we have been discussing so far. But before drawing the implications, let us first dwell more on Arendt's discussion of her highly original notion of action, directly connected to her notions of natality and process attitude.

NATALITY AND THE PROCESS CHARACTER OF ACTION

Arendt starts her exposition in *The Human Condition* by distinguishing among three basic human activities—labor, work, and action. Labor is an activity sustaining the daily existence of a human being, her or his metabolism with nature. It is an activity whose products are for immediate consumption. By contrast, work is an activity that makes durable products that constitute the world of objects inhabited by humans. Action in Arendt's sense of the word—following Greek usage, Arendt relies on the term *praxis*—may be defined as acting in concert with others without the mediation of things at all. *Praxis* is political action par excellence.

Most of this political action, of course, concerns the world of things that exists between men, the world of durable goods created by work. As Arendt writes, this world so understood simultaneously unites and separates humans as a table unites and separates a group of people sitting around it: the world saves them, so to speak, from "falling over each other."[23] However, there exists also "the second, subjective in-between" that is not tangible and consists —as opposed to the objective world of things—of deeds and words that cannot solidify into things. Arendt calls it the "web of human relationships" and writes: "for all its intangibility, this in-between is no less real than the world of things we visibly have in common."[24] Thus political action is *about* the world, but it acts *into* the web of human relationships, changing them as a result of its appearance. The three human activities—labor, work, action—are rooted in three corresponding human conditions—life, worldliness, plurality —but all these activities and their corresponding conditions are tied to "the most general condition" of human existence—birth and death, natality and mortality. Out of the three activities, action is most closely related to natality because "the new beginning inherent in birth can make itself felt in the world only because the newcomer possesses the capacity for beginning something anew, that is, of acting." Arendt uses the term "action" to designate political activity, and natality may be, in her opinion, the central category of political thought.[25]

Political action is linked so intimately to natality because genuine politics —although always directed to worldly concerns—also always discloses a unique "who" worthy of remembrance, the story of a great deed. Natality, thus, is conceived here as a fundamental capacity to bring new phenomena into existence. It is important to stress, however, that to act in Arendt's sense is not only to begin something new; rather, action is also the beginning of "disclosure of who somebody is," that is, action is a disclosure of the "who" rather than of the "what." Another curious detail of action is that it may not disclose the "who" of the actor immediately. It only starts "a new process which eventually emerges as the unique life-story of the newcomer" that affects life-stories of all others with whom s/he comes into contact. However, in certain cases "the process of a single deed can quite literally endure throughout time until mankind itself has come to an end."[26]

This process character of genuine political action is most obviously seen in its difference from sovereign rule, an activity usually taken to be "politics." Following Arendt, one sees that rule and governance, since they are modeled on making, *poiesis,* should not be called "politics" at all—they are hardly related to what the early Greeks called *praxis,* genuine political action. Indeed, acting in Arendt's sense is different from making in that it does not result in a finished product (for example, a table or a vessel), it is the performance of the word and deed *par excellence.* Even more important is the fact that an actor cannot control the processes s/he unleashes in the way a maker can control the making of a product, strictly following the plan of creation, and beating recalcitrant matter into shape if it resists the planned fabrication. Since an individual acts in the presence of the plurality of equals, and genuine political action always has an aspect of disclosing a "who" of the actor to equal others, s/he has no control over the process of disclosure: an actor can only initiate political action, whose greatness or failure will be judged by the *polis.* That is why a political actor is the originator and sufferer of the consequences, but never an "author" of his or her action. The story of a deed will emerge as a result of the complex interaction with others, with the help of storytellers, who will record the deed as they see fit, and so on. Action, therefore, is irreversible and unpredictable: once set into motion, its consequences will persist through time; and the final story of the deed that will emerge eventually is beyond the actor's personal control.

Also, genuine political actors emerge by acting against "the overwhelming odds of statistical laws." When it happens, action actualizes the human condition of natality, by bringing a radically new life-story into the world, and affecting all other connected life-stories. Natality, thus, is a fundamental capacity to give birth to the new: a new deed and a new "who" of the actor and the change in the "whos" of all other actors. Action, "an infinite improbability that occurs regularly" intercepts the inexorable procession from life to death, and almost seems like a miracle to those who are bound by the sight of this inexorability. "The miracle that saves the world, the realm of human affairs, from its normal, 'natural' ruin is ultimately the fact of natality, in which the faculty of action is ontologically rooted."[27]

This "process character of action," rooted in natality—its ability to unleash the unpredictable processes of the emergence of the new "who"—should be distinguished from what, following Arendt, one may call the process attitude of modern man. The process attitude is a phenomenon of modern times and is concomitant to the forgetting of the true character of political action. This amnesia is brought about by the modern substitution of making for acting. The essential "frailty" of political action, its unpredictability and irreversibility—the fact that we can never control the "who" that emerges as the result of our action—makes humans seek solution in conceiving of politics on the model of making, fabrication, and in attempting to control the consequences of political action. The substitution of making for acting ushers in the vision of politics as rule, as mastery or household governance, when constant control and use of violence are employed to achieve the pre-set goals of a politician.

However, this transformation also has another corollary—people forget about the process character of human action and develop a process attitude instead. The process character and the process attitude are linked: an attempt to substitute making for acting, writes Arendt, leads to "the channeling of human capacity for action . . . into an attitude toward nature," when nature, rather than only action, is conceived as a process. Heretofore humans observed what nature offered to their eyes and manufactured things out of natural materials according to observed laws of nature. Now, following a "process attitude" people "act *into* nature," "unchaining elemental processes": they provoke processes within nature, so that products appear or reactions happen that would have never existed without human intervention.[28]

It is not always clear whether Arendt considers the triumph of the process attitude to nature a wholly negative development. On the one hand, her text is filled with indictments of the process attitude. For example, she suggests that the spread of the process attitude made life itself being viewed as a set of biological processes. "And since this biological life, accessible in self-observation, is at the same time a metabolic process between man and nature," men forget about their distinct political qualities and start treating themselves as only one living organism among others.[29] That is, remembrance of the great qualities of genuine political action dissipates and human beings are viewed as mere living creatures, primarily concerned with sustaining their life rather than with producing great deeds. Correspondingly, labor that supports metabolism between nature and a human is taken to be the highest human activity, while "an everlasting life process of the species mankind" becomes the only remaining constant in the modern world. Action is barred from this world of natural processes where. following Marx, even thought is seen as natural process, and individual life is considered as just an element of a generic life process itself. The process attitude has extended so far and wide that what humans are doing on earth now appears "not as activities of any kind but as processes, so that, as a scientist recently put it, modern motorization would appear like a process of biological imitation in which human bodies gradually begin to be covered by shells of steel."[30]

On the other hand, the process attitude, since it was originally linked to the process character of action, may have some positive features as well. For example, the residues of a genuine understanding of action that unleashes processes it cannot control are still manifest in the fact that natural sciences have also become the "sciences of process." They thus preserve some aspects of political action that was initially alone capable of starting "new unprecedented processes whose outcome remains uncertain and unpredictable whether they are let loose in the human or the natural realm."[31] Modern humankind has generally forgotten what genuine political actions are, but this memory may be eventually restored, given the fact that modern science still retains residual process-initiating elements of action.

Arendt does not specifically say anything on how the spread of the process attitude affects natality. However, one may suggest—developing her argument—that natality too becomes conceived in accordance with the process attitude. People forget that natality is the most general human condition of existence, in which a capacity for action is rooted. Instead, natality becomes viewed now as an inexorable biological process, as a recurrent link in the everlasting life process of mankind. The consequences for this forgetting of the deep existential significance of natality as the birth of the new are dire. Concepts of nation and nature, subject to process attitude and linked to what one might call the "process view of natality," now present themselves as inexorable processes as well. Nature is seen in the "realist" sense, as a set of deep structural processes that humans cannot influence. A nation almost obviously seems to be a community tied by a continuous chain of biological births.

Could this conceptualization be put aside, and another one suggested, based on Arendt's understanding of natality as the most general human condition? Perhaps the process attitude may be repelled and the action-related vision of natality be restored? Indeed, nation then could be understood differently from the currently predominant vision of an unending chain of births, a continuous sequence of constant birth labors, or a community linked by this process of inexorable descent. Furthermore, a link between nation and nature may be re-established on a different ground, making a habitual justification of nation through its "naturalness" seem out of place from the start. A critique of the process attitude to nation may thus be more successful in changing commonsense perceptions of the nation than a scholarly exposition of its "unnaturalness."

NATION AS A COMMUNITY OF ACTION

Nation, linked to natality conceived in Arendt's terms, is a community of people living together to give birth to novel deeds. This redefinition of the nation radically unsettles its currently dominant ethnic definition. Nation becomes a community of people that remember what is a genuine political action, people tied by shared natality of the new rather than by a common parental origin. Furthermore, the standard modern civic definition of nation, which is currently in retreat under the assault of ethno-nationalism, may be redefined to give new strength to the civic impulse. Indeed, the standard civic definition of nation—all citizens inhabiting a given state and consenting to its laws are a nation—is not enough to be considered a civic nation understood as the one united by the human condition of natality. As Arendt claims, modern nation-states emerge when common affairs are started to be run as a household: "We see the body of peoples and political communities in the image of a family whose everyday affairs have to be taken care of by a gigantic, nation-wide administration of housekeeping."[32] Therefore even in a civic nation, understood in a standard way, people may merely work or labor together without any resort to action.

By contrast to ethnic and standard civic definitions, nation as a community of action—nation as *polis* or *civitas,* one could say—brings together neither a community of procreation, nor a national household, but all those humans who remember that their stories may reveal their unique "who" and affect the life-stories of others, redrawing the web of human relationships. Of course, not all should necessarily do novel deeds or excel in "infinitely improbable" actions: this nation is not a community of compulsory and endless experimentation with each citizen striving to be unique. Rather, it is a community of people who remember genuine political action, are capable of recognizing novelty once it appears, and who would thus generate a story about it as "naturally" as fabrication generates tools.

Thus conceived, the nation is gathered around a common world of humanly made objects and shares a web of human relationships—a common subjective in-between, in which stories are generated. In a sense, this nation may be closer to what are now called subcultures tied by shared objects and a common web of recognition and distinction. Perhaps contemporary state borders seem obsolete for this nation because, as one rock musician has put it, motherland "is . . . where my friends are."[33] Ethnicity, language, religion, territory—all these bases for exclusive self-definition become irrelevant for a civic nation conceived as a stage for the recognition of the novel deed, as a set of shared practices to create objects that "gather" people around them and protect people from falling over each other, and to recognize the newcomer born into this world when s/he appears. The Greek *polis* was created as a solution to the problem of frailty of human action, according to Arendt, so that deeds deserving fame would not be forgotten, and everyone would have an opportunity to excel and distinguish oneself. Nation can now be seen as a Greek *po-*

lis in this sense: as an arena for the natality of the new that should allow each exceptional deed to be registered and recognized. *Natio qua novatio:* this is a vision of a community united by natality conceived as giving birth to new deeds, rather than as a process of the endless reproduction of bodies.

NATURE AS A COMMUNITY OF ACTION

This vision of nation based on the human condition of natality may seem highly idealistic in its practical implications. Arendt's original concept of natality does not have much support in everyday life still guided by the mundane conception of natality as a process of physical birth. In order for our criticism and alternative proposal to be effective, one has to challenge the idea of "natural" natality in the minds of the millions. How could the link between the nation and the process of physical birth, a link so intuitively obvious that it resists any criticism of its naturalness coming from social science, be broken? How could this most "obvious" link become most obviously problematic?

Here, perhaps, a corollary redefinition of nature—also based on Arendt's concept of natality—could help. Indeed, nature viewed in connection to natality (conceived as giving birth to novel actions) might become a curious realm, where "birth" does not have "natural" qualities as opposed to those humanly contrived. Two consequences follow. First, birth of novel actions becomes central to nature thus redefined, and nature is freed from the process attitude imposed on it by modernity: it is not seen anymore as a set of inexorable processes. Second, biological birth stops being "natural" in that nature has human action at its core, and the intuitive notion of nation as a "natural" community of birth cannot be entertained even on an everyday level since birth most obviously becomes "unnatural", contrived, artificial. Consequently, all seeming naturalness of linking people by birth or descent becomes suspect: descent is achieved by unnatural means, what was before an inexorable biological process is now a humanly controlled fabrication, or—a wilder possibility—political action in its own right.

This view of nature as *polis* is a possibility as never before. Paul Rabinow, reviewing recent developments in microbiology, repeats the opinion of Francois Dagognet, an intriguing French philosopher of science: if for the last two centuries culture was modeled on nature, with positivism and behavioral sciences being the latest reincarnation of this yearning for mimicry, now nature can be modeled on culture.[34] Creation of biological organisms with pre-set qualities gives an opportunity to set cultural mechanisms working directly in the very creation of nature, rather than through the mediation of the cultural construction of scientific facts and theories. Nature may become a human practice, blurring the hallowed distinction between human and non-human.

But if one extends Rabinow's argument and recognizes in some aspects of cultural practices—working now at the heart of the production of new natural organisms—aspects of action in Arendt's sense, then one suddenly finds *a polis* working at the very heart of nature.

Arendt's writings themselves hint at a possibility that political action might one day become central to natural processes. Indeed, in her opinion, scientists constitute the only extensive contemporary group of people residually capable of action in the Greek sense of the word:

> The capacity for action, at least in the sense of the releasing of the processes, is still with us, although it has become the exclusive prerogative of the scientists, who have enlarged the realm of the human affairs to the point of extinguishing the time-honored protective dividing line between nature and the human world.[35]

That scientists are residually capable of action may mean two things. First, they perform such great deeds that affect everybody living on earth (discovering nuclear reaction, for example), that these deeds, although not strictly political in Arendt's sense of the word, still merit the title of action more than the base competition for power of the so-called politicians. Second, scientists still release processes as human action is supposed to do when it releases into the web of human relationships deeds that will eventually emerge as life-stories. This second possibility makes scientists particularly close to practicing action in the Greek sense.

However, mentions Arendt, even if they unleash processes, scientists do not practice genuine political action since they unleash natural processes rather than processes for an emergence of a unique "who," a process of formation of a memorable or lamentable life-story. In other words, scientists do not act into the web of human relationships, they act into nature; they do not possess the revelatory quality of action since they do not necessarily produce stories about the "who" of actors, which will supply meaningfulness to human existence.

This judgment seems somewhat unjustified. Of course, Arendt primarily speaks here about processes released in the material world, but in a preceding passage she also speaks of the "code of honor" of scientific organizations and scientists acting in concert,[36] and must be aware that scientific reputation is the "who" that is disclosed with each great work of a scientist. "Invisible colleges" of scientists of a given branch of knowledge, to use the term of Derek De Solla Price, supply the most demanding arena for recognition of both the professional and the moral qualities of a scientist. Furthermore, a brilliant innovation frequently threatens reputations already established in the field, and thus a novel deed of an experimenter or researcher affects the life-stories of those linked by the web of relationships within a given invisible college, eliciting multiple counter-reactions, which sets up a frequently unpredictable and irreversible process of the eventual emergence of the "who" of the new-comer.[37] Still, Arendt could object, unleashed processes that lead to the emergence of the life-story of great scientists are limited in scope: frequently they rest within a given invisible college and do not penetrate the wider public. The "who" revealed is relevant for only those who are "in," who can understand the discovery and appreciate the greatness of an achievement.

Therefore, acts of scientists, in order to become political actions in Arendt's sense, would seem to need to have boundless, rather than bounded, implications: a process of establishing a great life-story should spill over the borders of the invisible college and be recognized as such by the whole public. For example, in a recent case in Russia, the brilliant life-story of a geneticist Timofeev-Resovskii has emerged into the public realm with the help of a renowned writer who made a story worthy of remembrance, although Resovsky's reputation among the scientists was already well established.[38]Therefore, in order for scientists to perform a genuinely political action, their acting into nature should also be an action that directly affects every life-story in the web of human relationships. This seemed to Arendt to be an exception rather than a rule; the same conclusion seems to apply to the contemporary situation as well: very few scientists are capable of action in the Greek sense of the word.

CONTEMPORARY SCIENCE AND POLITICS

There is one difference between Arendt's time of writing and ours: she wrote her book while witnessing the launching of the sputnik, which signified that radically changing the human condition by leaving earth became possible. Now another change in the human condition is almost as manifest: natality and mortality have lost their "naturalness." Both are administered by huge technical networks, while the problems of euthanasia, cloning, rights of embryos or use of fetal tissue and the like are the problems brought about by this technologization of birth and death. Leaving aside death, let us concentrate on the changes in natality. One looks with simultaneous interest and apprehension at the new possibilities offered by the latest birth techniques. This apprehensive curiosity is based not so much on a realization that a technical possibility to reproduce humans has appeared, but on the prospective changes in the human condition that this change may possibly offer.

Scientists are now becoming capable of aspects of action in Arendt's sense in three respects. First, their scientific discoveries, "extinguishing the time-honored dividing line between nature and the human world," have such broad repercussions that it would seem that life-stories of great biotechnologists or of the developers of the cloning technique threaten to eventually touch every life-story on earth. Second, the processes they unleash in nature may now also directly unleash the unpredictable and irreversible processes in society. The uproar caused by the statement of doctors that they would clone people notwithstanding the ban on such activities manifests an understanding that acting into nature may bring consequences of a radically new kind: human beings may not ever be the same; the human condition itself may be altered irreversibly and unpredictably.

Third, scientists now seem to be able to affect the web of human relation-ships by unleashing processes for the creation of life-stories "second-hand", so to speak—by means of produced others. Since scientists are becoming able to produce new people on a mass scale, they might contribute to releasing new "whos" potentially capable of unique deeds. What work of a scientist may affect the web of human relationships more than unleashing a "natural" process that will bring a human being into existence? Thus, a cloning scien-tist directly acts into nature but also indirectly acts into the web of human re-lationships by a powerful mediation, by contributing to a birth of a new hu-man being who may eventually act and affect this web directly. Producing bodies here implies more than just assisting the physical process of birth, it also means mediation in eliciting future actions. Nature becomes a site of po-litical natality: it is conceived less as a site for physical birth, than as a site for the birth of potential new great deeds.

However, it seems that all these new aspects of scientists' activities still cannot ensure that these activities will almost automatically generate mean-ing that illuminates human existence. A follower of Arendt should still look for actions that act into the intangible web of human relationships, rather than for creation of tangible works, of which scientists are capable. The problem is of decisive importance: how can making, formation, become action imme-diately, without the mediation of human products who would then act?[39] To put it rather differently: how can action become an integral part of fabrica-tion? How can action, squeezed out from human existence by the spread of making, be now found at the very heart of making? This problem seems in-soluble within Arendt's conception.

A solution to this problem may be unexpectedly suggested by the blurring of boundaries between human and non-human that contemporary science is rediscovering day after day. Perhaps, Arendt's distinction between an objec-tive world of durable things and the intangible web of human relationships is itself a product of modern yearning for separating the natural elements from the human ones. If Latour's hypothesis holds, Arendt's two entities, the "world" of tangible things and the "web" of intangible human relations, to-gether constitute one network of technical and cultural elements, which we would like to break into opposed parts according to a neat distinction—an objective hardly achievable nowadays, particularly in the world of biotechnology. Perhaps, a world of objects that unites people now contributes as much to providing meaning as the story that is woven around it, so that the two form a whole, a web-work.[40]

The prospects opened by the vision of nature as *polis* are intriguing, if hard to ponder, and we stop here in our exploration of this topic which merits another book of its own. What is undoubtedly important for the present chapter, however, is that concomitantly to the emergence of this new vision of nature as *polis*—nature as based on the natality of the new deed—the "naturalistic" prejudice of the blood ties that allegedly lie at the foundation of the nation may be effectively dispelled. Most simply put, new biotechnologies give ample grounds to question the naturalness of the birth link. Of course, cloning also offers to ethno-nationalism the possibilities it had never dreamt of, and thus new biotechnologies are potentially very dangerous and ominous. For example, current levels of cloning techniques that allow a clear choice of the genotype to be cloned imply the "blood tie" most obviously establishing congruence between the object and subject of cloning. This could contribute to the wildest fantasies of the purest "cloned" nations linked by the most evident descent and to the projects of most radical eugenics. But new biotechnologies also visibly upset the conception of birth as a natural process. For example, when the cloned ovum is put into the body of an ethnically unrelated and unknown person, or certain undesirable parts of the genotype (for instance, those making people susceptible to tuberculosis) are kicked out in the process of cloning, to what extent may a nation linked by this process intermingled with "traditional" birth techniques claim common descent or blood ties?

Let me stress once again this argument, which is a spin-off from our general consideration of nature and nation based on political natality. The standard civic definition of nationhood is under threat everywhere in the world. It kept many human communities together for the last two centuries, and is a feature one would be happy to keep in the future. Unfortunately, nowadays this is frequently impossible. The civic definition of nationhood seems to be losing ground because of the unstoppable spread of ethnic nationalism. Battling this resurgence of ethno-nationalism on the basis of the "irreality" or "unnaturalness" of a vision of descent-linked nation it espouses does not bear much fruit. However, a subversion of the currently predominant view of natality, in which the ethnic vision of nation is rooted, and a concomitant redefinition of the civic nation, may be more effective. Modern biotechnologies— whose development one should not always mindlessly support since they bring many as yet unknown and profound dangers—are at least interesting in one respect: they seem to put the old definition of natality in question for the most mundane of observers. One should not misunderstand the last sentence. Cloning is no solution to ethno-nationalism. But the questions that new technologies of life pose to us more and more insistently may help us, finally, decisively challenge the self-evidence of rooting nations in biological natality.

NOTES

1. Raymond Williams, *Keywords: A Vocabulary of Culture and Society* (New York: Oxford University Press, 1976), 213.

2. Liah Greenfeld, *Nationalism. Five Roads to Modernity.* (Cambridge, MA: Harvard University Press, 1993), 4–10.

3. Eric Hobsbawm, *Nations and Nationalism Since 1780,* 2nd ed. (Cambridge: Cambridge University Press, 1992), 17.

4. In late Soviet society, only children of mixed marriages could choose their ethnic nationality (between recorded nationalities of both parents) when they were issued internal passports at the age of 16. Originally, when internal Soviet passports were introduced in the 1930s, ascription of ethnic nationality to each citizen relied on self-designation and existing family names (Victor Zaslavsky, *The Neo-Stalinist State: Class, Ethnicity, and Consensus in Soviet Society* (Armonk, NY: M.E. Sharpe, 1982), 92). A memory of these two institutional practices seems to define the corresponding constituent parts of the contemporary "natality test."

5. Rogers Brubaker, *Nationalism Reframed: Nationhood and the National Question in the New Europe* (Cambridge: Cambridge University Press, 1996), 30–31.

6. Kate Soper, *What is Nature? Culture, Politics and the Non-Human* (Oxford: Blackwell, 1995), 110.

7. She distinguishes between three currently dominant conceptions of nature: these include metaphysical, realist and lay ones (Soper, *What is Nature?* 155—56).

8. Williams, *Keywords,* 219.

9. There are two standard overviews in English of the development of terms *physis* and *natura*: in Arthur O. Lovejoy and George Boas, *Primitivism and Related Ideas in Antiquity* (Baltimore: Johns Hopkins University Press, 1935), 103—16, 447—56; and in R.G. Collingwood, *The Idea of Nature* (Oxford: Oxford University Press, 1945), 43—48. I follow their exposition, but also draw heavily from Ya. M. Borovskii, "O termine *natura* u Lukretsiia" [On the Term *natura* in Lucretius], *Uchenye Zapiski LGU* [Learned Notes of the Leningrad State University], no. 161 (1952), since he pays more attention to etymological connections.

10. Sophocles, *Antigone,* st. 345, as quoted in Borovskii, "O termine *natura*," 229.

11. *Odyssey,* X: 303, quoted in Borovskii, "O termine *natura*," 225, who cites the Greek term. English translation according to Lovejoy and Boas, *Primitivism and Related Ideas,* 104.

12. Parmenides fragments from Diels 5, 28 B 16; quoted in Borovskii, "O termine *natura*," 226).

13. Borovskii, "O termine *natura*," 232—37.

14. See e.g. Lucretius, I: 628—33. He also distinguishes between human "semen" and "seminal" elements that nature mixes in order to produce existing things, but etymological connections are obvious. Of course, there is a long Greek tradition to conceive of natural generation as mixing the "seeds" of things. See Sobol's commentary in a Russian edition of *De Natura Rerum* (1947).

15. Soper, *What is Nature?* 37.

16. Stephen Toulmin, *Cosmopolis. The Hidden Agenda of Modernity* (New York: Free Press, 1990, 128.

17. Steven Shapin and Simon Schaffer, *Leviathan and the Air-Pump: Hobbes, Boyle, and the Experimental Life* (Princeton: Princeton University Press, 1985).

18. Bruno Latour, *We Have Never Been Modern* (Cambridge, MA: Harvard University Press, 1994), 111.

19. Latour, *We Have Never Been Modern*, 107. He does not call for the reestablishment of the initial innocence of the world of unseparated natural-cultural compounds since the successes of science are often indisputable. Rather, he calls for the open acknowledgment that this separation is constantly at work in modern societies, hoping that this appreciation may restore dignity not only to humans, but to things as well.

20. The term "fourfold" comes from Heidegger's essay *The Thing*. Latour frequently explicitly uses Heideggerian allusions.

21. Patricia Bowen-Moore was first to stress this particular concept of Arendt and to articulate links with existential analytics of Heidegger that explain the centrality of this category to her thinking. Heidegger concentrated on being-unto-death and the finality of human existence, thus a phenomenon of birth enters his writing only in discussion of an existential structure of thrownness into the world in *Sein und Zeit*. Arendt, on the contrary, provided an extensive phenomenological description of an existential beginning available in every human birth, according to this argument (Bowen-Moore, *Hannah Arendt's Philosophy of Natality* (Basingstoke: Macmillan, 1989), 5). Bhikhu Parekh claims that Arendt had even coined the term (See his *Hannah Arendt and the Search for a New Political Philosophy* (Atlantic Highlands, NJ: Humanities Press, 1981), xi).

22. Hannah Arendt, *The Human Condition* (Chicago: University of Chicago Press, 1958), 247.

23. Arendt, *Human Condition*, 52.

24. Also: "we call this reality the "web" of human relationships, indicating by the metaphor its somewhat intangible quality" (Arendt, *Human Condition*, 183).

25. Arendt, *Human Condition*, 9.

26. Arendt, *Human Condition*, 178, 184, 233.

27. Arendt, *Human Condition*, 184, 246—47.

28. Arendt, *Human Condition*, 231.

29. Arendt, *Human Condition*, 308. Here, as in some other places, Arendt seems to blur the distinction that she herself suggests—between a term "process" being strictly a feature of political action, and a word "process" as used in contemporary common parlance to describe whatever proceeds. For example, it is not clear whether the "metabolic process" in question really has a quality of unpredictability and irreversibility,

whether Arendt implies an extension of the "process attitude" on the sciences of life, or whether she just uses it incautiously, in the ordinary meaning of the word.

30. Arendt, *Human Condition*, 320–23.

31. Arendt, *Human Condition*, 231.

32. Arendt, *Human Condition*, 28.

33. Thomas Cushman, *Notes from Underground: Rock Music Counterculture in Russia* (Albany: State University of New York Press, 1995), 171.

34. Paul Rabinow, *Essays on the Anthropology of Reason* (Princeton: Princeton University Press, 1996), 107–8.

35. Arendt, *Human Condition*, 323–24.

36. Arendt, *Human Condition*, 323.

37. As recent studies of science have tried to show, this clash of newcomers and established scientists over what theory should be adopted as "truly" reflecting nature defines what is considered true as a result of these battles. The "who" of a newcomer will emerge only after the whole reconfiguration of the web of human relationships in a given branch of science, a complicated interaction between the emerging life-story and life-stories that seemed already established, and the myriad of reactions and lateral effects that this interaction elicits, is complete. See e.g. Bruno Latour, *Science in Action* (Cambridge, MA: Harvard University Press, 1987).

38. Timofeev-Resovskii, a subject of Daniil Granin's biographical sketch (Granin, "Zubr" [The Aurochs], *Novyi Mir* 62, no. 1–2 (January–February 1987)), was a controversial Soviet geneticist who was caught by the Second World War in a lab in Nazi Germany, but to everybody's surprise spent the war in experimentation there. Upon returning to the Soviet Union he was imprisoned but subsequently released, and became the central figure who opposed Lysenko's biology. Paradoxically, his absence during the purges of geneticists in the Soviet Union saved him from extermination, while close interaction with German genetics made him a principal actor in the rebirth of scientific genetics in the Soviet Union.

39. Also, it is not for nothing that "producing actors" sounds so ominous for a contemporary reader.

40. Recent French sociology of action resolutely strives at making objects the central part of investigation. For example, Luc Boltanski and Laurent Thevenot (in their *De la justification: les economies de la grandeur* (Paris: Gallimard, 1991)) single out six incommensurable worlds of everyday disputes on justice—which are all tied together not only by the distinct ways an argument is made within a world, but also by specific objects that "found" this particular world. See also Nicolas Dodier, "Action as a Combination of 'Common Worlds'," *Sociological Review* 41, no. 3 (1993).

Chapter Five

Friendship:
Early History of the Concept

The Russian language has a curious quality: the word for "friend," *drug*[1], and the word for "other," *drugoi*, are so closely linked that, while reading translations of Levinas' philosophy that speak of the relationship of the Self and the Other, a Russian reader might be easily misled to think that s/he is reading about friendship. Indeed, most Slavic languages have the same etymological link (in Ukrainian, Bulgarian, Polish, Slovenian and Czech, for example, *drugii, drugi* or *druhy*, respectively, all mean "the second"), which makes Russian postmodernists rejoice. When one has to explain in Russian a rather difficult thought of Blanchot and Derrida (based on Nietzsche's insight from *Human, All Too Human*, 376) — that friendship is not a warm proximate relationship of the similar but rather a union across the chasm that separates two existentially distinct, distant and profoundly dissimilar egos — one does not spend much time persuading the audience. This thought seems to be inscribed in the very structure of language: *drug* is *drugoi*, the friend is inescapably the Other. French *amitié* and English *friendship*, having developed from other Indo-European roots, do not offer the same possibility — loving and proximity seem to be inscribed in their etymology.

The following remarks will try to examine what this curious fact meant for the reception of Byzantian statements on friendship that arrived in medieval Russian together with the first translations of the XI–XIV centuries, and to evaluate what proto-Russians meant when they used the word *drug* and its derivatives, *druzhba* or *druzhina* (friendship).

1

First, etymology. There are two main competing theories. In the classic *Russisches Etymologisches Wörterbuch,* Vasmer finds that *drug* is closely linked

115

to Lithuanian *draugas* (companion, fellow traveler), to Gothic *driugan* and Anglo-Saxon *dreogan* (meaning "to achieve, to perform"), to Gothic *gadrauchts* (which translates Greek *stratiotis*), to Old East Germanic *trucht* (military detachment, retinue) or *truchtin* (commander, prince).[2] Predominantly military connotations are obvious here, and the military provenance of the word is supported by the fact that the very widespread ancient Russian word *druzhina*, derivative from *drug*, was often used to designate the group of close warriors that the prince lead. The second theory sees *drug* as developing from a common Indo-European root *dhreu-/*dhru- that in Russian also gave the word for a tree, *derevo*, while in middle German it gave *trauen*, "trust, believe," *Treue* "faithfulness," and in Lithuanian, *drovetis*, "to be ashamed."[3] The most recent dictionary adds that Russian *drug* is also linked to Old Icelandic *drjugr* (sturdy, strong, reliable), and suggests that Gothic *driugan* meant not only prevailing in combat but assisting someone in combat as well.[4] Here the connotations of sturdiness and reliability come to the fore, and numerous proverbs support this interpretation: *drug* is the one on whom one can always rely in a difficult situation. However, these two theories are not mutually exclusive, and we may hold both connotations (a companion fighter, on the one hand, and something or someone sturdy or reliable, on the other) in mind while reading the following exposition.

Analyzing the medieval term *drug* is difficult since the Russian language does not have its own OED, and there is no single authoritative dictionary. However, I will try to give an overview of its main meanings, by default using the most recent dictionary of usage from the XI–XIV centuries: citations from two other dictionaries, Sreznevsky or Barkhudarov, will mention their source.[5] The first and most widespread meaning is what the French would call *le prochaine*—that is, what the English speakers would call "neighbor" as it is used in the Christian injunction "love thy neighbor". For example, the famous first collection of didactic statements specifically written for the Kievan prince in 1076 has a translation of excerpts from the apocryphal Wisdom of Jesus, son of Sirach, one of which advises *dobro sotvoriti drugu*, "do good unto thy friend before thou die" in King James's translation, or *eu poei philoi* in the Septuagint (Sirach XIV: 13). The collection of canonic and didactic statements from the XIV c. called *The Righteous Rule* states the oft-repeated wisdom that a person who sacrifices his soul for his neighbor (*za druga svoego*) is under no human, but divine law. There are even rarer Russian usages when the root *drug*—is inserted into the complex word *drugoliubets*, "the lover of one's neighbor", as in the 1076 collection, or in the XIV c. *vita* of St. Theodore of Studion that uses this rather awkward term to translate Greek *philalliloi*. Barkhudarov also registers a rare dictionary entry for a later noun *drugoliublenie*, "love of one's neighbor", that appears in the list of desired Christian qualities in the XVI c. manuscript of *The Margarit* of St. John Chrysostom next to love of wisdom, in Russian—*liubomudrstvo*, i.e. Greek *philosophia*. The first undisputed usage of *drug* (in the meaning of "neighbor") outside of a translated text, as one might infer from Barkhudarov, is found in the First Novgorod Chronicle in the record for 1257: "It would be good if someone did good to one's neighbor (*dobro drugu chinil*), but if one digs the ditch for one's neighbor (*kopaia drugu iamu*), one falls into it oneself."

The second meaning was "companion, fellow traveler, accomplice", when the word was used to designate people on a joint commercial trip, in pilgrimage, military activities or conspiring to do something together. For example, the XIII c. *Prologue* (a compilation of *vitae* and didactic readings for a church calendar, a Russian variation of *Synaxarion*) recounts a story of a young traveler looking for a travel companion (*ishchiushchu druga*), since he himself did not know the route, while a XIV c. Russian translation of a Byzantian florilegium called *Melissa* ("The Bee") talks about a warrior who after glorious battle will be saved together "with comrades", *so druzi*, in the Greek original —*ton allon*. Barkhudarov offers an indigenous usage from Novgorod sources: in a record under 1338 in the First Chronicle archbishop Vassily is said to have ordered Isaac the Greek with companions (*s drugy*) to paint a church, while the XVI c. manuscript of a saintly "travelogue" says: "I, sinful Stephan . . . with my eight companions (*drugy*) have come to Constantinople to prostrate myself in front of holy places and kiss the relics of the saints." Also, it is rather curious that in the notion of a joint quest, next to pilgrimage or military expedition one included a trading expedition as well, which is well captured by the Russian word for "comrade", *tovarishch*—coming from the word *tovar*, meaning "commodity."

The third meaning—"a follower of, a defender of"—is singled out only by the XI–XIV c. usage dictionary, because it is linked to a stable construction (*drug* with a noun in the genitive case, designating the *drug* of what or whom), and it could be perhaps well subsumed by sections on other meanings. Thus, in a Russian translation of *The Pandectae* of Nikon of the Black Mountain (1296), one finds the first usage of a frequently registered phrase "friends of God," *druzi bozhii*, standing for Greek *philoi theou*, an expression found in many church authors (see, e.g., multiple usages in Damascene on the holy icons), and perhaps all linked to John XV: 14, "Ye are my friends (*philoi*), if ye do whatsoever I command you." The 1377 manuscript of the main Russian chronicle, recounting exchanges between Pilate and the Pharisees call him "Caesar's henchman," *drug kisarevy*, while prince Vladimir who had adopted Christianity for Rus' is addressed as "lover of Christ, defender of truth (*druzhe pravdy*)" in the first authored text in Russia, a homily on law and grace by metropolitan Hilarion (written between 1037–1050, with the first extant manuscript dating back to XIV–XV cc.)

The fourth meaning, *drug* as a special status in its own right—as a friend proper that is distinguished from a person of kin, a neighbor, a counsel—can be distilled also from very numerous examples. Thus, the XII c. tale of SS. Boris and Gleb, the first two Russian martyr princes, states: *predany budete rodom i drugy*, "you will be betrayed by kin and friends." The same distinction between kin and friends appears in the 1296 manuscript of *The Pandectae*, where *drug svoih* stands for Greek *tous philous*, which suggests a possible model for the earlier tale. In an interesting passage the XII–XIII c. manuscript of the monastery statute of St. Theodore Studite assigns the title of friends proper to monks linked by ties of love and unanimity. In the XIV c. translation of Gregory of Nazianzus *drug* is opposed to a mere counsel (*svetnik*), since a true friend will influence his friend to accept baptism and Christian life: "where is a friend (*drug*) here, when one ignores the death of a beloved one who departs unenlightened?" The XIV–XV c. manuscript of the *vita* of Barlaam and Joasaph names the beloved ones, kin and friends proper (in the Greek original—*hetaireias*) as three equally important but apparently distinct things in life.

The XI–XIV c. dictionary cites three treaties between different Muscovite princes (dating from the 1350–1351, 1367 and 1389) of the same format: he who is a *drug* to me, is a *drug* to you. This formal agreement on friendship, reminiscent of *philia nomike* in Aristotle,[6] serves as the basis for frequent contemporary assertions of the explicitly non-emotional character of friendship in medieval Russia. Indeed, this hypothesis of the predominantly non-emotional and contractual character of early Russian friendship has support in the sources, e.g. it is vindicated by the Barkhudarov dictionary, which cites a famous record for 968 in the Lavrentievsky version of the main chronicle of Russia as the first secular statement dealing with *drug* proper. The Pechenegs use the opportunity of the absence of prince Sviatoslav to besiege Kiev, which is saved only by one youngster successfully fleeing to inform Pretich, a commander of a portion of Sviatoslav's army, who was camping nearby. When Pretich arrives to save Kiev, the Pechenegs take off, fearing a fierce standoff. Before they do so, however, "the prince of the Pechenegs told Pretich: 'Be my friend (*budi mi drug*)'. Pretich answered: 'I will be', and offered his hand. The Pecheneg prince then gave a horse, a sabre and arrows to Pretich, while he gave him armor, a shield and a sword."[7] Apart from these ritualistic warrior contracts, reinforced by exchange of gifts, medieval Russians might have also practiced something reminiscent of *xenia*—friendship with aliens, whose help and services they used when they went to a different principality. For example, the famous lamentation of Daniil Zatochnik, to a more thorough analysis of which we will return in due course, mentions that "a rich man is known everywhere and holds friends (*druzi derzhit*) in a foreign country"[8]—a condition that poor people cannot afford, in his words.

Attention to these aspects of formal friendship is sometimes stretched beyond proportion, by claiming that all friendship proper in medieval Russia (as distinct from, say, relationships with neighbors or one's own kin) was of a contractual kind and imposed stern mutual obligations. Thus one Russian linguist writes about an expression *druzhe pravdy* mentioned above: "When Hilarion calls prince Vladimir, who accepted baptism, a 'friend of truth,' he means a contract that this man has concluded with this 'truth,' i.e. with Christian faith, and is thus no longer free in his relations with others; he is now a fellow warrior and a travel companion of this truth."[9]

To counter the formalistic interpretation of medieval friendship, one could cite a number of instances when emotion seems to be important. One could certainly take the quote from Nazianzus—regarding care for a dear friend (cited above)as one such example. In another instance, in one of Damascene's treatises on the holy icons, inserted into a Russian XVI c. multi-volume compilation of devotional readings (*Velikie Chetii Minei*, Barkhudarov cites it in the article for *druzhestvo*, "friendship"), one finds: "If one has a sincere friend (*druga*), then he amasses such love and friendship towards him, that he does not want to desert him neither during the day nor at night." However, these excerpts, hinting at our contemporary understandings of friendship as an emotional tie between private individuals, are rare finds and they are concentrated mostly in translations of or allusions to exquisite Athenian gentlemen theologians like St. Gregory of Nazianzus or St. Basil the Great. Even by the eighteenth century, when some texts began to stress and glorify the emotional aspect in friendship (this is easily noted, for example in Karamzin—"Do you know what most impresses me in friendship? Trustfulness that two hearts have in each other"[10]), the most widespread meaning for the word *drug* was "one who is tied by friendship." This meaning is illustrated by an example of XVIII c. usage from a book of translated ancient instructive stories called *Apophthegmata*: the best medicine from troubles and failures is to have a true friend.[11] Reliability and guaranteed help still mattered most in Russia even in the age of Sentimentalism.

2

However, one could perhaps hold in abeyance a rather tired discussion (though one that has been to some degree revived by David Konstan) of whether ancient and medieval friendship carried private and emotional elements or mostly had the quality of an open public agreement. With respect to Russian sources, this question is simply not very interesting, at least in heuristic terms. Medieval Russian usage reveals instead another important tension that should perhaps be addressed with more attention. This is a tension not between the public and private sides of friendship, or between formalistic agreement and sincere emotion, but between the term "friend" and the term "friendship." Briefly, one cannot find all the meanings of the term "friend" in the terms that stand for "friendship."

There are two main medieval words for friendship, *druzhba* and *druzhina*, with the former being far less widespread: one finds it 64 times in the source texts for the dictionary of XI–XIV c., while there are 600 mentions of *druzhina*. We shall start our analysis, however, with a less frequent term, because *druzhba* became the main term that means "friendship" in contemporary Russian, while *druzhina* lost this meaning completely. Also, *druzhba* is a more elevated and literary term, one used in translations to render the Greek term *philia*. Examples are too numerous, and I'll cite just a few of them. The first 1076 compilation of didactic writings for a Russian prince already has this term in a rendition of Sirach XXII: 20, "he that upbraideth his friend breaketh friendship" (*razorit druzhbu* in Russian, from the Greek *dialesei philian*). The XII c. vita of St. Theodore Studite says that he cultivated with the Patriarch ties of "warmest love" by means of *druzhba, philia*. The XIV c. Russian version of *Melissa* says of *philia*, "All things are better new—both vessels, and clothes, but *druzhba* is better when old." With this wealth of usages in translated literature, one is a bit surprised to learn that the Barkhudarov dictionary dates back the first usage in an indigenous Russian text rather late—to 1535 only, citing an account of *druzhba* between the Polish king and the grand prince of Moscow.

Still, this extension of the bookish term *druzhba* to cover what we would now call diplomatic relations might be expected. First, even Greeks used the term *philia* for relations between their city-states; second, a Greek idiom *philian poieisthai*, "to establish friendship," with a linked expression, "to accept (an offer of) friendship," has thoroughly infiltrated Russian translations. Thus the XIV c. version of *The Wisdom of Menander* says: "Evade a cunning man and do not accept his friendship," while the XIV–XV c. vita of Barlaam and Joasaph mentions that people may have a hypocritical friendship toward others; both sources translate *philia* into Russian *druzhba*. Scribes might have easily introduced this usage into indigenous sources. Thus, an earliest recension of the Ipatievsky version of the primary Russian chronicle (dating back to about 1425) uses the phrase *druzhbu imeiu k tebe*, "I have friendship towards you" when it describes relations with Lithuanian princes in 1252. Perhaps such an extension of these terms from church into diplomatic usage was natural, because Christian princes were supposed to love their neighbors, which is supported by extensive evidence from Barkhudarov on the XVI c. use of the terms *drugoliubie* and *druzheliubie* (originally linked to Greek terms like *philalliloi*, "loving one's neighbor") that applied to relations between rulers. Finally, Barkhudarov gives an example of an adjective, *druzhebnyi*, "pertaining to friendship, friendly" appearing in 1541 in the Lviv Chronicle in the following context: "And the grand prince started to will friendship with Caesar, and asked Caesar's interpreter to write a treaty of friendship (*gramotu druzhebnuiu*)."

However, most interesting for the meanings of *druzhba* is an almost total absence of usage that would render the term "companionship" or "joint travel or quest," that one would expect to have been formed, based on the second meaning of the term *drug*. Among entries of all three surveyed dictionaries we find only two exceptions that prove the rule. The *vita* of Studite gives a story about a returning man of great virtue invited to join by each comradeships or companionship (*druzhby* in Russian, *hetairias* in Greek), which were formed by splitting all people into these sub-units. And a first complete translation of the Bible, ordered by the Novgorod archbishop Gennadius in 1499 to fight the heresy of the Judaizers, renders *ekklisias tes apoikias* in I Ezra X: 8 as *druzhby preseleniia*, "congregations of those who moved."[12]

This is all the more surprising, given that another medieval word for friendship, *druzhina*, consistently translates excerpts that carry connotations of companionship or people on a joint quest, be it of spiritual, military or commercial kind. Thus, the term *druzhina* that is now taken by speakers of contemporary Russian to mean "a squadron of a prince's close warriors," was initially used to designate a widespread phenomenon (fellow travelers or just accomplices in a certain endeavor), while *druzhba* languished in use mostly for bookish renditions of *philia* that hardly touched on the everyday life of a medieval Russian person. For example, a treaty between Smolensk and Riga (1229 manuscript, Gothic recension) states that a commodity on a boat which had sunk should be extracted to the riverbank by the whole crew, *druzhina*. Such blunt commercial connotations that were important for indigenous concerns are of course fewer in translated sources, which used *druzhina* to designate people of one's congregation, i.e. *synodias* (in *Pandectae* of Nikon of the Black Mountain, 1296); people leaving Athens together with their spiritual father (Gregory of Nazianzus, XIV c.); travelers on pilgrimage suddenly meeting the Sarazenes (Miracles of St. Nicholas the Wonderworker, XIV c.); and in general—fellows of a certain martyr or saint (a formulaic expression in numerous sources). Notions of a spiritual joint quest prevail here, but even in translations one also finds usage that is more down to earth, for example, mentions of a *druzhina* of robbers (*Prologue*, XIII c.). All hints to skirmishes and dangerous travel point us to the fact that *druzhina* was frequently armed, and this links it to a meaning, most widespread in indigenous Russian sources—"people, closest to a prince, his council and his standing army."[13]

Judging from the chronicles, *druzhina* in this sense is a gang of armed people, personally committed to the prince, frequently of Varangian origin. They come to wage war when he calls them against someone (there are innumerable instances of such events mentioned), help him deliberate and even establish statutes and laws of the land (cf. Prince Vladimir in the 1377 Lavrentievsky chronicle, in a record for 996, and in many other places). Sometimes they push the prince to undertake a raid for booty: in 945, according to the Lavrentievsky chronicle, "said Igor's *druzhina*: the men of Sveneld have clad themselves in good armor and clothes, while we are naked. Come, prince, with us for tribute—we will get and you will get."[14] This understanding of *druzhina* is over-theorized in Russian historical literature, particularly in that Soviet commentators saw in it the origin of a future landowning aristocracy, and were thus keen on deciphering minute differences among the more or less propertied factions within this squad of warriors. However, the model for *druzhina*'s functioning, given the absence of documentary evidence, was inferred from Tacitus' comments on the barbarians' *comites* in I c. AD (*Germania*, chapter XIV): "In the day of battle, it is scandalous for the Prince to be surpassed in feats of bravery, scandalous for his followers to fail in matching the bravery of the Prince. But it is infamy during life, and indelible reproach, to return alive from a battle where their Prince was slain . . . The Princes fight for victory; for the Prince his followers fight. . . . In the place of pay, they are supplied with a daily table and repasts; though grossly prepared, yet very profuse. For maintaining such liberality and munificence, a fund is furnished by continual wars and plunder."[15]

Summing up: *druzhba* was more bookish, used for translations of the Greek term *philia*, and rarely—*hetaireia*. Thus, the notion of companionship or joint mission was largely absent from it, and the term *druzhba* made it into colloquial usage through diplomatic jargon that itself originated by incorporating the terms translating the Greek expressions linked to a famous injunction "love thy neighbor." In contrast to that, the term *druzhina* had the connotation of companionship as its primary point of reference, and was more colloquial since it could designate many proximate and understandable phenomena from indigenous Russian life. Of course, translated texts mattered here as well: for example, the now prevalent military connotation of *druzhina* seems to depend in its development on renditions of the Greek sources that had designated with the same term other—civilian and spiritual—types of joint quest or undertaking.

Thus, the meanings of *drug* seem to be polarized between these two abstract nouns that designate a condition of being a friend or refer to a group of friends. The meaning of *drug* as *le prochaine* largely fed *druzhba*, while the meaning of *drug* as a close companion in a joint undertaking largely fed *druzhina*. But these are just the first two meanings of the term *drug*. Where are the others? Given that the third meaning of *drug* is a rather special case, stemming from a stable idiomatic construction, one is not puzzled by the absence of such expressions as "friendship with God," with Truth or with Caesar: generic nouns were perhaps unnecessary to describe this rather singular condition, only available to a special few. But what about an almost total absence of attempts to use a generic noun that would employ the fourth meaning of *drug* (a special vocation in life that distinguishes it from kin, neighbors, counsels etc)? Once (in the *Prologue* from 1383) *druzhina* is used to designate a specific group of people different from kin, but that is perhaps all we might find. Why would not medieval Russian need a generic noun to designate a special condition of being a friend that would distinguish it from, say, love, or neighborly feeling? Why would it be content to have two terms that reflected Christian love of one's neighbor and a companionship, but would not have a term for friendship as friendship? Perhaps being a "friend" was a status, distinct from others, and captured in so many examples of usage, while "friendship" was not yet an institutionalized condition that would define it *qua* friendship.

3

This difference between the respective functions of the terms "friend" and "friendship" makes one wonder what was specifically achieved in medieval Russia by speech acts that involved terms for "friendship," *druzhba* and *druzhina*, rather than those speech acts that just employed the noun *drug*. In order to evaluate this, I shall examine the things—mostly of a mundane, material kind—that mediated the relationship between people called "friends" or, by contrast, the things that mediated the relationship designated as "friendship." This attention to things may offer us a useful heuristic tool to distinguish between the types of ties involved in an engagement.[16] Here we move from linguistics to sociology, from looking for the meaning of words employed in speech acts to evaluating their impact, felicitous or failing—that is, we try to re-enter a network of pragmatic and rather tangible concerns into which these words were woven.

Looking at these things, one easily realizes that a *drug* could either have separate things with another *drug* or share them, have them in common. Saying this, we do not distinguish between different meanings of *drug*; rather we look at how and which things bring phenomena designated by the term *drug*

together. Thus, in the XII c. vita of St. Theodosius Pechersky, a founder of
Russian monasticism, we learn that someone brought a precious object to be
temporarily entrusted for the care of monk Konon, *drugu sushchu,* i.e. since
he was known as a true Christian *drug.* The XIV c. Russian version of
Melissa tells about Alexander wishing to help his *drug* marry off his daugh-
ter and thus giving some gold to establish a dowry. In another instance, this
manuscript tells of a household master who distributes a silver coin to each
that produces discontent among recipients. The master tells one of the dis-
contented: "*druzhe* (in the Greek original—*hetaire*), I will not forego you."
Paleia, a Russian expostion of sacred history (1406), tells us about the Jews
who depart, having been granted by their *drug* some gold, silver and clothes.
The XIV c. manuscript of the miracles of St. Nicholas describes how he gave
6 gold coins to an elder, saying; "accept this, my *drug,* and give me the car-
pet." From our previous examples, one also readily recollects Kievan commander Pretich, who swaps arms with his new warrior *drug.* Gifts, exchanges, and even temporary loans structure this type of relationship between
drug and *drug.*

The second type of relationship is about sharing. From previously mentioned examples we remember how *drugi* (plural for *drug*) share work and
tribulations: Isaac the Greek paints the church with *drugi*; Stephan the Novgorodian goes with *drugi* to Constantinople. But there are more mundane
cases of sharing. A Russian version of the 1392 Niebuhr agreement on peace
between Novgorod and German merchants clearly stipulates that a charter
should be issued to "Ivan with *drugi*" for common possession, while another
sentence says: "On Neva river they [or we?—it is unclear from the context
O.Kh] beat up the robber the son of Matthew and his *drugi,* and confiscated
their property." Shared property from one group of *drugi* passes to another.
Cases of sharing more elevated goods do not escape mention also. *Melissa*:
"when a warrior does not spare himself or his arms while fighting for himself
and his *druzhina,* he will gain salvation and all his *druzi*" (the last word translates Greek *ton allon*). That is, salvation might be a shared good as well. And
my favorite quote from the Buddhist-influenced *Vita* of Barlaam and Joasaph
tells how to share things with friends when one is physically alone: "I think I
am already living for 45 years in the desert of Shinar, but I have *drugi* (in the
Greek of the original—*synagonistas*) that befriend me on my road of higher
procession (*puti vyshniago shestviia*) and teach me."

Now, in contrast to *drug,* the nouns *druzhba* and *druzhina* are hardly used
in situations that would imply separate possessions, exchange or gifts. They
are mostly about sharing. For example, in case of *druzhba* we learn from the
XII c. version of the Studite monastery statute that monks should be firmly
tied by common love and unanimity, because there is "an equality of friend-

ship" spread between them, Nazianzus speaks of sweet *druzhby sovokuplenie*, "the unity of friendship," while the XIV c. homily on lying teachers admonishes readers "neither to listen [to them], nor have *druzhba* with them, nor eat with them." There is only one dictionary example where *druzhba* implies separate fates or services for each other, but this usage is still rather ambiguous: "united in *druzhba*, overcoming hardships [literally—"carrying weights," O.Kh] for one another" (XIV c. *vita* of St. Theodore of Studion).

In the case of *druzhina*, examples of sharing are more numerous, as one would expect, and even more expressive than in the case for *druzhba*. We recollect the goods to be evacuated on a riverbank together (from the Smolensk 1229 treaty), as well as other commercial undertakings or common voyages mentioned in previously cited sources, but there are other startling instances: common robbery (XIII c. *Prologue*), or the following episode from a 1300 Riga charter: "As *druzhina* sat at the banquet drinking, they hit each other to death." The Barkhudarov dictionary also shows that in the XVI c. manuscript St. Saba's cenobitic monastery was called a *druzhina*, while Sreznevsky's dictionary (filled with common Slavonic usage, not necessarily practiced in Rus') gives examples of usage on *druzhina* travel to Jerusalem and Jordan and hints at the church origins of such usage: in the 1056–57 Ostromir Bible, Slavonic *v druzhine sushche* was used to say (Luke II: 44) that Joseph and Mary supposed Jesus "to have been in the company (*en te synodia*)."[17] This sharing in a *synodia* was supposed to be pretty intense, as we see in *The Pandectae* example (1296) registered in the XI–XIV c. usage dictionary: "I pray your mercy my Lord, so that you do not separate me from my *druzhina* [in Greek—*tes synodias*], not in the future, not any other way."

Exceptions to this representation of *druzhina* as concerned predominantly with sharing common things are found only in indigenous Russian sources. For example, there are two instances of usage from the Lavrientievsky chronicle (1377). In a record for 996 prince Vladimir ordered to forge silver spoons for *druzhina*, saying: "with silver and gold I will not get a *druzhina*, but with *druzhina*, I will get silver and gold." And in a record for 1197 a prince at war "does not collect gold and silver, but gives it to *druzhina*, because he loves *druzhina* greatly." Here, of course, love and the gifts of the prince imply reciprocal services in kind coming from his retinue. And the property acquired by individual members of warriors' *druzhina* is distinct from the property of the prince; there is no sharing here. Even when the member of *druzhina* dies without heirs, the most famous early legal code, *Russkaia Pravda*, prohibits the prince from taking it, in contrast to the property of a dead serf without heirs, which is given over to the prince automatically.

If in contrast to speech acts with *drug*, speech acts with both *druzhina* and *druzhba* almost never imply exchanges or separate possessions, and they mostly occur in the contexts of sharing (save for cases from indigenous chronicles and legal codes just discussed), then this might demonstrate how bookish translations from Greek sources tried (intentionally or unintentionally) to unobtrusively impose a new higher ideal of friendship on a largely ignorant and perhaps recalcitrant Slavic populace for whom the simpler word *drug* still could designate a very separate existence. That is, *drug* occurred in contexts of partial and privy interests where *druzhba* and *druzhina* almost never had.

Of course, often speech acts with *drug* could imply sharing, and if we put them next to speech acts with *druzhba* and *druzhina*, we can see that sharing in general was conceived on three levels simultaneously. One could share property: commodities, spoils and tribute. One could share activities (a more widespread type of sharing): eating together, drinking together,[18] traveling and fighting (sometimes—dying) together, deliberating together in a council and establishing laws and institutions together. On the basis of these two (what we would now call) rather pragmatic types of sharing one could talk in literary language about the sweet unity of friendship—sharing love, salvation, and even "roads of higher vocation." But this talk could not deny the obvious: the reality of medieval Russian friendship was as much about separateness and otherness as it was about sharing.

4

The lamentation of the unfortunate Daniil Zatochnik, a famous XIII c. example of an indigenous text of unparalleled literary force, says it all: "My *druzi* and the close ones turned away from me, because I do not put varied dinners in front of them anymore. A lot of people befriend me, putting their hands in my saltcellar, but when troubles come, they behave like enemies and try to make my steps falter; with their eyes they weep with me, but in their hearts they laugh at me. Thus do not have trust in a friend (*ne imi drugu very*), and do not put hope on a brother." This excerpt is rather revealing. Even sharing such a tangible and luxurious thing as a saltcellar is not a guarantee of your friends' help: each of them have their separate interests, including perhaps an interest in your own failure and demise. What could one say about a more mundane friendship that attempted to rely on sharing such obvious medieval objects as simple food, unpretentious drink or even letters themselves, one of which—a plea for help—Daniil is sending to his prince, i.e. a lordly friend?[19] Daniil seems to convey such remorse about the unbridgeable gap between separate and different egos in every friendship, that it is similar to Nietzschean ruminations on the same topic.

Zatochnik, however, is hardly ingenious in his insight on the otherness of friends, even if he is unbeaten by his contemporaries in style and force of expression. A colloquial speaker of Russian could always suspect that *drug* was *drugoi*, a friend was the other, even in the XIII c. In fact, the word *drugoi* was more widespread in written sources than *drug*: the database of the XI–XIV c. dictionary registers 590 usages of *drug* and substantially more than a 1000 instances of usage of *drugoi*; it even declines to count them. In written sources the word *drugoi* appeared simultaneously with *drug* and sometimes this adjective had a shortened form that was written as "drug" also, because in Russian it was and is possible to shorten adjectives by taking the ending away: *Kruglyi* (round) is equivalent to *krugl*; *krasnyi* (red or beautiful) is equivalent to *krasn*; *drugii* or *drugoi* (not this, another, second) is thus equivalent to *drug*. Sreznevsky even thinks that an example of this adjective *drug* (as a shortened form of adjective *drugoi*, not as the noun *drug*) appears in the following line of the 1229 Smolensk treaty with Riga that he cites in a dictionary article for *drugoi*: "Who hits another (*drug*) with wood and bruises or bloodies him, he should pay him one and a half grivna [monetary unit] of silver." The dictionary of the XI–XIV c. usage gives 6 primary meanings of the adjective *drugoi*: 1) not this one, not that one; 2) the other one, distinct from this one; 3) one that follows the first one; 4) second; 5) some. Curiously, it ends with singling out the special sixth meaning, when *drugoi* appears in the role of a noun and then is said to mean "any human, *le prochaine*, comrade." Some of the examples given are the following: "Avrilii, a bishop of that seat with his close ones (*drugyimi ego)*"—from translated Byzantine Nomocanon (XII c.); "Because you suffer yourself, understand your neighbor (*drugomu*, in Greek original—*allos*): if you help a suffering one, then while suffering you will be helped yourself"—in XIV c. version of *Melissa*. And a non-translated source, *Russkaia Pravda*, says: "if one takes money from others [or "neighbors"—*druzi* in Russian], and starts to negate this, then one should call the witnesses."

One hardly escapes the feeling that contemporary classifiers of historical linguistic material tried to uncover some neat logic behind the usage when there was, in fact, none to be found. *Druzii, drugyi, drugi, drug*—both what we now call adjectives and nouns—could be historically used to translate phrases that involved appeal to a relationship of proximity, i.e. a neighborly quality in the sense of *le prochaine*. It is only now that we segregate these similar sounding words according to their logically defined and thus mutually exclusive functions into different classes. And the three dictionaries we studied are not alone in this attempt to impute logic behind usage, while usage itself hardly supports a distinction between *drug* and *drugoi*. Thus, the only etymological dictionary (by Shanskii) that deals with the history of the word

drugoi next to the word *drug* (usually such dictionaries do not concern themselves with the historical distinctions between the two terms) claims that this
adjective (common to all Slavic languages) developed initially in idiomatic
phrases *drug drugu*, *drug druga*—meaning "one another". Only later the adjective *drugoi* allegedly decoupled itself from this reciprocal formation and
became independent.[20]

This hypothesis may be supported by some evidence, even if this account
seems too neat to be true, given the maze of historical ties between *drug*, *drugoi* and *drug druga*. In Russian manuscripts, the stable reciprocal construction *drug druga* used to translate the Greek term *allilon*, which is a doubling
of *allos*, meaning "the other." Thus, even in the first 1076 miscellanea we find
"pray one for another (*drug za druga*)" with no obvious Greek original underlying it. However, the same phrase in Russian translates *hyper allilon* in
the Pandectae from XIV c., and this repeats word for word Jacob V: 16:
"Confess your faults one to another, and pray one for another (*hyper allilon*),
that ye may be healed." Similar examples of *drug druga* translating *pros
allilous*, *tas allilon*, *allilois*, etc., pepper the pages of the Russian manuscripts
that conveyed Christian wisdom to the newly converted people.

One way to take this massive amount of linguistic evidence is to say that
the Christian notion of "neighbor" was taken over to designate this basic unit
of reciprocal relationship: the word *drug* was doubled to become *drug druga*.
Another would be to say that a notion of "friend" meaning *le prochaine*
was—on the contrary—distilled from the very structure of language that used
the word *drugoi*, "another" to now designate the reciprocal relationship between any Christians. This lead to the formation of the equation "other = thy
Christian neighbor" which also came to mean "other = thy friend," that is,
drugoi was reduced to *drug* in combinations like *drug druga*. These two easy
hypotheses are not the only possible ones. Instead of reducing one word to another, one might suggest points of parallel multiple generation and overlapping: after Derrida we tend to believe that there is hardly one origin of any
phenomenon.

I will leave exploration of this linguistic maze to professional philologists,
and will point only to yet another interesting development that might tell us
about medieval intuitions formulated against the background of this maze of
usage. The Russian word *vdrug*—which now only means "suddenly"—is first
registered in an indigenous Russian source, according to the Barkhudarov
dictionary, in 1379, in the form *s drug*, meaning "with a *drug*", that is, "together", or by implication, "simultaneously": "He departed simultaneously
with (*drug s*) Mityai—at the same time, but by a different road." It is impossible to decipher—as a contemporary yearning would push us to do—whether
the departing one was traveling with a real friend, or just a Christian neigh-

bor: the difference was perhaps not there yet. But this XIV c. inscription of the word "friend" into the very term that would capture the structure of simultaneous time—togetherness in its pure form—goes against the previous, more basic XI–XIV c. inscriptions that inseparably linked friendship and the dissimilar. Perhaps, Russians have been finally learning how to live with the basic intuition that a friend is always and inescapably the other. You go a different road, but are still together—*s drug*—if you depart at the same time, *vdrug*: time conquers space. Time is an attempt to bridge the spatial and existential chasm that inescapably separates the self from the other.

NOTES

1. Pronounced as "droog."
2. Max Vasmer, *Etimologicheskii slovar'russkogo iazyka* (Moscow: Progress, 1964), vol. 1, 543.
3. Nikolai Shanskii, ed., *Etimologicheskii slovar'russkogo iazyka* (Moscow: MGU, 1963–1982), article on *drug*, which exposes Trubachev's theory.
4. Pavel Chernykh, *Istoriko-etimologicheskii slovar' sovremennogo russkogo iazyka* (Moscow: Russkii iazyk, 1999), vol. 1, 271.
5. Of the three source dictionaries, each has its own problems. A first preparatory 6 volume set, which collected registered usage from most sources that were easily accessible to a single scholar in the end of the XIX c., was prepared by Izmail Sreznevsky (*Materialy dlia slovaria drevne-russkago iazyka*, (St. Petersburg, 1893–1912)). His dictionary is very suggestive since it frequently gives parallel Greek and Latin terms, but it was criticized by later scholars precisely for that reason —since it either relies on translated South Slavic texts that were not characteristic of indigenous usage up north and thus stayed an aberration for Eastern Slavs, or it relies on manuscripts existing in very few recensions. The ambitious Soviet multi-volume dictionary of the Russian language of the XI–XVII c., which was being published since 1975 and is still unfinished (Stepan Barkhudarov, ed.-in chief, *Slovar' russkogo iazyka XI–XVII vekov)*, tried to look for purely indigenous and allegedly widespread and secular usage. Thus, it purged many Church Slavonic texts from its source base as non-important, and tried to register the first usage found in a non-translated source. The advantages and disadvantages of this dictionary come from the fact that it is the result of a huge collective work: it covers many sources, but usage appearing in a dictionary article is a result of the arbitrary choice of people reading through the sources and then of the chief editors—Barkhudarov *et al.* The most recent dictionary (Ruben Avanesov, ed., *Slovar' drevnerusskogo iazyka (XI–XIV v.)* (Moscow: Russkii iazyk, 1988–)) tried to correct this non-exhaustive character of the previous dictionary compilation, and to reintroduce church literature of the non-liturgical kind back into the source base. It also narrowed the sources to manuscripts of XI–XIV c., thus expanding but clearly circumscribing the set of them (784 as opposed to 402 in Sreznevsky

and even smaller amount in Barkhudarov), and exhaustively scanned all appearances of a given term in these 784 sources, counting the frequency of usage. The drawback here, of course, is what may be considered to be an arbitrary choice of the 784 sources (e.g. manuscripts of the Old and New Testaments were excluded, as were the sources that were defined as Bulgarian, Serbian, or of generic East Slavic origin). I will be using the Avanesov dictionary, adding usage from Sreznevsky and Barkhudarov when they highlight something useful that Avanesov may have omitted.

6. This is one of two kinds of friendship for gain, the other being *philia ethike* when there are no clear written stipulations on mutual obligations; see *Nicomachean Ethics* 1162b21.

7. Barkhudarov cites only the central exchange, while I render the whole scene, following a website version of this Chronicle—*Lavrentievskaia letopis'*, <http://litopys.narod.ru/lavrlet/lavr03.htm> (22 Nov. 2004)

8. *Molenie Daniila Zatochnika*, <http://old-russian.chat.ru/14zatoch.htm> (22 Nov. 2004)

9. Vladimir Kolesov, *Drevniaia Rus': nasledie v slove* [Ancient Rus': Heritage in Words] (St. Petersburg: Filologicheskii fakultet SPbGU, 2000), 54.

10. Iurii Sorokin, ed., *Slovar' russkogo iazyka XVIII veka* (St. Petersburg: Nauka, 1992), vol. 7, 15.

11. Sorokin, *Slovar' russkogo iazyka XVIII veka*, article on *drug*.

12. The King James version is rather more polysemic, translating this as "congregations that had been carried away," which suggests transgression of the laws of God.

Interestingly, the 1499 Gennadius Bible also gives a unique stray usage of *druzhba* in the meaning of "people following one another and dancing" that translates Greek *choros* in Judith III: 7: "all the country round about received them [Holofernes's army] with garlands, with dances, and with timbrels." This meaning did not stick in Russian, but the archetypal force of this image of what friends do together can be seen from an illustration to the 1966 edition of *The Song of Friends* (first edition—1944), a rhyme for 3–5 year olds that reads: "We are moving, moving, moving to far away lands! Good neighbors and jolly friends! We are taking with us a cat, a siskin, a dog, a fighter cock! And a monkey and a parrot—what a great company!" The picture shows children in a dancing chain, as if forming a train. This verse, taught in families and kindergartens, was known by almost every Soviet child, having been written by a most popular children's poet, and also the author of the text of the Soviet (now—Russian) anthem. A poem thus inculcates a vision of a dance, linked to companionship on pilgrimage to exotic lands. See Sergei Mikhalkov, *Pesenka druzei* (Moscow: Malysh, 1966). This cornerstone of Soviet civilization—that offered to children habitual expectations and developed their moral intuitions—still awaits its deconstruction.

13. Apart from these two meanings of *druzhina* (companionship and prince's warriors), dictionaries mention the third meaning (a commune that pays for transgressions of one of its members) that appears in the first extant legal code of Russia, *Russkaia Pravda*. However, this usage is scarce and not characteristic of other sources. The full text of this document is available at <http://www.hist.msu.ru/ER/Etext/RP> (22 Nov. 2004).

14. Text for 945 from *Lavrentievskaia letopis'*, <http://litopys.narod.ru/lavrlet/lavr03.htm> (22 Nov. 2004).

15. This excerpt (actually, a substantially longer one, from chapters 13–15) is cited in a conventional account by Anton Gorskii, *Drevnerusskaia druzhina* (Moscow: Prometei, 1989), 15–16. English translation from *Germania*, <http://www.northvegr.org/lore/tacitus/002.php> (22 Nov. 2004).

16. This term comes from a category *mode d'engagement* in the sociology of Laurent Thevenot that grants objects a role in coordinating human interaction. The most radical version of ascribing agency to things is found, of course, in the sociology of Bruno Latour and Michel Callon. All of these new sociologies depart from treating networks as just nets of naked humans or disembodied subjects, and include objects as nodes of networks next to subjects. Accordingly, a study of friendship is then recast as a study of humans mediated by things, or a study of a human-non-human nexus that allows an appearance of a new thing (understood in a Heideggerian way as a four-fold assemblage of earth and sky, mortals and gods), rather than just a study of humans. Attention to things in and of friendship is intuitively widespread among historians, of course, see e.g. Peter Burke, "Humanism and Friendship," in *Friendship in Medieval Europe,* ed. Julian Haseldine (Stroud: Sutton, 1999), 267, on such objects as specifically drawn lists of "laws of friendship," friendly inscriptions in books and salon albums, and exchanged portraits.

17. Sreznevsky also cites the Slavonic XI c. manuscript of the Patericon of Synai where *druzhina* translated Greek *hetairous autou*, Latin equivalent being *ad socios suos*.

18. Eating and drinking together very often seem to be the two most basic founding acts of medieval friendship conceived as sharing. Thus, Barkhudarov cites a XII c. Russian version of *Chrysorroas*, an alleged collection of sayings from John Chrysostom; "Do not unite with them in eating, nor in drinking, nor in *druzhba*, in any thing."

19. We hardly know of the context of this lamentation, e.g. who Daniil was and whether he succeeded in receiving help. On letters as a substitute for a missing friend see Carolinne White, "Friendship in Absence—Some Patristic Views," in *Medieval Friendship*, ed. J. Haseldine, 72–73.

20. Shanskii, *Etimologicheskii slovar'*, article on *drugoi*.

Chapter Six

Friendship:
Classic and Contemporary Concerns

Issues of friendship might seem peripheral to the central political questions in Russia, which are usually seen as related to rebuilding the weak state, but this impression is misleading for a number of reasons. First, as I argued in chapter 2, because it is so important in structuring human relations, friendship offers important but underexploited resources for civil society and thus may shift the focus of political discussion from the problem of the weak state to the problem of strong society. Second, the central place of friendship in such classics of political theory as Aristotle. Cicero, and Augustine has only recently begun to receive the attention it deserves. Rather than relegating friendship to a politically marginal private sphere, these thinkers offer a discussion of the "political friendship" that may serve as a model for a project to address the troubles of contemporary Russia. Obviously, this possibility cannot be realized through a mechanical application of their work, but will require a rethinking based on a close examination of the actual practices of Russian friendship.

This chapter will describe the range of possible concerns of such a study, first by stressing the relevance of friendship as a means of cohesion and then by giving an overview of debates in political theory on the issue of friendship. Some conclusions on the relevance of political theories of friendship for contemporary Russian experience will be offered in the end.

IMPORTANCE OF FRIENDSHIP IN RUSSIA

My interest in thinking about friendship stems from the ubiquity of this phenomenon in post-Communist Russia since, as some observers would maintain, this may be a saving grace for the country. Indeed, with all other resources ensuring peaceful social cohesion severely depleted, friendship may turn out to be the only extensive resource easily available. Yet, the topic of friendship in Communist and post-Communist societies is severely understudied. For example, given its ubiquity and salience, there has been remarkably little scholarly analysis published on issues of friendship the Soviet Union. Perhaps in the only notable exception, Vladimir Shlapentokh described friendship as one of the most valued social relationships in the USSR. He cited data from one 1981 empirical study to stress the difference between Soviet and American perceptions of friendship and to highlight the extraordinary importance that Soviet people ascribed to friendship: 15.8 percent of Soviet respondents met friends every day, 32.3 percent—once or several times a week, and 31.2 percent—several times a month. For the US of the same period, the median was substantially lower: 4.49 times a month for young bachelors and 3.08–3.55 times for married couples.[1] Face-to-face interaction with friends surpassed all other leisure activites in terms of time spent, except for watching TV,[2] because friends played the role of confessors for each other, served as the means of communication alternative to official mass media, and helped each other in procuring scarce goods and services in the conditions of the economy of deficit. Hence, Soviet official sources never exalted friendship; *Pravda* never ran an editorial on it. The only scholarly Soviet study that directly addressed the subject was more concerned with expounding historical views and philosophical doctrines on friendship from Aristotle to Hegel than with actually examining the peculiarities of Soviet friendship. It hinted, however, that unconditional trust and the possibility of confessing and discussing personal problems at any time made Soviet friendship an unofficial moral value.[3]

My own work on the formation of the basic unit of Soviet society, a self policing work group of allegedly equal builders of Communism—the designation of which was conveniently transliterated into English as *kollektiv* to stress this specificity—has also shown that close interpersonal friendship was always suspect in the eyes of the powers that be because of its potential contribution to creating a "false *kollektiv*" that challenged the official ones. Friendship built informal networks that subverted official collective surveillance and discipline.[4] Bringing all these accounts together, one understands why friendship became a suspect value for the Stalinist regime: friends did not abandon each other even when the *kollektiv* attacked one of them. A friend, by definition, then, was an individual who did not let you down even under direct menace to himself or herself; a person to whom one could securely entrust one´s controversial thoughts since he or she would never betray them, even under pressure. Friendship thus in a sense became an ultimate value. produced in

resistance struggles in the Soviet Union: any ascribed category of human relationship could crumble under the threat of terror—children denounced parents,
wives betrayed husbands or vice versa, and so on. By contrast, "friend" was
not an ascription but an achievement; it was a definition forged by terror and
thus represented a dearly earned status.

This value of close interpersonal friendship in informal life developed, however, not only as a result of terror but also because a friendship network became the main arena for unofficial individualization, for revelation of knowledge about oneself and the formation of self-identity. This function of Russian
friendship, one may argue, did not disappear even in the current conditions of
the radical weakening of the repressive state, and the contemporary salience of
friendship in Russia is not a result of strong or weak state institutions.

My book suggested that one of the sources of centrality of friendship for
Russian life lies in the fact that friends form an arena for existentially important
communication through which the sense of a given individual self emerges. Curiously, submitting to a periodical review by relevant others—upon which Soviet citizens habitually relied in their everyday lives in order to establish the
sence of their selves and check previous self-evaluations—was an unintended
spin-off of the uniform purge practices in the official sphere, themselves an heir
to the penitential techniques of self-cognition practiced by Orthodox Christianity for ages.[5] That is, a network of close frends was instrumental in the establishment of the sense of an individual self through voluntary submission to a review by relevant others in such situations as birthday parties or famous regular
"kitchen" discussions of ethical concerns.

In other words, in later Soviet society, friendship as a moral value was
tested in milder but more widespread struggles, while it also served as the
arena for the emergence of selfhood. Still, the obligation to withstand pressure in order to be called a true friend and to be admitted to rituals of construction of the self of your friend persisted. Dyadic and triadic interpersonal
relationships and larger networks of friends constituted the unseen underpin-
ning of everyday life in the Soviet Union. These relationships made life simultaneously tolerable and intriguing for Soviet citizens, as well as for the
Sovietologists doomed to do research amidst the grayish landscapes of Soviet
life: who would live in a society consisting of obedient automatons, duped
into submission by ideology and terror?

FRIENDSHIP AS A MEANS OF CIVIL COHESION

After the collapse of the Soviet regime, Russia has inherited friendship ties as
a very important part of its social terrain. Friendship spans a complicated set

of transformed elements of the Soviet society and new social entities that together constitute post-Soviet society, as I argued in the end of Chapter 2 of this book. Friendly networks that formerly existed as if on the obverse side of society have emerged into the open. On the one hand, they have become an obvious part of the post-Soviet business world and of what some observers call clan politics. At least, some friends' networks, transformed and institutionalized to a certain extent in assigning related government or business positions, lie at the core of many power groups. In stating this, one needs to be doubly cautious, however. First, the term "clan" came into wide mass media usage after a famous article by David Stark, "Privatization in Hungary: From Plan to Market or From Plan to Clan?"[6] Successful as a rhyming catchword, the metaphor of a clan is somehow misleading: it would be far-fetched to model relationships of dependence and patronage in contemporary Russian politics on Scottish kinship lineages. Rather, following an initial set of distinctions proposed in a classic article by Eric Wolf, we may envisage a spectrum of interpersonal relationships that may develop from a friendship into a clique and then into a patron-client relationship.[7] A former friendship network that united equal partners in the Soviet days might be transformed upon entering joint pursuit of wealth or power in the post-Communist days into a clique, which is defined as the group tied, not by polyvalent and multifaceted interests in each other, but by "a set of roles associated with the particular job". In short, a friendship network abandons existentially important communication and is transformed into a simple group of more or less equal political or economic entrepreneurs, which makes this group rife with potential conflict and accusations of betrayal.[8] If further developments bring obvious differences in status, a clique might devolve into a patronage network, when a "big man" moving from one office to another carries with him (or her) a whole following of loyal clients.

Neither pattern of group arrangement is novel to twentieth century Russia: T.H. Rigby attracted attention to cliques in the internecine fight for power and promotion in the "crypto-politics" of the late Soviet system,[9] while patron-client relationships were clearly one of the ubiquitous phenomena of the Stalinist system: see accounts about a whole army of middle managers arriving with a new director of the new industrial plant[10] or of Stalin's attempts to root it out.[11]

In contrast to cliques and clienteles, friendships are polyvalent networks of equal and close partners who are genuinely interested in an unspecified number and types of concerns of each other,[12] rather than only in job-related concerns as in cliques or in an exchange of power for loyalty as in a clientele. Thus, those friends' networks that withstood the temptations of jointly pursuing wealth or power seem to retain the functions they inherited from the old days: they provide the most fundamental means of social welfare and defense for the individual, but—more importantly—ensure the maintenance of the arenas of existentially important communication contributing to personality formation among their members.

As I argued in Chapter 2, the post-collectives and the recently created business groups are tied into post-Soviet society by means of semi-private and semi-public protection providers that use the threat of physical violence to maintain the predictable behavior of civil bodies. The weak state has brought into existence a whole plethora of entities that use violent non-civil methods to ensure the more or less smooth functioning of businesses. However, all of these bodies, civil and militant, are penetrated by the networks of friendly concern, mutual help, and nonviolent influence. The central problem of contemporary Russian civil society thus may consist in transforming the relations of uncivil violence according to the principles of friendly networks.

OBJECTIONS AND RESEARCH QUESTIONS

There are a couple of objections usually immediately raised against this type of argument. The first objection holds that what people most frequently call friendship in Russia is actually something else, and that the rhetoric of altruistic friendship is just a disguise for obvious relations of gain. Another objection is that, even if we ever find genuine altruistic friendship in Russia, it is exclusive by definition: it links a few private individuals in an exercise in mutual benevolence, opposing a broader society. Thus, it would seem impossible to link the whole society employing the principles of contemporary private friendship. These objections, however, are not insurmountable obstacles. Recent thinking on friendship may provide us with grounds to adequately address both of them.

Let's take the first objection. On the one hand, "clan politics", which are so often pointed out as the main feature of political struggles in Russia, can be described as friendship only with a great deal of conceptual stretching. In fact, as I have argued, these "clan politics" are either clique politics that are inherently unstable and rife with conflict, or patronage politics. Now, no matter what people accustomed to ordinary usage of the term "friendship" in Asian or African villages are prone to see in Russia, a stable exchange of material benefits for personal allegiance and political support is hardly ever called "friendship" in contemporary Russian parlance. The blatant inequality of a patron-client relationship prevents people from calling one's patron or superior "my friend".

On the other hand, exchanges between more or less equal partners very often merit the title of friendship, and here the analysis of such sociologists as

Pierre Bourdieu and Luc Boltanski looks very appropriate, because it helps us to carefully dissect the intricate mix of utilitarian and altruistic components of a typical modern friendship between equals. For example, the work of Bourdieu suggests that people linked in networks tend to misrepresent their own relationships of equivalent exchange of gifts and services in normative terms of altruistic friendship. They rely on these terms to make the functioning of exchange relations smooth and unproblematic.[13] In his corrections to Bourdieu's theory Boltanski has shown, however, that many human relationships we cherish do not employ the critical capacity of a suspicious social scientist who uncovers acts of equivalent exchange allegedly disguised by altruistic language, nor should this capacity be used at all if we are to keep these very relationships going. That is, according to Boltanski, what he calls relations of *agape* and what we may call "authentic friendship" may develop out of a regular gift exchange after participants in this exchange consciously stop monitoring the value of gifts exchanged.[14]

Friendship then becomes sharing in active forgetting, that is, jointly stopping the act of critically evaluating inputs brought into the relationship. In her recent work on the informal exchange of favors in Russian society Alena Ledeneva used some concepts of Boltanski but for some reason did not employ this very idea.[15] On the basis of her and Boltanski's work, one can show how relations of authentic friendship may emerge from the most widespread relation of everyday equivalent exchange of favors in Russia. The Soviet phenomenon of *blat*, for example—the exchange of services of access to scarce goods in the conditions of the economy of shortages—may have frequently given rise to genuine friendship when participants in the *blat* network ceased habitually monitoring the value of services exchanged and thus started acting for the sake of their friend himself or herself. Even in the Soviet days, the most cynical relationships may have engendered the most altruistic. This mass potential for altruistic behavior survives in post-Communist Russia as well.

The second typical objection—stressing the exclusive character of modern Russian friendship at the expense of broader society—may be challenged on different grounds. Modern friendship seems to have become an exclusive private relationship involving a few individuals only after the epochal transformation brought about by the appearance of the impersonal market and bureaucratic mechanisms in the Western world. For example, as Allan Silver has persuasively argued, thinkers of the Scottish Enlightenment, who were among the first to theorize this change, thought that only after commercial exchanges between individuals had become subject to transparent market evaluation did pure, disinterested emotional ties between individuals become possible. Without the need to procure favors, gifts, or services by means of others—since people could now get them in the open market—were people expected to be drawn together by genuine interpersonal sympathy.[16]

However, until this great transformation that rendered friendship and enjoyment of interpersonal communication a private pastime, there was a wholly different classical tradition that viewed friendship as a public virtue and a common good for the *polis*. Classical political theory thrives on discussing the issue of friendship. Recent studies by Alasdair MacIntyre, Bernard Yack, and Jacques Derrida,[17] to name just a few, have rediscovered this overlooked tradition of theorizing "political friendship" that started with Aristotle and went through Cicero and Augustine almost to Montaigne: ancient Greeks—and early Christians, to a lesser extent—knew how to befriend each other in the thousands, and this experience can shed some new light on our modern problems. That is, in Classical Greece, Greeks talked of *hetaereia* (tight interpersonal networks, effectively being groups of male peers who grew up together and fought and participated in city politics together), different types of *philia* or *xenia* (different types of well-wishing), and political friendship proper, *politike philia*. This last concept will concern us more than the others in the exposition that follows.[18]

Political friendship was looked upon as a species of friendship for gain (utility friendship) that presupposed equal exchange of contributions and gifts. That is, among the three types of friendship (for pleasure, for gain, and virtuous friendship), political friendship clearly had a very specific transitional status between the second, middle and third, higher form of friendship. Briefly, political friendship had one peculiar feature that neither friendship for gain nor virtuous friendship possessed. Although Greeks thought that befriending many was impossible as a rule—in utility friendship this led to too many quasi-contract obligations, in virtuous friendship this led to necessarily ignoring the demands of your dear friends and thus to a decrease in your own virtue—in political friendship, one could be friends with many other citizens without servility or loss of virtue.[19]

Getting slightly ahead of the exposition, I would like to mention another curious quality of *philia politike*. At least according to one influential interpretation, partners in political friendship banded together for material gain, but they also gained in virtue as a result of this friendship. In other words, equal exchange and a common pursuit of the shared goal remained, but these gain-oriented relations contributed to the growth of virtue among all the people involved in political friendship.[20]

These theoretical considerations seem to offer some promising avenues of thought on using the potential of friendship relations in Russia to ensure public order and develop civil society. However, many questions still remain unanswered. How does one reconcile in practice the principles that tie small interpersonal networks at the expense of the broader society with the demand to integrate these networks together in this very society? How does one transform the ancient ideal of common undertaking in the pursuit of virtue to fit the realities of present-day Russia, where virtue hardly seems to be a word to ever be used? Which principles of friendship can be employed in transforming the vast terrain of uncivil life, if one is not just naively trying to make everybody befriend everybody else? Answering all of these questions would require at least a painstaking study of the classical sources and of contemporary works that rethink the classic experience, an objective for future study. What will follow now is a preliminary attempt to map possible approaches to dealing with such questions.

ARISTOTELIAN RUMINATIONS

Communitarian thinkers have demonstrated a marked interest in the problem of political or civic friendship. Many have noted one of the starting sentences of the eighth book of Aristotle's *Nicomachean Ethics*: "Friendship also seems to hold cities together, and lawgivers seem to be more concerned about it than justice . . . [For] when people are friends, justice is unnecessary, but when they are just they need friendship as well."[21] MacIntyre, who explicitly brought this quote into the central debate of communitarian thought, seemed to represent friendship as a prerequisite of any community, whether just or unjust. In practical terms, he depicted friendship as a series of sets of personal friends or their overlapping networks that together constitute a sharing of all in the common project of creating and sustaining life in the city, a sharing incorporated in the immediacy of an individual's particular friendships. Of course, he stressed that political community envisaged as a set of friends' networks was alien to a standard liberal individualist model; but, insisted MacIntyre, that is how many Americans still tended to think of such social endeavors as schools, hospitals, and philanthropic organizations. Thus, friendship is an affection that arises in common allegiance and common pursuit of goods.[22]

Bernard Yack has made an especially illustrious attempt to challenge this communitarian vision and show the purely instrumental, self-interested character of political friendship in Aristotle. He points to barter and market exchange, which Aristotle describes as a kind of political friendship, and notices no element of close personal emotion in them. A thin well-wishing needed to qualify the relationship as friendship is preserved in these relationships only to the extent that there exists "the disposition of human beings to develop a sense of concern for the good of individuals with whom they share goods, identities and activities."[23] When political friendship, not mediated by clearly

stipulated obligations—which Aristotle calls *"ethikon* friendship for gain"—
develops, emotions based on accusations of betrayal of these obligations
threaten the very existence of the polis. Yack therefore concludes that Aristotle is a realist who is in favor of the minimal well-wishing that exists in stable political friendships like those based on clearly formulated exchange
agreements.

The majority of those writing on friendship in Aristotle dispute this rather
thin notion of political friendship. The influential interpretation of John M.
Cooper uses a discussion of the goal of political regimes to shed more light
on Aristotle's sparse lines dealing with civic friendship as such. His argument
then rests not only on all direct elaboration on the topic of political friendship
in the various *Ethics* (such as 1161b13, 1163b34, 1167b2, 1171a17, 1242b22)
but also adds a discussion in *Politics* (1280b5–38) on why citizens have to
care about each other's good life so that no vicious or unjust person takes part
in politics. A *polis*, in this excerpt, is said to care about the *eunomia* (the good
character) and virtue of its citizens. Cooper writes: "According to Aristotle,
then, a city is a kind of community that depends upon the friendly interest that
the citizens take in one another's qualities of mind and character," as well as
in their economic interests.[24] In Cooper's opinion, political friendship does
not require the deep empathy that Yack ascribes to a communitarian position,
but it does require goodwill and concern for the moral qualities of other citizens. Thus, he rejects the common undertaking model of MacIntyre, but also
rejects the minimal well-wishing model of Yack; a shared concern for the
virtue of others becomes central for Cooper.

Sibyl Schwarzenbach, who follows Cooper's exposition on Aristotelian
friendship, tries to adapt this interpretation to the needs of modern Swiss democracy. After freedom of conscience was established by the Reformation,
the notion of "thick values" that unite people in political friendship based on
religious unanimity should be abandoned, she says. Schwarzenbach proposes
to tone down the radical intensity of any similar kinds of political friendship
and to introduce a consensus on what she calls "second-order values," instead
of the Aristotle-inspired common pursuit of shared "thick values." These second-order values would include well-wishing toward the other, tolerance,
abiding by the law, acknowledgment of the universal principle of respect for
others, and perhaps the new value of care and friendship. Also, given the professed liberal ideal of the impenetrability of the borders of private life, she
proposes that people caring about the virtue of others should concern themselves only with the "public political character," rather than with the comprehensive moral qualities of fellow citizens.[25]

This project retains a stress on virtue, but it aims at checking the moral
virtues of others, a project of dubious quality. At least in the case of post-

Communist Russia, Cooper/Schwarzenbach's paradigm seems very queston-able. One could argue that the USSR was an example of repressive Aris-totelianism: concern for the virtue of a fellow citizen was best exemplified in the procedure called the purge, in which the comprehensive moral character of each Communist and later, each Soviet citizen, was checked at periodic in-dividual screening sessions staged by every work collective. The state cared about the virtue of citizens, all of whom were officially called "comrades," and all of whom shared the same goal of the good life, defined as the radiant ideal of Communism. The end result of this politics of state-promoted friend-ship based on unanimity and care for virtues was disastrous.

FRIENDSHIP AS COMMUNICATION BETWEEN THE DISTANT AND DISSIMILAR

Two recent theorizations seem to try to recover the radically different Greek experience of political friendship, and in so doing they distance themselves from the classical formulations of the Aristotelian theory of friendship. The Aristotelian system, according to one of these theorizations, is based too much on the model of enforced rulership rather than on the contest among equal friends for excellence in the eyes of relevant others. This is the position of those who follow Hannah Arendt's stress on pre-Socratic friendship as a model for free politics. Another theorization is linked to the works of Jacques Derrida and Maurice Blanchot and tries to transcend the Aristotelian view of friendship as a reciprocal symmetrical relationship of a similar ego and alter ego. It aims at recasting political friendship as non-reciprocal and at intro-ducing radical dissimilarity between friends to the point of eliminating any symmetry in their relationship.[26]

Let us first see what the followers of Arendt have to say on matters of friendship. She rarely mentioned this category in her written work—an ad-dress on Lessing, a few lines in *The Human Condition,* and the transcript of the 1954 lectures at Chicago are almost all we have. But her commentators consistently point out the centrality of friendship in her life and for her think-ing.[27] Shin Chiba, for example, stresses the persistent concern of Arendt's writings: a search for the new *vinculum,* a bond that would tie people together in a truly human, political, rather than a natural way, and would thus distin-guish them from herd animals or gods.[28] The Latin term in question comes from Augustine, on whose concept of love Arendt wrote her first dissertation. But she deemed Christian love for a neighbor unpolitical, and thus she later opts for another bond—fellowship based on debate and deliberation that al-lows immortal deeds to be registered. As she states in the 1954 lectures, what characterizes friends is an unending debate on how things appear to them. Just saying the *doxa*—how things appear to you—without the need to come to a final resolution and absolute truth, is what makes a conversation between friends so special. By discussing the different perceptions of the common world that lies between them, uniting and separating them simultaneously, friends establish and sustain this in-between, a world as some phenomenologists would understand it: a unity of shared things that set up the coordinates for prospects for meaningful action. Acts of immortal quality acquire an arena in this world, while debate and deliberation produce stories of great deeds as automatically as fabrication produces artifacts.

Friendship thus is not modeled on joint commercial pursuit or dividing something, it is about being partners in establishing and maintaining the common world.[29] One could say that the central feature of friendship for Arendt is its background quality: she does not discuss it very often, concentrating rather on attracting attention to the agonistic character of pre-Socratic politics, on the constant striving to perform an immortal deed of superior excellence, but friendship is what makes all this agonistics possible. Friendship is "the common regard for the in-between," friendship sets up this background—the world that serves as the arena for struggles and contests in the foreground.[30] Without friendly discussion, a world would remain inhuman, says Arendt[31]—one could almost take that to mean that no humanity is possible without a fundamental friendship in discourse that founds the common world.

Her approach is pre-Socratic, of course, in that she abandons the need for a Platonic absolute truth or correct world-view imposed on all. All citizens are equal in expressing their different views of what lies in between them, and the greatest virtue of a statesman, a *primus inter pares*, is to be able to bring all of these different views (*doxai*) into one unified *sensus communis*, a common sense of the world, shared by all but perceived differently. The appearance of a philosopher-ruler breaks this background friendship and establishes a state with one philosophical truth imposed on all. The genuine political friendship is then lost, together with love for the common world; the struggle is unleashed to tame the fundamental condition of human plurality and unpredictability by forced rule that makes actions predictable. Concomitantly with the substitution of rulership for politics, a warm feeling develops among the oppressed that gives rise to the notion of fraternity, so poeticized by Rousseau some time later. This is no equivalent for friendship, however, in Arendt's opinion: people linked by fraternity have no responsibility for the world that they have lost. Once freed, these former pariahs do not become friends who build a free politics in a common world; rather, they remain worldless and cannot master their newly acquired freedom.[32]

In Arendt's view, friendship is what makes people constitute the world between them; it is a background quality of debate and common deliberation that allows distinct and plural partners to establish and maintain a shared world without violence and direct rule over one another. Friends in this *polis* do care about the virtue of others, but they do not care about enforcing these demands of virtue by orderly communal pressure. Rather, an on-going contest decides who is most virtuous, while friendship sets the stage for this contest.

A second recent theorization of friendship—that proposed by Jacques Derrida —also stresses the background quality of political friendship. Derrida provides his own Aristotelian exegesis, discussing the relevant quotations on civic friendship contained in *Nicomachean* and *Eudemian Ethics*, but then shows how the usual characterization of political friendship as a mutual advantage friendship is destabilized by a famous remark, ascribed to Aristotle, "O friends, there is no friend." Derrida points out that this classic rendition of the phrase from Diogenes Laertius that was used in many commentaries (most notably, by Montaigne and Nietzsche) can be also interpreted in a more conventional way: "He who has many friends, has no friends." This last interpretation is in line with Aristotle's assertions that friendship of virtue is impossible with the many. But the undecidable condition of two competing interpretations—a paradoxical appeal to friends that tells them they are no friends, and a logical statement that better fits what Aristotle wrote in other places—is less interesting than the aspect of appeal to friends inherent in every version of interpretation. If the first interpretation has an appeal "O friends" right before our eyes, the second has it in an implicit form, since Aristotelian treatises were directed to his friends—disciples in the Academy, for example—and thus may have the same emotional invocation attached in the beginning even of this seemingly most dry theoretical statement.

In other words, there is a performative aspect in both sentences that we tend to overlook if we look for constative meaning only. Following Hanna Pitkin, one could say that both interpretations are quasi-performatives, in that they have a part that conveys a constative meaning and a part with implicit or explicit performative (illocutionary or perlocutionary) effects.[33] In Derrida's approach, an interlocutor in discourse on friendship becomes a friend himself or herself by at least being willing to listen and understand the enunciation produced by the other. This well-wishing present in the agreement to understand is very thin, but it is there nevertheless:

> This request for friendship, this offer of friendship, this call to coming together in friendship, at least to hear, the time it takes to hear, at least to finally agree, the time it takes to agree on the meaning of the sentence, is . . . an inflexible *hyperbole* of philia, . . . because its featherweight vulnerability would offer no foothold for a

reversal of any kind . . . And if politics were at last grounded in this friendship, . . . the politics of this hyperbole, would this not be the break with the entire history of the political, this old, tiring and tired, exhausted history?[34]

This performative politics of friendship also concerns Maurice Blanchot. Writing on Bataille's death, Blanchot states that only the death of our friend makes it clear to us that we can hardly speak of him. During his life, we could always speak to him, but we cannot speak of him now, since a radical existential abyss separates us from his unique experience. We shall never breach this abyss, no matter how hard we try. During his life we could afford to overlook this abyss and stress similarities between his experience and ours; his death now makes this illusion impossible. The only thing we could do now, in the radically asymmetrical relationship with our deceased friend (since he is dead, he cannot reciprocate), is to provide incessant but always incomplete answers to the question "Who was Bataille?", based on his remaining works. But this question is doomed to remain unanswered.[35]

This asymmetrical relationship is characteristic of any literary community that ties together the deceased writer and his latter-day-reader friends and would not surprise us. The point of Blanchot's philosophical analysis of this posthumous friendship, however, also has a direct political bearing: in his opinion, this is the generic structure of what he calls the unavowable community. Friendship established in performative effects of a speech act, friendship as a background feature of any literary community, is, in his opinion, also at the heart of such politics as exemplified by the May 1968 events in Paris. A community of friends that gathered on the streets and barricades of Paris was "a community denied community": this friendship ultimately toppled De Gaulle, but once the crowds disbanded, nobody could easily grasp what had brought these people together.[36] The radical alterity of these friends engaged in May 1968 politics, the absence of any common ground that could justify their being together, is akin to the radical alterity and insurmountable difference that is stressed by Blanchot in his friendship with the deceased Bataille. Literary communities united by friendship (which serves here as a background condition of a successful speech act) and political communities of a novel kind share the notion of friendship as a non-symmetrical relation of radical alterity between its parties, rather than a symmetrical reciprocal relationship between similar ego and alter ago that Aristotelians like so much.

Derrida's and Blanchot's notion of political friendship embodied in performative effects of each understandable utterance might seem very strange and alien to us, or so thin that it does not merit being called friendship at all. However, it is precisely so strange and alien because it carries some features of Greek *philia politike*, which moderns would hardly characterize as close to our habitual notion of private and personal friendship. In a sense, we are all Greek in that we retain this capacity to befriend another with a help of performative effects of a special type of speech acts. Thus, perhaps we should not be looking at the ancient texts to find what they might tell us about friendship. We should better explore how they embody friendship in their very functioning, how they establish friendship between an author and a reader, this minimal *philia politike* that we would hardly call friendship now. Not all texts would qualify, however: we should first explore only those we are more or less sure embodied friendship in their form—and here classic texts about friendship are our best example (our best friends, one is tempted to say): most of them provide a reader with an offer of befriending an author as the prerequisite for a correct understanding of this text.

FRIENDSHIP AS A CONFIGURATION OF DIVERSE PRACTICES

A brief overview of attempts at establishing a background friendship as offered by a text provides an exhilarating sense of many as yet unexplored possibilities. The first rendition of the topic of friendship in the form of a philosophical dialogue, Plato's *Lysis*, provides us with a description of friendship among boys and of love for boys (both captured, of course, by the same word *philia*).[37] Ignoring what Plato says on friendship and concentrating on the performative effects of the text, one might propose that this dialogue offered a temptation to a young reader: enchanted by Plato's words and thrilled by the lack of resolution of the problem discussed in the dialogue, a reader was expected to come seek the answers in personal communication with the author and, as a result of this encounter, to fall for Plato's ideas and style, to befriend him, and to befriend wisdom. This strategy of offering friendship by means of the text, though not as obvious as in *Lysis*, is manifest in other classics as well.

I shall not comment here on Aristotle's texts and their addressees in the Academe, since we have already briefly touched on this topic. Suffice it to say that later philosophical schools (of the Hellenistic age) similar to his are frequently taken to be the only true remaining embodiment of the tight interpersonal friendship of classical Athens.[38] Friendship served as the background quality for producing philosophical truths, including truths on friendship itself. Later, in Cicero, we encounter a similar but very curious friendship offered to the reader. His dialogue *Laelius. De Amicitia* opens with an address to his friend Atticus that clearly "bares the device" of performative strategies employed in the text. Cicero says that he has imagined this dialogue so that truths stated in it seem more persuasive and so that Atticus recognizes himself while reading it. Obviously, Cicero means that Atticus will identify with one of the virtuous characters of the dialogue and thus will see himself mirrored in the text. However, he may also imply that Atticus will perceive the skillful and virtuous hand of Cicero himself, who has been arranging the text in a very specific way, and thus perceive his alter ego.[39] In both cases, however, the reading of *Laelius* is supposed to raise the virtue of Atticus and also of us, modern readers, taking his position centuries later. Befriending Cicero is a background act that is required from the reader in order to understand the text in all its intricacies.

Augustine also expects his reader to befriend him, although this friendship would be different from the one with Cicero. In his texts, Augustine is always with friends and disciples, he is hardly ever alone. Even in his famous scene of conversion, he abandons his friend Alipius, with whom he has been spending time reading the Bible, just for a short moment of time and after prostration and crying under a tree in an orchard, goes back to him to read yet another line, which solidifies him in his conversion. As it turns out, Alipius has been experiencing the same thing. Having congratulated each other on such an event, they go to share their joy with Augustine's mother, another devout believer.[40] Now they are all friends in Christ. A new type of friendship is born: turn away from former fallen friends, turn yourself to God in solitude, but then immediately look for new friends in God, those friends who have experienced the same conversion. In this exposition on pagan friendship turned Christian, the story also gives a clue on how one should be reading this text itself: to become a friend of the author, to become Augustine's alter ego, a reader should abandon the world and turn to God—only after this exercise will he or she join the circle of the elect that truly understand this text.

Nietzsche requires a similar conversion, in a sense. In the introduction to *Human, All Too Human* he gives advice on how to become a "free spirit" by means of training and revelation. The truth to be revealed, however, is the opposite of Augustine's—God is dead, and free spirits linked by this truth are friends linked by a loss. Indeed, Nietzsche is looking for friends, but for as yet non-existent friends, as he asserts,[41] hence his attempt to create them by advising potential free spirits who read his books. These spirits will therefore enjoy a friendship that is based on the experience of a double loss: a loss of God and a loss of Nietzsche himself. Nietzsche's text is a reaching out towards future friends, bridging the gap of his death as well. Perhaps one might say that faith in God is replaced in Nietzschean writing by faith in a friend; but this new faith in friendship is necessarily predicated on a loss—Nietzsche explicitly makes friends only with those who will come after him.[42]

A loss as a central feature of any friendship, a radical abyss that separates friends no matter how close they are, was already mentioned in the discussion of Derrida and Blanchot, who took on these Nietzschean topics. Aphorism 376 from *Human, All Too Human* seems to nicely sum up this conception of friendship as a non-symmetrical and radical alterity: just think about the different opinions we have and the many reasons for misunderstanding, and you will see how fragile is the ground on which our friendships rest. Friendship resides in self-delusion: to remain your friends, people have to deceive themselves concerning your nature. Also, would not any of us be deadly offended if we for a minute realized what our friends knew about us deep in their hearts? But let us be tolerant to others the way we are tolerant to ourselves, writes Nietzsche, and the old Aristotelian maxim will be recast: "O enemies, there are no enemies." Alterity highlighted in this Nietzschean aphorism can be dealt with by jointly forgetting the precarious basis of friendship, a remedy proposed by the aphorism. Also, this alterity can be overcome by reaching out for a friend who will come afterwards, a strategy that Nietzsche employed by offering his texts to his future reader-friends. Derrida and Blanchot noticed what Nietzsche not only said in his texts but also did with the help of his texts: his offer of background friendship.

Let us sum up. So far I have given some examples of strategies of befriending a writer and a reader that different classic texts on friendship imply. I have tried eschewing the analysis of what these texts said about friendship, not taking these texts to be containers of a blueprint to be implemented in reality. I have concentrated on the "how" of these texts rather than on the "what": how do authors establish friendships with their readers, necessary for the understanding of their utterances? Applying to the texts of Derrida and Blanchot such an analysis becomes very complicated: their strategies of befriending the reader relate to Cicero's attempts at befriending as higher math relates to simple calculus. Suffice it to say that Derrida and Blanchot are intentionally opaque and paradoxical, eloquently stressing the unbridgeable alterity of our friend the author. They are intentionally non-symmetrical, so that almost any trace of reciprocity is abolished: readers can hardly identify with Blanchot as their alter ego, and hardly any reader could write in the same manner—thus friendship with him is difficult if we are looking for similarities and symmetries. Another hint on Blanchot's strategies of befriending the reader, even if this friendship is of a very special kind and may seem rather strange to many of us, is offered by one of his rare direct political remarks. In his words, a community of friends conceived akin to a literary community is "a war machine" that has a goal of destruction of society.[43]

That the May 1968 events, which Blanchot gives as an example of the unavowable community, might have been a revolution against mass society and the conformism attending to it is a well-established platitude. Thus, one would expect that the community of friends that appeared briefly in 1968 was against "society" understood as Heidegger's *das Man*, that it was based on radical alterity that defies groupings based on common norms and mores, that challenges symmetry and reciprocity—indeed, any type of commonality at its core. But one may go further and suggest that *philia*, or *amicitia*, or *l 'amitié* should defy not only *societas*—a specific recent way to arrange human practices —but any dominant type of configuration of practices that we have historically witnessed so far.

Paul Rabinow has shown that only by the 1830s did the French word *Société* started to habitually designate all those living in France and concomitantly sociology became possible as a science describing all people joined in this entity.[44] Vadim Volkov has investigated a similar development in the Russian case[45]—only after the 1860s' reforms that had liberated the serfs and the concomitant development of the mass press did the Russian word *obshchestvo* cease to designate the public of the salons of the opening pages of Tolstoy's *War and Peace*, where the "good society" of Russian aristocrats engaged in polished conversations in French, and came to express the notion of the reading public and later the notion of all people living in the same country, tied by a system of norms and laws applicable to all. Heretofore, the Russian nobles and the Russian peasants could hardly be described by a single term *obshchestvo*: this joint description presupposed a profound effort of bringing together their lifestyles and mores and molding a universal standard of civilized behavior. Some would say that this epochal break was completed only by the Bolsheviks, who imposed the universal structure of Soviet *das Man* on each citizen or, better, socialized everyone in accordance with the demands of this set of unobtrusive norms guiding everyday behavior.

But if *société, obshchestvo, societas* is a historical and a very specific configuration of practices, it might wane or even disappear one day, like other previously dominant configurations of practices—for example *polis, imperium, Christianitas*, to name but a few. Bringing together people in their radical alterity and plurality without a mandatory common ground, rather than striving for the *homonoia* (unanimity) of the Greek *polis*, *concordia* of the Roman Empire, or *caritas* of Christendom, might introduce friendship as a novel and influential form of *vinculum*—this very important tie that Arendt was studying all of her life.

INCONCLUSIVE CONCLUSIONS

But what might this discussion of Aristotelian and post-classical friendship possibly mean for the present-day concerns of Russia? Conclusions are difficult to draw now, but here are some interim remarks.

First, I have to discuss the obvious mapping of ancient experience onto contemporary Russian political reality. As Hutter and many others have noticed, friendship became coequal with the structure of the *polis* not because of the extension of the ideals of a tight group of personal friends (*hetaereia*) to cover the whole *polis*, but because these powerful factions competed for power in Athens and finally ruined democratic life there. One *hetaereia* vanquished all others and became the set of people controlling main power positions in the *polis*. The Roman version of the same model demonstrates that eventually one patronage group (or a group of *amici*) could manage to gain total control of the offices of the Republic, with Sulla first realizing the power of provincial armies by installing his *amici* to rule Rome. The ideal of the universal friendship of the Stoics—their *philanthropia* among the sages—was formulated against this background of the formation of the ruling elite based on one winning group of friends that came to control the whole empire and thus, for the Romans, the whole known world.

Now, this is hardly a desirable development in contemporary Russia, even though it seems very possible. The current president could attempt to transform one group of his former Petersburg colleagues from local bodies of state security or mayoral offices into the backbone of his administration. This would allow this clan of *amici* to vanquish opposing clans and run the whole country, recruiting new members to run distant places and recalcitrant localities. This power structure is reminiscent of the ancient *hetaereia* and may even use the rhetoric of friendship as a state ideology, but would hardly be close to an alternative vision of politics. Also, a vast resource of everyday friendship that Russians enjoy in their ordinary exchanges would be left untapped—only the few would be able to join the select circle of "friends" ruling the country and jointly diverting the anti-oligarchic sentiment of the disgruntled masses from the real oligarchs that would rule them.

Another straightforward application of the discussion above would be to heed Cooper and Schwarzenbach and to advise reintroducing care for the moral character of the citizen as a central concern of the polity, although in an attenuated form. Schwarzenbach actually proposes an experiment for Switzerland: replacing a regular but largely useless army with a "care corps" in which both women and men would engage in community service. As a result of this, the army as a school of male bonding in joint violence would be replaced by a school of caring service, in which new mores of concern for the other would be inculcated and would change the political system eventually. This community service would have more far-reaching consequences than just helping the needy or fulfilling unpleasant citizen tasks; people united in the care corps would also learn to care about each other's moral qualities, even if looking for second-order rather than thick values.

In the Russian context, a rebirth of this type of politics of caring friendship could have another cultural resource already available: a purge ritual, when the moral qualities of each person are evaluated by the relevant community, a ritual that has a very bloody history. Now, paradoxically, banned from the political sphere, it is represented by the firmly entrenched benign rituals of everyday life, like birthday celebrations, when people toast the celebrant with special speeches, implicitly evaluating his or her moral qualities, which are subject to a caring communal review once a year.[46] Nietzsche has shown that the origins of many great things, including the highest moral ideals, lie in the most bloody and lowly of endeavors. Elements of human sacrifice and partaking in the flesh and blood of the killed become the central ritual of Christian morality. Thus, practices are frequently remolded to suit different aims and goals and may bring sublime achievements as well as debased and horrible results. To give another example: concern for the Christian virtue of your neighbor meant an almost total communal surveillance in Calvin's Geneva, and the Consistory might have been as ferocious as the Russian purge commissions in the 1930s, had it been given the same orders and the same technical means to carry them out.[47] Nevertheless, Schwarzenbach can now call for a care for friends' virtues, stressing the attenuated form of a similar practice, that is, insisting on the inviolability of individual rights and on the need to eschew a single thick definition of the religiously conceived good. As a result, the practices may be similar, but the outcomes to which they are directed are different.

In an analogy, a call for the reestablishment of a periodic communal review that would evaluate the second-order virtues of Russian citizens need not be considered a reestablishment of bloody pure commissions, but a remolding of the formerly terror-ridden practice to achieve noble and humane goals, by introducing necessary safeguards. This could make befriending each other in hundreds, rather than in small tight networks, possible. However, more research would then be needed on how one could integrate the mechanisms of communal review of excelling deeds (that exist in sports, arts and sciences, within business community and even within the networks of virtuosos of violence) with mechanisms of existentially important self-review and thus transform the former without endangering the latter.

The third and final proposal that I shall discuss here—to model political friendship on anti-Aristotelian patterns, be they of the pre-Socratic or postmodern types, is interesting but is much too radical and looks very unrealistic once we descend from the heights of theory to the mundane details of configurations of humans, objects, and practices. This third proposal implies transcending state borders and thus spells death for a national community as traditionally conceived. A literary community of writers and readers, or a political community based on this background friendship model, or an Arendt-ian community of debate and deliberation on issues of the common world—all of these hardly fit existing national borders.

Russia recast as this type of political friendship would look more like a net-work of spaces linked by discourse in the Russian language than like a nation with physical territorial constraints. Language thus might become a Heideg-gerian "house of Being" in a very immediate, demetaphorized sense, particu-larly if technology enters the picture and the common world becomes linked through the Internet. Might then a friendship network called Russia be de-fined as a set of carriers of definitive texts of Russian culture and the inter-pretive community around it? Or might national culture itself be envisaged as a network of political acts produced by quasi-literary communities of friends, so that the common political arena is constantly shaped and redefined?

I will stop here, with no ready solutions for Russian problems and with no unified interpretation of what political friendship as a new configuration of practices—replacing the old configuration called society—might look like in everyday life. This is a doxic statement, I guess: this is how things appear to me in an on-going debate. If readers accept this claim as an initial move set-ting the stage for concerned discussion, joint deliberation will help us clarify other aspects of this common world.

NOTES

1. Vladimir Shlapentokh, *Public and Private Life of the Soviet People* (Oxford: Oxford University Press, 1989), 171.

2. Vladimir Shlapentokh, *Love, Marriage and Friendship in the Soviet Union: Ideas and Practices* (New York: Praeger, 1984), 240.

3. Igor Kon, *Druzhba. Etiko-psikhologicheskii ocherk* [Friendship. An Essay in Ethics and Psychology], 2nd ed. (Moscow: Politizdat, 1987), 324.

4. Oleg Kharkhordin, *The Collective and the Individual in Russia: A Study of Practices* (Berkeley and Los Angeles: University of California Press, 1999), esp. chapter 7.

5. Kharkhordin, *The Collective and the Individual*, chapters 2 and 5.

6. *East European Politics and Societies* 4, no. 3 (1990).

7. Eric R. Wolf, "Kinship, Friendship, and Patron-Client Relations in Complex Societies," in *Friends, Followers and Factions: A Reader in Political Clientelism*, ed. Steffen Schmidt *et al.* (Berkeley and Los Angeles: University of California Press, 1977), 172–75).

8. The best literary account of what happens with the Soviet friendship network, when it enters business, is a famous novel by a former top Logovaz manager—Yulii Dubov, *Bolshaia paika* [A Big Serving] (Moscow: Vagrius, 2000).

9. T. H. Rigby, *Political Elites in the USSR: Central Leaders and Local Cadres from Lenin to Gorbachev* (Aldershot: Edward Eigar, 1990),

10. Stephen Kotkin, *Magnetic Mountain: Stalinism as a Civilization* (Berkeley and Los Angeles: University of California Press, 1995), 76.

11. Sheila Fitzpatrick, *Everyday Stalinism. Ordinary Life in Extraordinary Times: Soviet Russia in the 1930s* (New York: Oxford University Press, 1999).

12. Beate Volker and Henk Flap, "Amitié et inimitié sous communisme d'Etat. Le cas de l'Allemagne de l'Est," *Revue francaise de sociologie* 36, no. 2 (1995).

13. Pierre Bourdieu, *The Logic Of Practice* (Stanford: Stanford University Press, 1990), esp. chapter 6.

14. Luc Boltanski, *L' amour et la justice comme competences* (Paris: Metailie, 1990).

15. Alena Ledeneva, *Russia's Economy of Favours: Blat, Networking and Informal Exchange* (Cambridge: Cambridge University Press, 1998).

16. Allan Silver, "'Two Different Sorts of Commerce'—Friendship and Strangership in Civil Society," in *Public and Private in Thought and Practice*, ed. Jeff Weintraub and Krishan Kumar (Chicago: University of Chicago Press, 1997).

17. Alasdair C. MacIntyre, *After Virtue: A Study in Moral Theory* (London: Duckworth, (1981); Bernard Yack, *The Problems of a Political Animal. Community, Justice and Conflict in Aristotelian Political Thought* (Berkeley: University of California Press, 1993); Jacques Derrida, *The Politics of Friendship* (London: Verso, 1997).

18. There is voluminous literature on each of the terms. See a useful overview in David Konstan, *Friendship in the Classical World* (Cambridge: Cambridge University Press, 1997). Some interpreters make the experience of *hetaereia* most important for the rebirth of the politics of friendship: see, for example, Horst Hutter, *Politics as Friendship: The Origins of the Classical Notions of Politics in the Theory and Practice of Friendship* (Waterloo, Ontario: Wilfried Laurier University Press, 1978). However, this type of interest group struggle over the control of the state recalls current Russian clique or patron-client politics so much that Hutter's argument could hardly serve as an alternative to the status quo. I'll get back to *hetaereia* politics in the last section of this chapter.

19. Aristotle, *Nicomachean Ethics*, 1171a15.

20. John M. Cooper, "Political Animals and Civic Friendship," in *Friendship: A Philosophical Reader*, ed. Neera Kapur Badhwar (Ithaca, NY: Cornell University Press, 1993).

21. *Nicomachean Ethics*, 1155a22–27.

22. MacIntyre, *After Virtue*, 155–56.

23. Yack, *Problems of a Political Animal*, 36.

24. Cooper, "Political Animals and Civic Friendship," 318.

25. Sibyl A. Schwarzenbach. "On Civic Friendship," *Ethics* 107, no. 1 (October 1996), 113.

26. Peter Fenves, "Politics of Friendship—Once Again," *Eighteenth-Century Studies* 32, no. 2 (Winter 1998–99), elucidates these points very succinctly.

27. The most extensive treatment of friendship is in Hannah Arendt, "On Humanity in Dark Times: Thoughts about Lessing," in her *Men in Dark Times* (London: Jonathan Cape, 1970); and Hannah Arendt, "Philosophy and Politics," *Social Research* 57, no. 1 (Spring 1990). For the role of friendship in Arendt's life, see Elisabeth Young-Bruehl, *Hannah Arendt: For Love of the World* (New Haven: Yale University Press, 1982).

28. Shin Chiba, "Hannah Arendt on Love and the Political: Love, Friendship and Citizenship," *The Review of Politics* 57, no. 3 (Summer 1995), 508.

29. Arendt, "Philosophy and Politics," 82–83.

30. Patricia Bowen-Moore, *Hannah Arendt's Philosophy of Natality* (New York: St. Martin's Press, 1989), 145.

31. Arendt, "On Humanity in Dark Times," 24.

32. A condition of Russia after 1991, one is tempted to remark.

33. Hanna Pitkin, *Wittgenstein and Justice: On the Significance of Ludwig Wittgenstein for Social and Political Thought* (Berkeley: University of California Press, 1972).

34. Derrida, *Politics of Friendship*, 218.

35. Maurice Blanchot, *Friendship* (Stanford: Stanford University Press, 1997).

36. Maurice Blanchot, *The Unavowable Community* (Tarrytown, NY: Station Hill Press, 1988).

37. *Lysis* is generally considered to be an "early" dialogue, different in form and effect from such mature expositions as *The Symposium*, for example. This makes its performative strategy less intricate and more visible. For recent debates on this dialogue, see Don Adams, "A Socratic Theory of Friendship," *International Philosophic Quarterly* 35, no. 3 (September 1995).

38. Hutter, *Politics as Friendship*, 49.

39. Atticus, as we know from historical records, was selling Cicero's letters and thus served as a small publishing house, a kind of machine for immortalizing the great deeds of Cicero—a final service to his deceased friend.

40. St. Augustine, *Confessions* 8.12.

41. Nietzsche, *Human, All Too Human*, section 2 of the introduction.

42. A more detailed and accurate analysis of friendship in and with Nietzsche can be found in Oleg Kharkhordin, "Druzhba svobodnykh umov: vozmozhno li nitssheanskoe soobshchestvo?" [Friendship of Free Spirits: Is a Nietzschean Community Possible?] in *Nitsshe i sovremennaia zapadnaia mysl'* [Nietzsche and Contemporary Western Thought], ed. Viktor Kaplun (St. Petersburg, Moscow: Letnii Sad, EUSP, 2003).

43. Blanchot, *Unavowable Community*, 48. In this very excerpt he talks about the community of lovers, but earlier compares it to the May 1968 crowd, in which everyone could "mix with the first comer as if with an already loved being, precisely because he was the unknown-familiar." (30)

44. Paul Rabinow, *French Modern: Norms and Forms of the Social Environment* (Cambridge, MA: MIT Press, 1989).

45. Vadim Volkov, *The Forms of Public Life*, unpublished Ph.D. thesis, Cambridge University (UK), 1995.

46. Olga Kalacheva, "Den' rozhdeniia: prazdnichnoe ustroistvo i osnovnye znacheniia" [A Birthday Party: The Setting of Festivities and its Main Meanings], in *Problemy sotsialnogo i gumanitarnogo znaniia* [Problems of Social and Humanistic Knowledge], ed. Nikolai Vakhtin *et al.*, vol. 2 (St. Petersburg: Bulanin. 2000).

47. See similar points in Michael Walzer, *The Revolution of the Saints. A Study in the Origins of Radical Politics* (New York: Atheneum, 1968). 226, 230–31, 305.

Chapter Seven

Virtue

Western students of Soviet morals for a long time characterized the specificity of this ethical system as aimed at training certain traits that constitute a model moral character rather than at learning and applying universal ethical rules. For example, an analysis of the 1961 Moral Code of the Builder of Communism, adopted by the XXII Party Congress together with the last version of the Party Program, shows that though the Code enumerates certain "principles," the "emphasis clearly is placed on morally praiseworthy attitudes, sentiments and predispositions, making it a statement of exemplary character rather than of conduct rules."[1] Indeed, such principles as proletarian internationalism can be seen as a re-statement of the virtue of *caritas* — love for other Christians, no matter what their ethnic origin -while unflinching Communist resistance to enemy doctrines has its corollary in Christian enmity toward devilish machinations, no matter what their provenance. According to standard analyses of Soviet ethics, the ultimate criterion of the morality of an act was whether it contributed to the building of Communism or not, that is whether and to what extent it corresponded to the ultimate goal of political development. The Moral Code of the Builder of Communism, then, was a "device of the party leadership to promote those *traits* which it deems more important to molding society in the direction it wishes."[2]

In her work Katerina Clark described Socialist Realism as a system not of aesthetic but of didactic concern par excellence, which aimed at moral transformation rather than at aesthetic insight. She has also recently outlined a set of personal features of the fearless leader, captured by standard epithets of the Socialist Realist novel, that were intended to be emulated by readers of the novel (and, by extension, by viewers of the Socialist Realist film as well): these included temperance and perseverance, then sternness of faith, and,

finally, care for the masses. Hot-headedness was allowed as well, but such
passionate outbursts were usually ascribed to disciples who would eventually
master their intemperance and would come to be self-possessed and self-
controlled believers.[3] Although Clark registers the preponderance of two
character traits—temperance and love/*caritas*—other virtues, such as prudence, courage and justice, can be found in didactic novels as well. Learning
these qualities was easy. As my own analysis of Communist books of guidance has demonstrated, the main way to fashion one's self was to choose and
follow an exemplary hero, resolving difficult moral situations with the help
of personal identification with this model figure: what s/he would have done
in such a case? Preaching by example, stemming from the medieval *imitatio
Christi*, rather than its corollary—preaching by word—came to dominate the
arsenal of moral practices of Soviet civilization.[4]

1

This attention to model character traits suggests that Soviet morality was a
morality of virtue rather than a morality of principle. Alasdair MacIntyre's *After Virtue*, and the ensuing discussion of how the ethics of virtue are opposed
to the ethics of principle, articulated the now famous distinction between the
morality of appropriate action that eschews general rules and the morality of
law that is predicated on the application of a standard universal rule to any
situation of everyday life.[5] If Aristotle and Aquinas are key figures for the
first type of morality, Kant and Rawls would be central for the second. In this
respect, Soviet morals were more Aristotelian than Kantian. They encouraged
attention to particularities of the case in consideration, rather than to a general rule that was to be applied to all cases; exemplified a yearning for narratives that depicted model virtues rather than theorizing about them; and finally, placed an emphasis on desirable character traits rather than internal
values.

    For example, Soviet people grew up habitually criticizing the "coldness
and inhumanity" of laws. They demanded instead that a judicial decision
"takes into consideration the particular condition of a given individual"
(*voidet v ego polozhenie*), that it should show its full humanity in accounting
for all minute details of the situation of the act and individual considered.
Harold Berman noted long ago this intense personalization of Soviet justice
by comparing the criminal codes of the Anglo-American world and the
USSR. Thus, in the Soviet case, negligence was defined as a criminal failure
to consider consequences by the specific defendant, while in the USA a person could be indicted for negligence if s/he failed to consider those factors

that any rational person should have taken into account.[6] In the Soviet case, this American standard was clearly not enough—judicial investigation was supposed to determine whether this particular standard of rational behavior could be applicable to the person in question, given his or her education, background, standpoint and mood at the time of the crime, and so on.

Thus, a feeling of total appropriateness underlay the functioning of justice; it was not possible to satisfy the people's sense of justice simply by appealing to the equality of the application of predetermined rules. Everyone was sure that such a general application could not guarantee real equality of treatment, given the differences between individuals. The same applied to moral judgment in everyday debates—no single general criterion could be used to evaluate the morality of a given action. Only a consideration of the context of an act, particularities of the person who had carried it out and the specificity of consequences, could provide a totally just evaluation of an act. In short, the appropriateness of action for a given context, not its conformity with a general rule, was the main way to assess its moral rightness. Soviet ethics was a form of virtue ethics.

Soviet politics was no less Aristotelian than Soviet morals since it relied on elements of a quasi-Aristotelian reasoning to an unprecedented extent, and it is surprising that so many political theorists overlooked this basic fact of Soviet civilization. At the least, it relied on those elements that Hobbes thought to be Aristotelian when he decided to scrap them for good. One can briefly enumerate these three pre- or anti-Hobbesian features that clearly distinguish the Soviet political system from that of modern liberal democracies. First, this politics had a clearly set goal, a *telos* of political development that Aristotle sets up for the *polis* by saying that people get together to live in city-states not just in order to live but in order "to live well." Hobbes, who represents the foundation of our modern understanding of politics, singled out this very definition as the root of all evil. In his opinion, because some vicious philosophers (and here he implies Aristotle and Aquinas) had posited a certain *summum bonum* as the goal of development of politics, seditious ministers of the English revolution—who had their idea of the good for the country— fomented dissent and then open rebellion by clashing with the royalists who had another vision of the good. Hobbes argued that a modern state was different from the previously conceived types of political union in that it eschewed imposing the desired goal of development. In short, modern politics is about avoiding the sum of bad things, *summum malum*, rather than seeking *summum bonum*, that is, the modern state should guarantee the pursuit of the good to every citizen, but specifically in the private sphere, while its public activity should simply guarantee law and order, thus preventing the "war of all against all."[7] Thus, post-Reformation Europe guaranteed freedom of conscience and the pursuit of religiously-defined good in the private realm, while no common perception of the good life as a shared goal of society's aspirations was to be pursued by public authorities. Now, this is exactly opposite to the Soviet understanding of politics—the Soviet Union had a clearly defined goal, the building of a Communist society, and thus considered itself morally superior to the liberal West, where politics was all about lowly motives of self-preservation and ensuring for each an opportunity for the private pursuit of avarice and similar sins.[8]

Second, the Communist project relied on a decisive feature lying at the foundation of the teleological politics of the common good -what Aristotle called *homonoia*, his Latin detractors translated as *concordia*, and what in Russian became *edinoglasie*, unanimity—which, given the Bolshevik fear of factional strife, ushered the intense effort to weed out all types of schismatics and factionalists. Third, given that Aristotle often insisted that friendship was more important than justice,[9] one is hardly surprised that citizens of the Soviet Union were supposed to be friends in a common undertaking of building a better future. No other major modern country besides the USSR officially ascribed to its citizens the title of "comrades."[10] Of course, this link to the Aristotelian model came through a long chain of descent. The Bolsheviks copied the vocabulary of West European Socialism of the 1830s–40s and of the French Revolution, with both these vocabularies and their shared notion of *fraternité* being heavily indebted to Rousseau's vision of people united in the general will. This vision itself was inherited from Montesquieu and Machiavelli and their notion of republican virtue, which was itself a handy redefinition of Aquinas's notion of the Christian virtue of the prince, which was in its turn a product of the medieval interpretation of Aristotelian politics. Of course, Aristotle did not demand the periodic review of the virtue of comrade-citizens (even though some commentators define care for citizens' virtues as a central feature of the Aristotelian view of the *polis*[11]), but when the Bolsheviks institutionalized regular purges, they may have brought this logic to its practical conclusion.

Given these Aristotelian qualities of the Soviet system, one is puzzled by two questions: where did these qualities come from, and do they still matter after the collapse of Communism? Let me first provide brief remarks on historical aspects of these questions before moving on to an evaluation of their current implications.

2

The Bolsheviks were never enamored with Aristotle *per se*, since he was just one small part of the ancient heritage they were supposed to make available to each person in his or her individual development. Their language was mostly suffused with appeals to Robespierre, Gironde, Thermidor, and to other rhetoric of the French Revolution, which relied on Rousseau and the notion of civic virtue, a point well argued almost fifty years ago by Jacob Talmon.[12] But I would suggest that their version of the discourse of civic virtue, which in its theoretical form was incomprehensible for the masses of illiterate peasants, managed nevertheless to strike a chord with these masses because it reached a certain bedrock level of the popular discourse on virtues — a discourse familiar from church liturgy, catechistic expositions of the basics of the Orthodox Christian faith, and transmission of stories from saints' *vitae*.

Russian Church literature is replete with discourse on virtues all the way up to 1917, and after, while secular works with the word *dobrodetel'* in their title tend to become scarce after the end of the eighteenth century. Checking computer catalogues of major libraries reveals that theatrical plays with titles like "Virtuous French Lady" or "Virtue Rewarded"[13] and secular books with titles like "Virtuous Soul, or Rules of Moral Guidance"[14] become fairly rare by the beginning of the nineteenth century and almost disappear entirely by mid-century. Perhaps, translations of Kant and the spread of German idealism in general (with its ethics of principle) contributed to this development. Perhaps Russian revolutionaries and the learned society of the nineteenth century wanted to stress that they were radically distant from the stale discourse on virtues of the official church, or from the Masonic interpretation of virtues characteristic of the eighteenth century Russian Enlightenment. Perhaps attention to the inner life of the individual was replacing the usual didactic enumeration of visible personal qualities called virtues. All of these different reasons may have been true, but the end result is the same: while virtue survived as a moral concern, this survival was confined predominantly to church discourse.

But where did the Russian church get this discourse on virtues? To answer this question, one has to engage in a detective story similar to Umberto Eco's *Il Nome della rosa*—trying to discover the traces of a villain who introduced an Aristotelian type of ethics into mainstream Russian church culture. In Latin Christianity everything seems more or less straightforward: Thomas Aquinas wrote a commentary on Aristotle's *Nicomachean Ethics*, and in so doing added a list of three theological virtues (faith, hope and love), to the ancient list of four so-called cardinal virtues (prudence, justice, temperance, courage). In so doing, he authorized not only the subordination of pagan virtues to Christian ones, but he also attempted an integration of these pagan virtues into a Christian view of life as an open-ended quest for salvation. And who was the Russian or Slavonic Aquinas? Given the prevalence of discourse on virtue in the Russian church and the many texts of the Greek Church

Fathers translated into Slavonic in the XI–XIV centuries, how and in what form did virtue make its entry into the Russian discourse on ethics? That is, who of the saintly authors adapted Aristotle's discourse on virtues for Christian use, and how was it then transmitted to the Slavonic world?

3

First, some words about a possible direct influence of Aristotle on Slavonic writing. Aristotle in Russia had a rather unhappy fate. Very few people, if any, could read Greek after the disintegration of Kievan Rus', so that in 1518 the grand prince had to invite to Muscovy a monk from Mount Athos, Maxim the Greek, to translate some Greek manuscripts into Russian. The first full versions of Aristotelian treatises became available in Latin translations only with the spread of Ruthenian literary influence in the mid-seventeenth century. These, however, because of their connection with Catholicism and Jesuit colleges in Poland, were viewed with suspicion by their contemporaries. For example, one of the leaders of the Schism, Avvakum, deliberately rejects philosophical syllogisms as "an external whore", *vneshniaia bliad'*,[15] arguing that checking a theological argument by the criterion of its logic and conformity to a syllogistic structure is a trick of the devil. Thus, in 1664 he writes: "Christ did not teach dialectic or rhetoric because a rhetor and a philosopher cannot be a Christian. . . . For Hellenic wisdom is the mother of all devilish dogmas."[16] His insistence that pagan philosophers are to be rejected as sources of Christian wisdom parallels the preoccupation of a majority of the early Church Fathers, who witnessed the uneasy coexistence of pagan philosophy taught in Byzantium's secular schools with the public preaching of Christianity in the churches. Indeed, the Fathers found many heretics of their day pushed into their mistaken stance by faithfully applying the syllogistic inquiry to the Scriptures. As a result of this, the Fathers knew Aristotle, but there was a tacit contract not to cite him when criticizing Peripatetic philosophy.[17]

Some quotations of Aristotle were available in *Pchela*—a medieval Russian translation of *Melissa*, a Byzantian collection of remarks and maxims of philosophers and Church Fathers. The Greek original was part of the florilegium tradition, but the Russian translation endowed this collection with a different function—it became a source of didactic wisdom on salvation of the soul, and was copied endlessly in the fifteenth-sixteenth centuries.[18] Thus, it would have been extremely difficult to guess the content of the *Nicomachean Ethics* simply on the basis of these didactic aphorisms. Also, some of these alleged citations from Aristotle reflected not his philosophy but Christian views ascribed to him later in order to employ his authority. But since Russian scribes frequently dropped names of authors when rewriting a manuscript, the problem of ascribing to Aristotle some of the pieties he did not pronounce died out in subsequent versions of this collection.

The main reception of systematic Aristotelian philosophy before the Ruthenian influence of the seventeenth century came through the interpretation of the works of St. John of Damascus.[19] His *Dialectics* contained a prolonged exposition on the categories of Aristotle, without ever mentioning the philosopher by name. But the book depended on Aristotelian logic rather than on his ethics, and virtues are discussed only *in passim*, as a small part of a chapter on the freedom of the will.[20] When prince Andrei Kurbsky translated Damascene's *Dialectics* into Russian in the sixteenth century, he mulled over the categories of logic, not of ethics, even though he may have read the *Nicomachean Ethics* as well.[21] His introduction to Damascene's translation, though, used Maxim the Greek's translations of excerpts of St. Gregory of Nazianzus's funeral oration on St. Basil the Great,[22] and this may show us a more effective route of transmission of Aristotelian ethics into Russian life.

Fedor Karpov, a sixteenth century boyar, famous for his learned exchange with Maxim the Greek on astrology and for some letters to the Moscow metropolitan Daniel where he quoted Aristotle on politics, is perhaps the sole example of direct knowledge of Aristotle on the part of a subject of Muscovy. He definitely used *Nicomachean Ethics*, book 10, and possibly *Politics*, books 9 and 5.[23] Karpov's exposure to Aristotle was exceptional within Muscovy; he was engaged in diplomatic service and could have encountered Aristotle in Latin translations in some of his contacts. Most of his contemporaries could examine only a pseudo-Aristotelian treatise, a Slavonic translation of a mirror of princes which is written as a collection of advice from Aristotle to his disciple Alexander the Great, and which came to be known in Latin as *Secretum Secretorum*. Curiously enough, the Slavonic version was translated from Hebrew in the end of the XV c. and was used by the first officially condemned heretics of Russian history—the Judaizers.[24] Given its Hebrew provenance, this version of *Secretum Secretorum* contained some added excerpts from Maimonides (another Aristotelian who adapted Aristotle for Judaism). The effect of this treatise on the morals of Muscovy is hard to evaluate, largely because the twenty or so extant copies of Slavonic *Secretum Secretorum* contain advice on medicine and divination together with advice on political or moral issues.[25] Here Russian history abandons its similarity to *The Name of the Rose* but becomes more like another seminal novel— Milorad Pavic's *The Khazar Dictionary*—and it requires a well-qualified researcher capable of doing work in Hebrew, Arabic, Latin and Slavonic to evaluate rival versions of what may have happened during this most curious episode of medieval cross-cultural translation.[26]

4

Dmitrii Bulanin, Viktor Zhivov and Francis Thomson noted the absence of documented traces of direct transmission of Hellenistic philosophy to Russia, since—according to a now widely accepted thesis first proposed by Georgii Fedotov—the entire corpus of Slavonic translations available to a Kievan and then Muscovite reader up until the seventeenth century and the Ruthenian breakthrough was roughly comparable to the collection of a typical provincial Greek monastery, such as the one of the monastery of St. John on Pathmos, for which we have the thirteenth-century records of its holdings.[27] Indeed, the majority of available literature in Slavonic was of a didactic and liturgical character. But even the first translations carried with them a description of some doctrine of Christian virtues. The first *Izbornik* from 1073 (a book of Christian wisdom allegedly addressed to prince Sviatoslav, but actually just a Kievan copy of the text translated from the Greek original for the Bulgarian king Simeon in the end of the X c.) already carries a description of ancient cardinal virtues. Sreznevsky even mentions it in his dictionary (article on *doblest'*, courage): "There are four types of *phronesis*: prudence (*mudrost'*), justice (*pravda*), temperance [or, rather, in its Christian version, "chastity" in the sense of not submitting to one's passions—O.Kh., i.e. *tselomudrie*], courage."[28] The *Izbornik* from 1076 includes St. Basil the Great's exhortation "How should a man live?" which details monastic virtues, but was mistakenly addressed by a Kievan scribe to the laity.

The most popular genre of medieval Russian literature was miscellanea, which copied quotes from various older books and put them side by side in a new book. Precisely because each such book was almost an encyclopedia of Christian knowledge, a monk with such a book in his possession could go and found a new hermitage of saintly living. William Veder calls the structural principle of these books kaleidoscopic[29], but they may be also called constellations (to use the term of Walter Benjamin): these books are products of authoritative quotation where hardly anything was added by the fallen hands of a scribe, the only resemblance of authorial intention being an arrangement of cited sources. Thus, we cannot find a single Russian-authored treatise commenting on *Nicomachean Ethics*, but we find scores of manuscripts faithfully copying the original set of Slavonic translations together with citations from some added translations, mainly done in the XIII–XIV centuries. Postmodernists would marvel at this death of the author: the Aquinas effect was achieved by a mass of hardly identifiable scribes who managed to adapt and integrate the Aristotelian ethics as thoroughly as he did, but without any dogmatic treatises. They merely copied simple sets of exhortations and admonitions originally translated from Greek, frequently broken into smaller sets of quotes or even into one-liners, with all these new elements being regrouped into new constellations.

Of course, a manuscript might have been used for other purposes than learning virtue. Furthermore, the presence of a book, even in a substantive number of extant manuscripts, does not mean that it was read. Evidence of efforts of authorial creativity and direct appeal to individual morals appears only with the development of sermon writing for elite audiences in the mid-seventeenth century. Paul Bushkovitch documented the usual concerns of such popular sermon writers as Epifanii Slavinetskii and Simeon Polotskii. Both of these Ruthenians-turned-Muscovites had dropped the ascetic list of virtues and exhorted listeners (or readers) to fight two main vices of the Muscovite court—pride and greed, opposing to them the Christian virtues of humility and charity. That is, they copied their Ruthenian predecessors, but dropped from their consideration ancient cardinal virtues such as justice, concentrating on the Christian virtues most important for court life. However, the cardinal virtues of the Aristotelian epoch were not forgotten altogether: thus, in a rare sermon he directed to monks in the 1650s, Epifanii enumerates the usual four Hellenistic virtues, and then adds a Christian one—humility (*smirenie*),[30] in effect doing what Aquinas did to the set of virtues when he added three theological virtues to the four ancient ones. Now, one should not take Epifanii to be a grand innovator, since his spiritual teacher, bishop Petr Mohila, the founder of the first religious Academy in Kiev, already included the three theological virtues of Aquinas—faith, hope and love—in his version of the Orthodox catechism published in the 1620s.[31] Mohila, of course, was just incorporating into Orthodox thought what he had learned from his Catholic teachers in Poland, where he had picked up both Aquinas and Aristotle. Once Ukrainians and Belorussians firmly set themselves up in Moscow, Aristotle (in Latin and in Catholic interpretation) became part of the staple diet for at least two generations of the elite of the Russian clergy, until the "St. Petersburg coup" tried to purge this Muscovite spirit and to introduce elements of Protestantism into Orthodoxy instead.[32]

But, one might argue, sermons of the Ukrainians would not have struck such a cord with the Russian soul if it were not already prepared to listen to exhortations to virtue and to denunciations of vice. Indeed, the Zealots of Piety, a group from the 1630–40s, many of whom were very suspicious of the Catholic overtones of the Ukrainian faith and its syllogistic form, prepared the soil for the reception of the Ukrainian onslaught nevertheless. Their appeal to restore the corrupted morals—the parlous condition of which had been revealed by the Time of Troubles—relied on intense interest in virtue and piety, and based itself on reading the extant massive corpus of translations and miscellanea. The pre-seventeenth century sources of exhortation to virtuous living are more or less clear: the two most widely cited and excerpted Church Fathers in Russia were St. John Chrysostom and St. Ephraim the Syrian, both preoccupied with virtue.[33] According to Fedotov, the latter was loved more for his poetic style and vivid imagery rather than for content. The former was presented in Russian sources not as a Byzantian nobleman with sound Hellenistic learning (his teacher Libanius, an undisputed authority in secular rhetoric, is quoted in saying that he would have nominated him as a successor to head his school, had it not been for the fact that Chrysostom had been already stolen by the church), but rather as an ascetic monk. In fact, the seventeenth century Russian edition of Chrysostom specifically tried to reestablish the image of St. John the nobleman by translating his sermons *in toto*, without omissions and other editing.[34]

Apart from this, one could have access to miscellanea, three different types of which—*The Golden Chain*, *Izmaragd*, and *Pchela*—are prevalent. Let us take a closer look at the first version of *Pchela* in comparison to later ones.[35] It is especially interesting since its opening sections follow the order of cardinal virtues. The first section, a general introduction on virtues, lists quotes from Solomon, St. Gregory of Nyssa, Socrates, Diogenes and Aristotle. In chapter 2, on prudence, we have didactic sentences from an unnamed Apostle, Jesus of Sirach, Socrates, Diodorus, Aristotle, and Favorinus; on chastity (temperance) we have Job, Plutarch, Alexander the Great, Epictetus, Menedemus, and Xanthus; on courage—Socrates, Alexander the Great, Leonidus king of Spartans, Aristotle; on justice—Philip of Macedon, Menander, Hyperides, Pythagoras. Chapter 5 is about the virtue of friendship (yet another Aristotelian topic), and only then comes a chapter on charity. Now, in the later version this florilegium was transformed into a very pious reading, by changing the order of the presentation of chapters and sending all sentences on cardinal virtues into the end of the manuscript: of the 68 chapters in the second version, justice is mentioned only in chapter 12 (rather than chapter 5): all other Hellenistic virtues and the general introduction are almost in the end of the book. Instead the book opens with chapters (taken from the back of the first version) on power, charity, grace, prayer, providence, laudation, war and peace, memory, and so on. The rearrangement, one might guess, suited the goals of an ancient scribe presenting the book of wisdom now to the Christian prince, concerned with problem of rule and piety, rather than to a Byzantian student of rhetoric.

What about discourse on virtues in epistles on spiritual guidance? Maxim the Greek writes to the young Ivan the Terrible admonishing him to exemplify five virtues of justice, meekness, restraint [temperance? O.Kh.], generosity, and obedience. Not a particularly neat list of virtues, since neither the four cardinal nor the three theological ones are represented in full, but at least the

Aristotelian virtue of generosity is finally mentioned here—perhaps the only time in the course of early Russian history. A famous exchange between metropolitan Daniel and Fedor Karpov centers on whether one has to have endurance (*terpenie*) in living under any ruler, or should one expect justice (*pravda*) from a ruler. Daniel himself writes to boyars, admonishing them to moderation [temperance? or prudence in the sense of *sophrosyne*? O.Kh.], chastity and love, which interestingly means for him the absence of quarrels among the boyars, who were quite prone to starting disputes over affairs of honor in this period.[36]

A separate document of epochal significance, which may have been available to the Zealots, is the Statute of St. Nil Sorskii, elaborating the stages of spiritual struggle of a monk. It has a great deal to say about 8 virtuous deeds (fasting, chastity, poverty, charity, faith, endurance, modesty and humility), which he copies from the list of St. Nilus of Sinai.[37] This demanding set of virtues was a high point achieved only by the spectacular few and could not be recommended for the community at large, but it was linked to monastic standards of the *Philokalia* (5 volumes that assembled ascetic writings of Eastern monks in both Russian and Greek, though this appeared only at the end of the eighteenth century), and to Evagrius Ponticus' first standard enumeration of the eight deadly sins (in its Catholic reception, the number was slashed to seven[38]). A more widespread monastic treatise on spiritual ascent, *The Ladder* of St. John Climacus (XIV c.), could be taken as the most rigorous presentation of the practice of monastic virtue in Eastern Christianity, since it presents spritiual growth as a sequence of orderly stages: "Just as Aristotle's work begins by establishing many 'goods' and then the one good of life, *eudaimonia*, and continues by establishing the practices and virtues that allow for gaining the good life, so *The Ladder* begins by locating God as the supreme good for humanity, and continues by describing the virtues that are necessary to move toward that end."[39] However, if progression towards ultimate perfection starts with familiar worldly virtues—e.g. different versions of renunciation and penitence (which provide some equivalents of the classical Greek virtues of endurance and courage)—it ends with steps of *apatheia* and love of God, when the ascetic disengages himself from the world. Hence this treatise was not of much use for the laity.

Georgii Fedotov, who tried evaluating how the secular audience received these writings on virtue, suggested considering the XII c. epistle of Vladimir Monomakh. Of course, it is clear that only the tiny elite thought about Christian virtues at that time, and this famous grand prince of Kievan Russia is one of our best examples of this very selective reception. Only in the seventeenth century would many people start caring about what Monomakh cared about in the twelfth; still the pattern of reception is interesting. Monomakh repeats what he could get from the 100 words of pseudo-Gennadius included into the *Izbornik* of 1076, that a prince should have virtues of obedience, humility, repentance, and mortification.⁴⁰ But then he shifts his attention to justice, a main concern for a ruler, and advises his sons on this most important of princely virtues, adding a secular flavor to an otherwise trite Christian exposition. Now, one of the reasons why Aquinas had to tolerate cardinal virtues and deal with Aristotle in XIII c. Western Europe was that the Church had to somehow accommodate the barbaric peoples of Northern Europe, who still lived according to the heroic virtues so well described by Homer, and more or less successfully adapted by Aristotle for Athenian society. By merging such heroic warrior virtues as temperance and courage with such theological virtues as charity and hope, Aquinas was opening the way for successfully integrating Germanic tribes into the new Christian order.⁴¹ Monomakh might be said to be doing the same, by adapting strict monastic concentration only on matters of faith to fit his princely concerns.

The last question that one has to address in this section—in a very preliminary way—is this: from where did the Greek Fathers get their knowledge of Aristotle and the virtues? Plato and the Stoics are mentioned more frequently since they could be rather well-integrated into Christianity (for reasons that should not concern us here). Aristotle, on the contrary, became suspect after the first heretics, as I already noted, and so many Christian authors discuss Aristotelian topics without mentioning his name. Some early authors—like Clement of Alexandria (III c.), an originator of apophatic theology and the first to seriously concern himself with a discursive justification of Christian morals—could still be open in their use of Aristotle: "It is in the area of ethics that Aristotle most directly influenced Clement. Here Clement does not parade Aristotelian theories and distinctions simply to display his erudition, rather they form an integral part of his thought. In two broad areas of ethics, that concerning the 'good life' and that dealing with volition and wrongdoing, Aristotle's influence is clear."⁴² Later Fathers could hardly do the same.

Werner Jaeger agrees regarding the Aristotelian influences on Clement, but in his opinion the most decisive introduction of Aristotle into Christian morals happens in the writings of St. Basil the Great. But in Basil's multivolume *oeuvre* the name of Aristotle appears only three (!) times. In *Contra Eunomius* (1.5.43) he says that a Christian does not need the syllogisms of Aristotle, and in 1.9.8 he adds that Eunomius used them. In epistle 135 he evaluates Aristotle and Theophrastus as literary pragmatists who in his opinion were better in this respect than Plato—without any further comment. Still, St. Basil "had postulated a Christian ethics, and his commentary on the Psalms shows clearly that he wanted to use them as such. On closer inspection we see that behind this interpretation there stands Basil's own experience with Aristotle's *Nicomachean Ethics*, that he had no doubt studied carefully during his stay at the school in Athens. He then felt the need for a Christian equivalent and thought that the Psalms came closest to it."[43]

One of many questions for future study is the transmission of discourse on ethics from the Alexandrian school (Clement of Alexandria and Origen) to the Cappadocians (Basil the Great, Gregory of Nazianzus and Gregory of Nyssa). Festugiere noted that only Athens and Alexandria had Aristotle in original manuscripts, rather than in doxography—that is, in collections of concise statements on the opinions of philosophers popular in Byzantium. Thus, it is highly doubtful that anybody but Origen read Aristotle's treatises in manuscript. Runia adds Clement to this list. However, these two were virtually unknown in Russia, while the Cappadocians were a favorite object of quotation pilfering, while some of their works (like Basil's "How should a Christian live?") were copied by generations of scribes. Clearly, the task of tracing down the hidden Aristotelianism of the Fathers is a daunting task.

5

In 1926, Emelian Iaroslavskii, then the head of the Central Control Commission prosecuting Party crimes, edited the book entitled "What Should a Communist Be Like?" The book was part of the current discussion on Party ethics, and included a number of articles on Communist morality, notably the discussion between West European Communists and their Russian counterparts, together with some articles of popular Communist zealots like Smidovich, Krupskaia and Liadov. In 1935, a similar book, but with the title "What Does the Party Demand from a Communist?" (republished in 1936 in a corrected edition) already ceased to present the issues as a discussion and thus opted for the catechistic style of a clear, concise discussion of the moral qualities of the Communist. The 1943 edition, "What Does the Party Demand from a Communist During the Great Patriotic War?" shifted emphasis in that it added warrior virtues to the list of theological ones (*soznatel'nost'* and *skromnost'* were moved a bit to make way for *muzhestvo*), but it did not change the essential character of appeal: St. Basil the Great was speaking through the lips of St. Emelian Iaroslavskii, who by that time had already published 5 (!) volumes of writings against Christianity, an *Anti-Philokalia* of sorts.

Parallel to high moral discourse that hardly influenced the masses, a more effective way was to integrate Bolshevik moral precepts into the standard secondary school program on Russian literature. Thus, a Mayakovsky verse for children, started with a line known by generations of Soviet citizens: *Krokha syn prishel k otsu. . . .* "A kid came to his father and asked, 'Father, what is good and what is bad?' " The father then enumerates a series of typical situations that detail virtue and vice. A more advanced version of Mayakovsky was offered for teenagers, in the famous poem "Lenin": *Iunoshe, obdumyvaiuschemy zhitie, sdelat' by zhizn's kogo* . . . — "To a youth thinking about a model from which to make his own life, I say: Make it from that of Felix Dzerzhinsky!" The structure of setting up and following a moral exemplar is clearly outlined here. In short, a list of virtues is given by a father to a son not in the form of doctrinal treatise but in a series of model characters (with rhymes to make it all easier to remember!). St. Pavel Korchagin replaces St. Paul, while St. Oleg Koshevoi replaces Prince Oleg — the alleged founder of Kievan Rus'. The new society is based on Communist virtue, obvious moral exemplars, and educative Socialist Realist *vitae* and sermons — saintly zeal rules the day.[44]

Could these ways of moralizing, deeply impregnated in everyday life, disappear in twenty or so years after the collapse of the USSR? Given that the Aristotelian ethics of virtue was integrated into Russian culture only after centuries of insistent effort, it would be hard to believe its erosion could occur so quickly. Let us consider the two implications of this conjecture.

First, attention to virtues rather than stale survey studies of values may allow us to refocus Russia's quest for a new type of ethics that may found a better future. For example, a study of the ethos of those whom contemporary Russians call "bandits" and whom Vadim Volkov has analyzed as "enforcement partners"[45] shows that these virtuosos of violence share a certain way of life that cherishes personal qualities rooted in sports teams' activities of the Soviet past. Self-restraint in talk and action, courage sometimes bordering on total disregard of death, friendship in helping a warrior-comrade — all these qualities are part of the ideological self-representation (that is, misrepresentation) that these communities share.

Now, instead of unmasking this bandit discourse as misrepresentation (the task for a conventional critical sociologist), a virtue theorist might try doing what Aquinas did to the Christianity of the XIII c., founding Christian virtues on the bedrock of the cardinal virtues of the hero-warrior that suited the Germans and the Irish of those times so well. In a twelfth century society with the absence of institutional mechanisms of conflict resolution (as Macintyre notes), this was an ingenious way of integrating warring tribes into the world of Christian morality and more or less predictable behavior. One can imagine that a new ethos can be articulated in a similar way in post-Communist Russia.

The second implication of this study for contemporary concerns is an opportunity to compare radical virtue regimes and their sequels on the basis of a single common denominator — the reception and adaptation of Aristotelian ethics. One of the reasons for Aquinas's creativity in adapting Aristotle to

Christian purposes was the need to contend with the main intellectual weapon from the Arab conquerors—a serious threat at that time. Indeed, Al-Farabi and Al-Ghazali made Aristotle palatable to Islam long before he became part and parcel of Western Christianity, and Maimonides did the same for Judaism. Now, given that the ethics of virtue was a common denominator of all these moral traditions, a well-founded comparative study of the revolutionary politics of virtue (and a concomitant reconceptualization of certain contemporary problems, such as the Israeli-Arab confilct) becomes possible. It was not for nothing that the preeminent Taliban government agency was called the Ministry of Virtue and Vice.

NOTES

1. Kit R. Christensen, *The Politics of Character Development* (Westport, Conn.: Greenwood, 1994), 118.

2. Richard T. De George, *Soviet Ethics and Morality* (Ann Arbor: University of Michigan Press, 1969), 103.

3. Katerina Clark, "Socialist Realism *With* Shores. The Conventions for the Positive Hero," in *Socialist Realism Without Shores,* ed. Thomas Lahusen and Evgeny Dobrenko (Durham: Duke University Press, 1997).

4. Caroline Walker Bynum, *Docere verbo et exemplo: An Aspect of Twelfth Century Spirituality* (Missoula, Mont.: Scholars Press, 1979). Oleg Kharkhordin, *The Collective and the Individual in Russia* (Berkeley and Los Angeles: University of California Press, 1999), chapter 6.

5. Alasdair MacIntyre, *After Virtue* (London: Duckworth, 1981). See also John Horton and Susan Mendus, eds., *After MacIntyre* (Notre Dame: University of Notre Dame Press, 1994).

6. Harold Berman, *Justice in the USSR*, 2nd ed. (Cambridge, MA: Harvard University Press, 1962), 258.

7. See, e.g., Norberto Bobbio, *Thomas Hobbes and the Natural Law Tradition* (Chicago: University of Chicago Press, 1989).

8. This heroic ethic and positing the common goal of the good life is not uniquely Soviet, of course. In the twentieth century another notable example is the Third Reich, but this chapter eschews consideration of their complicated relationship, as well as a question of an Aristotelian community defined in terms of racial purity.

9. As he, for example, says in the beginning of chapter eight of *Nicomachean Ethics*: "Friendship also seems to hold cities together, and lawgivers seem to be more concerned about it than justice . . . [For] when people are friends, justice is unnecessary, but when they are just they need friendship as well." (1155a22–27)

10. One other example is of course the Nazi notion of *Parteigenosse*, but it applied only to party members, and was never universalized to cover all citizens of Nazi Germany.

11. John M. Cooper, "Political Animals and Civic Friendship," in *Friendship: A Philosophical Reader*, ed. Neera Kapur Badhwar (Ithaca, NY: Cornell University Press, 1993).

12. Tamara Kondratieva, *Bolcheviks et Jacobins: itineraire des analogies* (Paris: Payot, 1989). J. L. Talmon, *The Origins of Totalitarian Democracy* (London: Secker & Warburg, 1952).

13. Anne de la Roche-Guilhen, *Dobrodetelnaia frantsuzhinka, ili istoriia o Agnese Soro, zhivshei vo vremia Karla VII* (St. Petersburg, 1791). Liubov' Krichevskaia, *Slepaia mat', ili nagrada ispytannoi dobrodeteli: drama* (Kharkov, 1818). See also e.g. *Dobrodetelnoi volshebnik: dramaticheskaia opera v piati deistviiakh* (Moscow, 1787).

14. Aleksei Artemiev, *Dobrodetelnaia dusha, ili Nravouchitelnyia pravila v polzu i nauchenie iunoshestva* (St. Petersburg, 1777).

15. Victor Zhivov, "Religioznaia reforma i individualnoe nachalo v russkoi literature XVII veka" [Religious Reform and the Individual in Russian Literature of the Seventeenth Century], in *Iz istorii russkoi kultury* [From the History of Russian Culture], vol. 3, (Moscow: Iazyki russkoi kultury, 2000), 477.

16. Francis J. Thomson, "The Distorted Russian Perception of Classical Antiquity: the Causes and Consequences," in his *The Reception of Byzantine Culture in Mediaeval Russia* (Ashgate: Variorum, 1999), chapter VII, 347.

17. David T. Runia, "Festugiere Revisited: Aristotle in the Greek Patres," *Vigiliae Christianae* 43, no. 1 (1989).

18. Dmitrii M. Bulanin, *Antichnye traditsii v drevnerusskoi literature XI–XVI vv.* [Traditions of the Antiquity in Ancient Russian Literature of the XI–XVI Centuries] (Muenchen: Otto Sagner, 1991), 62–66.

19. See V. P. Zubov, *Aristotel'* (Moscow: AN SSSR, 1963), 332. W. F. Ryan, "Aristotle in Old Russian Literature," *Modern Language Review* 63, no. 3 (1968).

20. Ioann Damaskin [St. John of Damascus], *Polnoe sobranie tvorenii* [Complete Works], (St.Petersburg, 1913), 237.

21. Vasilii Kalugin, *Andrei Kurbskii i Ivan Groznyi* [Prince Andrei Kurbsky and Ivan the Terrible] (Moscow: Iazyki russkoi kultury, 1998), 100, repeats Kurbsky's statement that he had read Aristotelian ethics, but there is scarce evidence to prove this point. See Bulanin, *Antichnye traditsii*, 81; Georgii Florovskii, *Puti russkogo bogosloviia* [Ways of Russian Theology], 3rd ed. (Paris: YMCA-Press, 1983), 32.

22. Dmitrii Bulanin, *Perevody i poslaniia Maksima Greka* [Translations and Epistles by Maxim the Greek] (Leningrad: Nauka, 1984), 39, fn. 39.

23. Aleksandr Klibanov, *Dukhovnaia kultura srednevekovoi Rusi* [The Spiritual Culture of Medieval Russia] (Moscow: Aspekt Press, 1994), 210, 214.

24. W. F. Ryan, "Aristotle and Pseudo-Aristotle in Kievan and Muscovite Russia," in *Pseudo-Aristotle in the Middle Ages*, ed. Jill Kraye et al. (London: Warburg Institute, 1986), 106, comes to the conclusion that it was a "dominating text ascribed to Aristotle in the Muscovite period."

25. Ryan claims that unprecedented autocratic rule of Ivan the Terrible can be explained by adherence to advice contained in this mirror of princes that he owned. Czar Alexei Mikhailovich, father of Peter the Great, also had a copy of this work. W. F.

Ryan, "The *Secretum Secretorum* and the Muscovite Autocracy," in *Pseudo-Aristotle: The Secret of Secrets*, ed. W.F. Ryan and Charles B. Schmitt (London: Warburg Institute, 1982).

26. Moshe Taube has approached this problem with adequate skills, but there is no publication yet; see "Literature of the Judaizers or Literature for the Judaizers?" <http://www.aatseel.org/program/aatseel/1998/abstracts/Moshe_Taube.html> (22 Nov. 2004). The so-called "Judaizers' literature" also included a Russian version of Al-Ghazali's *Intentions of Philosophers*, another treatise with Aristotelian themes.

27. Georgii Fedotov, *Russian Religious Mind* (Cambridge, MA: Harvard University Press, 1946–66), vol. 1, 49; vol. 2, 30–32; Bulanin, *Antichnye traditsii*; Zhivov, "Religioznaia reforma;" Thomson, "The Distorted Russian Perception of Classical Antiquity."

28. Izmail Sreznevsky, *Materialy dlia slovaria drevne-russkago iazyka* (St. Petersburg, 1893–1912), vol. 1, 672.

29. William R. Veder, "Old Russia's 'Intellectual Silence' Reconsidered," in *Medieval Russian Culture, vol. II*, ed. Michael S. Flier and Daniel Rowland (Berkeley and Los Angeles: University of California Press, 1994).

30. Paul M. Bushkovitch, *Religion and Society in Russia: The Sixteenth and Seventeenth Centuries* (New York: Oxford University Press, 1992), 152.

31. Florovskii, *Puti russkogo bogosloviia*, 49.

32. Florovskii, *Puti russkogo bogosloviia*, chapter 4. Gregory Freeze also states that up until 1760 students of diocesan seminaries, who managed to master Latin grammar and made it to the end of the normative six year program (their number was pretty miniscule, though), learned Aristotle's logic and Aquinas's theology. After the 1760s seminaries began using a philosophy textbook by Baumeister (essentially an adaptation of Christian Wolff) instead of Aristotle, while Prokopovich and new Russian church hierarchs' treatises replaced Aquinas. (Freeze, *The Russian Levites: Parish Clergy in the Eighteenth Century* (Cambridge, MA: Harvard University Press, 1977), 93–94.)

33. This was an opinion of Fedotov, shared by many others; however, he hardly gave grounds for this largely intuitive claim (*Russian Religious Mind*, vol. 1, 46). Interestingly enough, these two were among the three ancient Church Fathers (the third one was Gregory of Nazianzus) that autodidact peasants perused in their reading groups in 1904; see Vera Shevzov, *Popular Orthodoxy in Late Imperial Russia* (PhD diss., Yale University, 1994), 656, 661.

34. Bushkovitch, *Religion and Society in Russia*, 228.

35. Translated in XII–XIII c., the earliest manuscript is from XIV c., and there are about 20 extant copies. See Dmitrii Bulanin *et al.*, eds., *Slovar' knizhnikov i knizhnosti Drevnei Rusi* [The Dictionary of Bookmen and Books of Ancient Rus'] (Leningrad, Nauka, 1987) vol. 2, part 1, 382–84. Full text appears in V. Semenov, ed., *Drevnerusskaia "Pchela" po pergammenomu spisku* (St. Petersburg, 1893).

36. All quotes from Bushkovitch, *Religion and Society in Russia*, 17, 45, 46.

37. Quoted in M. N. Gromov and N. S. Kozlov, *Russkaia filosofskaia mysl' X–XVII vekov* [Russian Philosophical Thought of XI–XVII Centuries] (Moscow: MGU, 1990), 145.

38. Louis Bouyer, *The Spirituality of the New Testament and the Fathers* (London: Burns & Oates, 1963), 384.

39. Joseph Woodill, *The Fellowship of Life. Virtue Ethics and the Orthodox Christianity* (Washington, DC: Georgetown University Press, 1998), 36. Lamentably, I have discovered this book far too late to fully integrate it into the argument of this chapter.

40. Fedotov, *Russian Religious Mind*, vol. 1, 245–57.

41. MacIntyre, *After Virtue*, 165–67.

42. Elizabeth A. Clark, *Clement's Use of Aristotle: The Aristotelian Contribution to Clement of Alexandria's Refutation of Gnosticism* (Lewiston, NY: Edwin Mellen Press, 1977), 27.

43. Werner Jaeger, *Early Christianity and Greek Paideia* (Cambridge, MA: Belknap, 1961), 59, 96.

44. See an enthusiastic account in Ella Winter, *Red Virtue: Human Relationships in the New Russia* (New York: Harcourt, Brace and Company, 1933).

45. Vadim Volkov, *Violent Entrepreneurs: The Use of Force in the Making of Russian Capitalism* (Ithaca, NY: Cornell University Press, 2002).

Chapter Eight

Res Publica

Cicero constantly mentions tangible things in his political works: they are important for the maintenance of the republican regime, as we would say now, but the mere presence of these public things is clearly not enough for him. Thus, he writes in *De re publica* III: 43: "Syracuse, with its admirable citadel, its harbors, its broad streets . . . , its porticoes, temples, and walls, could not be a commonwealth in spite of all these things (*ut esset illa res publica*) while Dionysus was its ruler, for nothing belonged to the people (*nihil enim populi*), and the people itself was the property of one man."[1] The idea behind this statement is by now well-entrenched in political philosophy: in the absence of just laws ruling the republic, there can be no decisive defense from the threat of despotism or tyranny. Cicero's concern is thus to describe those types of political arrangements (*res publica*) that are not worthy of this high title. For example, concludes Cicero, "wherever a tyrant rules, we ought not to say that we have a bad form of commonwealth, as I said yesterday, but, as logic now demonstrates, that we really have no commonwealth at all (*nullam esse rem publicam*)."[2] In *De officiis* Cicero describes the fallen republic after Caesar took power as something that preserves only a republican carcass of sorts: "And so only the walls of the city (*parietes modo urbis*) remain standing, and they themselves now fear the excesses of crimes; we have utterly lost the republic (*rem publicam amisimus*)."[3]

But did not the need to make such arguments stem from the fact that many people of Cicero's time would believe that, given the presence of obvious, tangible *res publica*—durable shared things, like porticoes and city walls—Syracuse and Rome were republics in any case? Is it not that because of such widespread belief Cicero had to insist, time and again, that the existence of a common theater, squares and sculptures, contrary to popular intuitions, does not ensure the presence of *res publica* automatically? Thus, he writes: "Where was there any 'property of the Athenian people' (*Atheniensium res*) when . . . the notorious Thirty most unjustly governed their city? Did the ancient glory of that state, the transcendent beauty of its buildings, its theatre, its gymnasiums, its porticoes, its famous Propilaea, its citadel, the exquisite works of Phidias, or the splendid Pireaus make it a commonwealth (*rem publicam efficiebat*)?- By no means, since nothing was the 'property of the people' (*quidem populi res non erat*)." And he says the same about Rome under the rule of the Decemvirs: "There was no 'property of the people' (*populi nulla res erat*); indeed the people rose in revolt to recover their property (*rem suam recuperaret*)."[4] *Res publica* here are interpreted as things being in someone's possession: they are, however, very tangible, as their enumeration shows.

The property connotations of the expression *res publica* are important, as many commentators have duly noted, but this should not obscure another interesting fact: a frequent lack of terminological difference between the designations of what we would now call institutions (e.g., republican regime as opposed to monarchy) and tangible things (like porticoes, walls and citadels in the examples above). This conflation of institutions and simple durable public things may not be characteristic of Roman life only. Other republics may have enjoyed a similar life with *res publica*—and here I will suggest examining the case of the medieval republic of Novgorod, which existed for about three centuries until it was conquered by the grand prince of Moscow in 1471. It left hardly any exquisite or complicated texts, there is no established code of its laws, and we have to fathom its institutions from chronicle records and archeological findings. However, some of the things that brought the Novgorodians together are still there, while those gone are well-studied by generations of historians.

Of course, every schoolkid in Russia knows that the main feature distinguishing Novgorod from its last chief enemy—Muscovy—was *veche*, a public assembly or gathering that deliberated on the most important concerns of public life. Phonetics relentlessly suggests to us that there must be something in common between this word and the Russian word for "thing," *veshch'*. Many have noted this curious fact[5], sometimes explicitly referring to Heidegger, who famously pointed out the "gathered" character of a pre-modern thing—a thing that does not wage the existence of an object perceived or instrumentally used by a modern European subject. Indeed, the word "thing" in old German and Scandinavian languages meant *ding*, or *dinc*, a public gathering to deliberate and decide on the matters of a tribe or a settlement, and in Iceland they still use the word *Althingi* to designate the national parliament. Heidegger would say that before modernity things—not only the councils I mentioned but any thing existing as a thing—were able to reveal their capacity to bring what he calls in his poetic language the "fourfold" of mortals, Gods, earth and sky together.

Similarly, *veche* could be very neatly interpreted as the Heideggerian *veshch'* that brought the mortal Novgorodians together with their gods, and opened up their common destiny in uniting the prospects of their earthly affairs with heavenly concerns. Lamentably, such statements are not corroborated by linguistic studies. Etymologists would insist that *veshch'*, "thing," and *veche*, "gathering" or "deliberative council," are unrelated, with *veche* coming from the hypothetic common Slavic root **vetio*, that also gave in Russian the word *sovet* that famously designates the form of direct democracy in 1917–18, but also the privy council of a medieval prince. By contrast, *veshch'*, the thing, allegedly comes from another common Slavic root **vektio*, traced to the Indo-European root **u-e-kti*. This root engendered in Polish the word *rzecz*, "thing," thus *Rzecz Pospolita*, the official title of the Polish-Lithuanian kingdom, was a translation of *Res Publica*. In Gothic the same root gave the word *waichts* (thing), in old Icelandic—*vettr* (thing), and in English—*wight*.[6]

Given that the intuitive candidacy of *veche* to be the main public thing in Novgorod does not pass the strictures of linguistic analysis, and we have too little reliable historical data to reconstruct its institutional life, one could perhaps point our gaze to the many tangible things that the Novgorodians shared. In the absence of a public treasury or unified public records of *veche* decisions, one nevertheless finds the churches, the bells (the most famous captured and deported to be installed in the Moscow Kremlin as a sign of decisive victory), and the stellar case of the woman who was wisdom and temple at the same time. This is St. Sophia, who united all Novgorodians, so that they used to say "where Sophia is, there is Novgorod"—perhaps the only clear instance of self-designation that the chronicles give us. But instead of these elevated and difficult examples of shared things, I choose to concentrate on a seemingly very simple one, which is most frequently mentioned in the First Novgorod Chronicle—the bridge that linked the two parts of the city together.[7]

The bridge is an obvious example of a thing shared by the entire city, i.e., an example of *res publica*, common affairs or concerns. First of all, in conventional parlance, this bridge is a prerequisite for city politics: it is the only multi-season bridge in all of Novgorod (and in all of Russia until the late XVII century). But also the bridge involves and invokes other entities when it brings people together, and thus it cannot be described as a passive object that only human subjects use, if one truly follows what medieval chronicles say about it, or if one lives with the bridge of medieval icons. There this thing called the bridge is not yet broken by modern scientific analysis into natural, technical, political, religious and social aspects. Thus one can hardly take it as just an object, i.e., something that is thrown in front of the viewer as an *object*, opposing the viewer as *Gegen-stand*. That is, chronicles and icons involve the bridge as part of different Novgorod endeavours, and they hardly mention any qualities that this bridge might offer for individual perception. Hence one cannot find adjectives that would describe the bridge of the chronicles as red, bulging, sacred or whatever else. Its only designation is Great, and sometimes—given it has a life of its own—as new or old. The bridge links the people, the elements, and God in their intertwined fate and serves as an arena for their struggles.

In the First Novgorod chronicle we first meet the bridge in the record for 1133, which says that the Novgorodians "have renovated the bridge that collapsed, and two wooden churches have been cut." After that repairs and renovations are mentioned as a major part of the city's history, usually as an event of central relevance in a record for a given year, next to a description of either heavenly omens such as comets or sun eclipses, or God-glorifying activities like (most frequently!) churches being built or renovated. Of course, fights within the city, between the city and surrounding principalities, or among principalities comprise most of events in the chronicle, but if something happens to the bridge, this is recorded with due diligence, surprising a contemporary reader: why should bridges have the same prominence as matters of religion, power and warfare? A typical full record of events worthy of inclusion into the chronicle as an entry under a given year comes from 1144: "A whole new bridge over Volkhov was being built, next to the old one. The same year Archbishop Nifont has painted all the ceilings in the cathedral of St. Sofia. Then also the post of city *posadnik* was given to Nezhata. That same year the stone church of the Virgin Mary was built in the Merchants' borough." And that's it: there are no more events to report, since God did not act, and also there was no factional strife within the city, nor any military crusades beyond its walls.

The central significance of the bridge is revealed in several ways. First, since the public assembly of all free citizens meets only after one part of the populace has crossed the bridge, the decisions of this assembly are frequently put into effect with the help of the bridge. Literally, those found guilty or proclaimed ostracized are physically tossed into river water from the bridge.[8] Immediately after the Volkhov bridge is first mentioned in the First chronicle, it performs this function the next year, in the opening sentence for the year 1134: "The Novgorodians have started discussing the war with the principality of Suzdal', and killed some of their own men and threw them from the bridge on Pentecost Saturday." Later, records mention those executed as being thrown from the bridge in 1141, 1186, 1291, 1316, 1398, 1418 and 1442.

In 1209 the citizens even made an attempt to toss the remains of a much-hated former *posadnik*, brought back into the city for reburial some years after he had fled from the people's rage. In 1141 and 1418 those thrown managed to survive the fall (a religious sign?) and saved their lives by either swimming or being picked up by fishermen. In the second case, the house of one of the fishermen is stormed and ravaged by the indignant crowd. In the first case, God's intervention is recognized, so after the person thrown from the bridge reaches the shore, he is merely fined an immense sum of money, and put into the dungeon for the rest of his life, with his hands chained around his neck.

This brings us to a second very important role of the bridge: it is what helps God say His word. Not that it is just a tool of God's providence, rather, very often, it is a space, or a part of an arena where God can speak and reveal His will. In 1251 the flood after "great rains" displaces the whole bridge, and in 1299 a fire engulfs it. In 1230 unattended corpses of people dead from an unknown disease fill public spaces — "city streets, the market, and the Great bridge" which thus serve as a theatre of death. In 1228, 1335 and 1388 God also enters the scene at the decisive moment, though not to punish, but to save. He acts when city inhabitants from opposing factions or sides of the city stand in full armour, ready to cross the bridge and fight to the death, rather than compete in discursive warfare at a joint public gathering. As the record for 1228 says: "God did not want to see bloodshed among brothers, neither did he want to allow the devil to rejoice". Hence God unleashes the elements. In 1228, for example, "lake Ilmen' was frozen for three days, and then the southern wind blew and tore the ice, and brought everything into Volkhov and tore 9 sections of the Great Bridge." After God intervenes, the people disband and elect a different *posadnik*, which satisfies everyone, and thus the cause for internecine warfare is eliminated. The same pattern is demonstrated in 1335: when ice and snow enter Volkhov and displace 15 sections of the Great bridge, the chronicle concludes: "God did not allow for bloodshed among brothers to happen, though after the devil's tricks one side pitted itself against another, and in armour stood each half of Novgorod, but God took care of these, and citizens came together in love."

The devil wins, however, at least temporarily, when God's interventions around the bridge are unable to stop warfare from breaking out. Thus, in 1218, when the weaker party in the city's conflict managed to destroy sections of the bridge, the other side crossed the river in boats and bloodshed ensued — "O brothers this miracle was done by the cursed devil," says the chronicle. In 1342, the archbishop is present at one of the two contending public assemblies vying for power and nominations of the *posadnik*, and then goes to broker the deal with the leadership of the other assembly. While he is doing this, the city splits into two armies on opposing river banks, but somehow the bishop manages to end this in peace, and "the Cross was glorified, while the devil was put to shame." Similar events happen in 1358 and in 1384.

In the most spectacular case, from 1418, divine power intervenes to stop bloodshed which has already started on the bridge. Archbishop Semeon "ordered that the Holy Cross and the icon of the Virgin Mary be taken, went on the bridge, and after him went the priests and clergy and Christ-loving people. . . . And he came and stood in the middle of the bridge, and blessed both sides with the life-creating cross, and they—seeing the honorable cross— wept." After that the bishop sent emissaries to both sides, and—what a good miracle!—both sides disbanded, "and calm arrived in the city."

The central role of the bridge as a space for key events that link God and mortals is obvious here. God speaks by disrupting the space or events surrounding the bridge, and frequently by preventing conflicts among groups that might have clashed at the site of the bridge. Ice, water, wind, fire, the cross and the icons are other important agents with whom the bridge lives its life. Among the many people that the bridge brings together and affects, the chronicle singles out the bishop and the clergy.[9] All these people, heavenly and earthly elements and God together make the unique assemblage which is the true Great bridge itself, with all the *grandezza*, as Machiavelli would have said, that is, greatness and aggrandizement that is appropriate to it. Decompose this assemblage into social and physical elements, invite a modern bridge scientist to look at it, and one finds a frail, half-rotten wooden structure dangling so low over the water that a stray ice floe in spring can dislodge it from its place. But with divine intervention and the physical elements involved, this bridge leads the Novgorod people to greatness comparable, if one listens to the chroniclers carefully, to that of the Greeks.

Apart from the chronicles, the Novgorodian icons consistently employed the Great Bridge in their imagery. For example, it is part of the upper tier of the famous icon "The fight of the Novgorodians with the Suzdalians," where it allows the procession with the icon from the Church of the Savior on one side of the river to enter the Kremlin on the other. Historically, the prototypical event for this icon is the 1170 siege of Novgorod by the warriors of the grand prince of Suzdal'. The miracle-working icon was taken over to the Kremlin, installed on the fortress wall, and when one of the myriad arrows shot by the attacking army hit the miracle-working icon, it turned its back on the offenders and they were blinded. In the aftermath, a smaller army of the Novgorodians, headed by St. George, SS. Boris and Gleb, the first two Russian martyr-princes, and St. Alexander Nevsky—the locally venerated saint— rushed out of the city walls and vanquished the overpowering enemy.

Art historians long ago noted the differences between three extant versions of this icon, the earliest painted in Novgorod in the mid-XV century for archbishop Evfimii, a staunch defender of Novgorod's independence, and the latest one from the end of the XV c., painted under the influence of the Muscovite school of iconography, already after the fall of Novgorod in 1471.[10] Political events are important here since under Suzdalians the XV c. viewer could easily see contemporary Muscovy: in the XII century Moscow was a tiny settlement in the principality of Suzdal'. Thus, the Novgorod version spoke of the Novgorod prowess to withstand the Muscovite threat, while the Muscovite version had to explain the XII century failure by claiming that everything is in God's will. Apart from stylistic contrasts, the main pictorial differences of the Muscovite icon are the disappearance of the locally venerated saint in the lower tier, the less imposing image of the Novgorod fortress, and the opposite direction of the procession carrying the icon in the upper tier. These differences are usually explained by the political goals of the icon painters of the Muscovite version, but most curious for us is the complete absence of the bridge in the upper tier: an icon painter could have just taken it to be an unnecessary ornamentation, rather than the obvious arena where main events happen. Also, a static scene of genuflection in front of the icon substitutes for a central event of the earlier icon (people from the fortress meeting the icon procession on the bridge): submission rather than public life is put into the focus of the composition.[11]

The bridge appears also in another famous icon that may be dealing with the 1570 sack of Novgorod by Ivan the Terrible, as the latest interpretation suggests.[12] The icon allegedly depicts the apocalyptic visions of the Khutyn monastery bell-ringer Tarasii in 1505, just before plague, flood and fire overwhelmed the city in the next three years. This theatre of death is usually interpreted as a story of divine retribution, since the angels who guide the killing arrows carry the books where they read the names of the sinners. One of the scenes that happens exactly on the bridge[13], however, may be taken to be the allegorical rendition of a historical dishonoring of the archbishop of Novgorod that also symbolizes the sufferings of many other people executed on the bridge by the troops of Ivan the Terrible in 1570. During 10 days of executions, according to conservative estimates, 2,500 people perished, and according to other estimates—about 15,000. Finally, the bridge appears as part of the gold and silk embroidery on the XVII century scarf of a Russian patriarch. On two opposing sides of the scarf, one has depictions of the two main cities of Russian Orthodoxy: Moscow and Novgorod, with the bridge across the river still visible as an important detail of Novgorod only.[14] Thus, the bridge survived in Moscow's imagery of Novgorod long after Muscovy had crushed the liberties of this free city.

References to the contrasts between Novgorod and Muscovy have become commonplace since Radishchev, with the former taken to be the epitome of liberty, and the latter, of despotism. However, something allowed Sigismund von Herberstein to call his 1549 travelogue *Rerum Moscoviticarum Commentarii*, while Giles Fletcher penned down in 1591 an even more radical tile—*Of the Russe Commonwealth*. What pushed them to talk about *res Moscoviticae* on the model of *res Romanae*, or about a Russian Common Weal, when the main thesis of both books was that in Muscovy the monarch was an obvious despot? Fletcher modelled his book on Sir Thomas Smith's *De Republica Anglorum* (1583), itself based on the theory of the mixed constitution and Ciceronian republicanism, which should have prohibited him from designating Russia with the direct English rendition of Latin *res publica*.

The term "commonwealth," of course, could be taken simply as a convenient designation for a "countrie of Russia" at that time, when the term "state" was not yet used to designate the apparatus of government or political unit. For example, Fletcher talks in one chapter about "the state or forme of their [Russian] government," and another chapter comments "on the state of the Communaltie, or vulgar sorte of people in the country of Russia": here the word "state" means "condition." Even if this explanation is true, Fletcher rarely used the word "Commonwealth" in the body of the text, perhaps because the czar's rule was "plain tyrannical," as he concluded. In one of the rare exceptions, the term with capital "C" appears in an acerbic discussion of the lack of opportunity for meritocratic promotion for the commons: "This order that bindeth every man to keep his rancke, . . . wherein his forefathers lived before him, is more meet to keep the subjects in a servile subjection and so apt for this and like Common-wealths, than to advance any vertue, or to breed any rare or excellent qualitie in Nobilitie or Commons."[15]

Statements with the same term, but clearly split into two words and in a lower case, hint at why Fletcher had a hard time calling Muscovy a Commonwealth, but was still pushed to do so. Fletcher copied an indictment of the Muscovite political regime from Herberstein, as Samuel Baron has persuasively argued, but he also added certain subjects of discussion that Herberstein ignored. These additions included a detailed account of the central government administration, the ruler's council, and what Fletcher dubbed the Muscovite Parliament, a *sobor* of members of the ruler's council and the hierarchs of the church.[16] In a chapter on this quasi-Parliament we find the phrase "common wealth" two times: first in a discussion of the approval by the Patriarch and the top clergy of the czar's decisions because "the Emperor and his Councell are . . . far better able to judge what is profitable for the common wealth," and later in the description of the announcement of the *sobor*'s decisions when it is proclaimed that "His Highnesse with those of his noble Councell . . . have found the matters proposed to be verie good and necessarie for the common wealth of his Realme."[17] Clearly, it was the common good of the people—even if, in Fletcher's opinion, appealed to in a rather hypocritical manner here—that justified talking about the Russe Commonwealth.

Now, instead of repeating indictments of the tyrannical government in Muscovy, let us look at what physical things people could share there. In Novgorod, as we remember, it was the *veche* square and the bridge that brought all of the people together to make decisions. In contrast, Fletcher notices no physical grounds for common meeting or deliberation, where the commons, the czar and the nobles could be brought together: "and first touching their libertie how it standeth with them (the commons), it may appear this: that they are reckoned in no degree at all, nor have any suffrage nor place in their *Zabore* or high court of Parliament."[18] The deficiency of sharing the common thing called the Commonwealth is glaring: not only are there no "common consultations for the publique benefit," as Fletcher thinks there should be, but there is also no physical space where the liberty of the commons might stand. Attention to space is manifest in that the chapter on the Parliament gives us precise descriptions of spatial arrangements of the decision-makers: the czar sits on the throne, while "in the next place not far from him at a small square table (that giveth roome to twelve persons or thereabouts) sitteth the Patriarche with the Metropolites and Bishops, and certeine of the principall Nobilitie of the Emperours Councel," with the rest of the courtiers placing themselves on the benches around the room in order of precedence. [19]

In a nutshell, what we find in Muscovy is a certain deficiency of sharing common things in comparison with Novgorod. On the one hand, some sharing is there, and Fletcher points our attention to what in his opinion ties the people together. Because of "publicke affairs" and institutions he feels he has the right to call what he sees a Commonwealth: the Muscovites have a common ruler, whose treasury, policies and courts allegedly link them all together. On the other hand, this sharing is deficient. Given no strong laws or other defences against arbitrary power, one cannot call this regime a republic, a commonwealth in the narrow sense of the word, even if some servile subjects of the czar justify his rule by appeal to the rhetoric of the "common wealth of the Realme." Furthermore, another decisive element is the absence of tangible and durable common things in Muscovy. In Fletcher's time the commonality of sharing some physical things—something once enjoyed by the whole people of Novgorod—had already become in Muscovy the specific province of only one estate—a vulgar mix of lowly people, "the Communaltie." The czar, his servitors, and the top clergy do not engage in this tangible sharing, and they also do not admit the Communaltie into spaces for regal meetings.

It would be interesting to see whether contemporary republics—particularly those that call themselves representative democracies—eschew the need to have tangible *res publica* that was a feature of Rome, Venice and Novgorod.

NOTES

1. English translation by C. W. Keyes from Cicero, *De re publica. De legibus* (Cambridge, MA: Harvard University Press, 1928).

2. *De re publica* III: 43.

3. *De officiis* II: 29; English translation from M. T. Griffin and E. M. Atkins, eds., Cicero, *On Duties* (Cambridge: Cambridge University Press, 1991).

4. *De re publica* III: 44.

5. M. A. Isaev, *Tolkovyi slovar' drevnerusskih iuridicheskih terminov*. [Dictionary of Ancient Russian Juridical Terms] (Moscow: Spark, 2001), 24. Note also the translator's word choice in the Russian version of *Das Ding*—Martin Heidegger, *Vremia i bytie* [Time and Being] (Moscow: Respublika, 1993), 321.

6. The meaning of the Indo-European **u-e-kti*, however, is "to speak," so that apart from *veshch'* another Russian word is linked to it—*rech'*, meaning "speech." There are many questions here, to say the least. Some would doubt all these conjectures of the etymologists' community as just a temporarily accepted academic consensus on contrived Indo-European roots. For example, the alleged Indo-European root for common Slavic **vetio* is **ueik-* or **uoik-*, meaning "act, work," so that in Lithuanian it became *veikti*, "to do something, to work," in old east German *witgan*, "to fight," "to dispute," and in Latin—*vinco*, "to win, to successfully prove." The most strange conclusion to follow is that the Russian words for deliberative assembly or council, *veche* or *sovet*, come from the Indo-European root word for acting, while the Russian word for thing, *veshch'*, comes from the word for speaking. This overturning of usual expectations contradicts our linguistic intuitions so much that etymologists—who use rows of recurrent changes of combinations of consonants and vowels to justify their claims on alleged common roots—will have hard time proving their findings to the majority of users of colloquial Russian.

7. All quotes in the following section are taken from records for a given year from *Novgorodskaia pervaia letopis'* (Moscow: AN SSSR, 1950). Translations are mine.

8. Bridge execution scenes appear in miniatures of the Illustrated Chronicle (*Litsevoi svod*), made for Ivan the Terrible. The most famous image is the execution of heretics in 1375, see e.g. the reproduction in B. A. Rybakov, *Strigolniki. Russkie gumanisty XIV stoletiia* [The Strigolniki: Russian Humanists of the Fourteenth Century] (Moscow: Nauka, 1993), 5.

9. There is a curious parallel here, registered by the etymology of the word *pontifex* that Varro gave: "bridge-builder." This term that entered the title of the Pope, came from the title of the Roman priests, who periodically performed ritual sacrifices by throwing effigies from the bridge over Tiber in Rome.

10. N. G. Porfiridov, "Dva siuzheta drevnerusskoi zhivopisi v ikh otnoshenii k literaturnoi osnove" [Two Subjects of Ancient Russian Painting and Their Literary Ba-

sis], in *Trudy otdela drevnerusskoi literatury* [Works of the Department of Ancient Russian Literature], vol. 22, (Leningrad: Nauka, 1966), 113–14.

11. Tatiana Polekhovskaia, "O tolkovanii novgorodskih ikon XV veka" [Interpreting XV century Novgorod Icons], in *Trudy gosudarstvennogo Ermitazha* [Works of the State Hermitage Museum], vol. 15 (Leningrad, 1974).

12. Elisa Gordienko, *Novgorod v XVI veke i ego dukhovnaia zhizn'* [Spiritual Life of XVI c. Novgorod] (St. Petersburg: Bulanin, 2001), 397–99.

13. See the details of the bridge scene in a drawing published in P.L. Gusev, "Novgorod XVI veka po izobrazheniiu na khutynskoi ikone" [XVI c. Novgorod as Depicted on the Khutyn Icon], in *Vestnik arkheologii i istorii* [The Herald of Archeology and History], vol. 13 (St. Petersburg, 1900), 39.

14. E. V. Ignashina, ed., *Drevnerusskoe shitie v sobranii Novgorodskogo muzeia* [Old Russian Embroidery from the Collection of the Novgorod Museum] (Velikii Novgorod: Novgorodskii muzei-zapovednik, 2002), 28–29.

15. Giles Fletcher, *Of the Russe Commonwealth*, facsimile ed. (Cambridge, MA: Harvard University Press, 1966), 49.

16. Samuel Baron, "Herberstein's Image of Russia and Its Transmission Through Later Writers," in his *Explorations in Muscovite History* (Brookline, VT: Variorum, 1991), chapter XIII, 256.

17. Fletcher, *Of the Russe Commonwealth*, 24.

18. Fletcher, *Of the Russe Commonwealth*, 45

19. Fletcher, *Of the Russe Commonwealth*, 22–23.